YOUNG CHILDREN'S BEHAVIOUR

YOUNG CHILDREN'S BEHAVIOUR

Practical approaches for caregivers and teachers

LOUISE PORTER

MACLENNAN + PETTY
SYDNEY • PHILADELPHIA • LONDON

First published 1999
Reprinted 2000,2002

MacLennan & Petty Pty Limited
Unit 4/809 Botany Road, Rosebery, Sydney NSW 2018, Australia

National Library of Australia
Cataloguing-in-Publication data:

Porter, Louise, 1958–
   Young children's behaviour: practical approaches for caregivers and teachers
   Bibliography
   Includes index

   ISBN 0 86433 143 6

   1. Preschool children—Psychology
   2. Behaviour modifications
   3. Discipline of children
   4. Early childhood education
   5. Classroom management
   I. Title
   372.11024

Printed and bound in Australia

Dedication

For my parents, Pauline Porter and Jim Porter
and grandparents, Kalvina Porter and Norman Verity
who taught me that the purpose of life is a life with purpose.

Contents

List of illustrations

List of tables

Part one

• • • • • • • • • • •

Introduction

Child care and, to a lesser extent, preschool, is a 'home away from home' for the young children who attend. Over half of Australian children attend child care in their preschool years; some for as many as 12 000 hours, which is only 500 hours less than they will spend in primary and secondary school put together (National Childcare Accreditation Council 1993). These figures demonstrate that child care has become more than child-minding and instead contributes significantly to the nurturing and socialisation functions which parents and families used to perform alone.

In this book I aim to cover many aspects of working with young children which are important for the children's socialisation—that is, for helping them to grow to accept their responsibilities and exercise their rights in their community. This is not a book about programming as such—there are many other excellent titles on that topic. It is a book about how you can prevent most disruptive behaviour and deal with those episodes which do occur in a way that looks after everyone involved—you, the upset child, onlooking children, and any victims or recipients of the inappropriate behaviour.

The trouble with writing about 'behaviour management' is that even that term is pejorative. It makes it sound as if children are 'naughty' and need to be 'managed'. Yet it's a term which most of you will understand and so I have persisted with it. However, I need to say at the outset that I regard behaviour 'management' as mainly preventive rather than responding to crises. I believe that the most important aspect of 'management' is to prevent problems from occurring in the first place by providing a high-quality program and by meeting children's emotional and social needs, as well as satisfying their intellectual drives. This belief is reflected in the structure of this book, which places intervention with disruptive behaviour after the chapters on children's emotional and social needs.

This last sentence introduces another issue—namely, what to call behaviour which results in a disruption to the flow of an activity. Someone—perhaps the child him or herself, another child, or one of the adults—is harmed, or the activity is disrupted when a child acts on hurt feelings, or when a dispute occurs between some of the children. If I call these incidents 'disruptive behaviour' it sounds as if that was the child's intent when, in most cases, it will simply be the *outcome* of a child's immature actions, not their *purpose*. For this reason I have avoided using terms such as *misbehaviour* or *inappropriate behaviour*, which judge a child's actions and ignore the reasons for the behaviour; however, I have at times used the *disruptive behaviour* label, simply in the interests of ensuring that you know what I am talking about.

In the first part of this book I describe what I think discipline is and what it is not. I believe that children have automatic rights, but that adults have rights too. However, our society has a long history of thinking of discipline as an either/or phenomenon—*either* adults win *or* children will walk all over us. It seems that we think that learning appropriate behaviour is different from learning any other skill and, as a result, we believe that we can force children to learn how to behave, when we wouldn't use force to teach them anything else which is important for them to learn.

Our history also means that we regard children as being different—even deficient—when compared with adults. The result of this belief is that we feel that we have to teach them to be other than they are, as if being a child is not good enough. This hidden assumption of our discipline is reflected in the words which we use when we talk about disciplining children—such as that children are *naughty*, or manipulative or doing something 'to get at' us. We don't use these words for adults. A manipulative adult, for instance, may be seen to be astute at office politics.

The purpose of Part one, then, is to examine what adults are aiming for when they discipline children—do we want children to do as they are told—and, if so, why?—or do we want to teach them how to behave considerately? And what is the difference between the two?

In answering these questions, my interest is not only in what is better for children, but also what works best for adults, the wider community and the adult–child relationship. It is important for children's sakes that we respect where they are at developmentally, that we accept that they are children. It is equally important for our sakes that we uphold our own rights; and it is important that this mutual respect is the basis of a caring and educational relationship with children.

These last two terms introduce another dilemma about terminology—namely, the historical demarcation between 'caring' and 'education'. My aim is that this book will be useful to caregivers in child care centres and teachers in preschools and in the first grades of primary school. Therefore, although in this book I mostly talk about 'caring' for children, I believe that 'learning and care are inseparable' (Greenman & Stonehouse 1997, p. 16). Therefore, teachers 'care' for children as well as educating them. And it is axiomatic that child care professionals teach children who are in their care. So when I talk about the educational aspects of a program, I am including caregivers in that discussion and when I am talking about caring and nurturing, of course I am including the work of teachers.

Finally, I chose to resolve the dilemma about using male or female pronouns by alternating their use between main sections in each chapter. Naturally, when I use the male or female pronoun, I am referring to children of either sex.

1

• • • • • • • • • •

Quality guidelines

Behaviour management refers both to the prevention of behavioural disturbances, and to helping children return to appropriate behaviour once an upset has occurred. It is not merely an add-on task which you carry out when the children's behaviour demands your intervention and which interrupts your other duties. Rather, it is your responsibility as an early childhood professional to 'socialise young children so that ultimately they can become responsible, competent, and fully functioning members of their culture and society' (Rodd 1996, p. 6).

Despite the socialisation of children being one of the most important tasks anyone can do for the children themselves and on society's behalf, there is little guidance for early childhood professionals on how to go about this process. In many countries, early childhood associations have established guidelines for the quality of child care services (e.g. Australian Early Childhood Association 1986; Department for Education and Children's Services 1995; the National Association for the Education of Young Children 1984; the National Childcare Accreditation Council 1993). The purpose of these guidelines is to lay the foundation for the delivery of a high level of care to children, as is the children's right (Gotts 1988). In addition, the guidelines aim to spell out standards of care, the implementation of which will promote children's optimal development.

But in terms of behaviour management the guidelines offer little specific advice. They give some direction on the prevention of behavioural disturbances. The delivery of high quality care will make it possible to avoid many behavioural disturbances which are provoked— often unwittingly—by inappropriate conditions of care. As to intervention, the guidelines convey a spirit and offer some specific clues about how we are to respond when children's behaviour disrupts an activity or interferes with other children or adults who are part of the group. The spirit of the guidelines is extended by the code of ethics for early childhood practitioners. Therefore, this chapter will examine both of these sets of principles and offer an interpretation of what each principle implies for behaviour management practices.

Guidelines for high-quality care

Australian child care centres are accredited (licensed) if they meet certain criteria for high quality care (National Childcare Accreditation Council 1993). These principles are listed in Appendix A. A summary of each of the principles is presented below, together with a brief discussion of its application to the prevention of and intervention with behavioural disturbances.

Staff–child interactions

Prevention. More than any other characteristic of the centre, the quality of the interactions between staff and children will affect the overall quality of the care which children experience at the time. More than this, high-quality interactions between adults and children promote the children's language skills, intellectual skills and social skills, both in the short and long term (Doherty-Derkowski 1995).

Although observations show that adults spend the vast majority of their time interacting with children in care or education settings, when researchers observe individual children it appears that nearly one-third of them receive no individual attention on a given day (Kontos & Wilcox-Herzog 1997). This leads to two conclusions. First, because of the child–adult ratio in early childhood centres a high *quantity* of interactions is not possible, and so instead it is important that adult–child interactions are of a high *quality*. Second, it will be important that you are conscious of how you distribute your attention so that the same children are not regularly overlooked (Kontos & Wilcox-Herzog 1997).

High-quality interactions are defined in the guidelines. They state that when talking with children it is important that both what you say and how you say it conveys respect for children; accepts their individuality and promotes their autonomy; supports their social learning and is responsive to their needs. Your interactions need to be warm and fun, and offer opportunities for personal two-way discussions between adults and children in which you listen to what interests the children, rather than asking questions for which you already know the answers (such as, 'What colour are you using now?'), or giving directives.

In short, you need to be responsive to children's age, current needs and the present situation (Doherty-Derkowski 1995). This involves reacting appropriately and promptly to their signals, listening to children with attention and respect, initiating activities which reflect the child's developmental level and interests, and being sensitive to the child's current mood and situation (Doherty-Derkowski 1995). These behaviours tell children that they 'are cared *about* as well as cared for' (Doherty-Derkowski 1995, p. 36).

Intervention. From this guideline alone, we are already building up a picture that behaviour management is to be based on a protective, nurturing, encouraging and educational relationship between you and the children in your care (Rodd 1996). The National Association for the Education of Young Children (NAEYC 1983) requires staff to use positive disciplinary methods such as prevention of difficulties and acknowledgment of appropriate behaviour. Staff are to avoid punitive, humiliating or frightening disciplinary strategies (NAEYC 1983) and should not place unnecessary restrictions on children or be harsh in their responses to children (Doherty-Derkowski 1995). Unnecessary restrictions on children's activities—that is, controls for other than safety reasons—result in children's poor language and cognitive development and behaviour problems at later ages, while harsh and critical responses to children have been related to aimless wandering in a centre, lack of attachment to caregivers, and stress in children (Doherty-Derkowski 1995).

A child-friendly environment

Prevention. The physical arrangement of the centre has many behavioural effects. First, the environment affects the participation of the children by its level of stimulation, attractiveness and fun. When children are actively engaged they are less likely to find disruptive things to do. Second, the environment can help children to feel safe and it can give them confidence that they can exercise choice and be independent and so have control of themselves during their play. Third, the layout of the centre communicates to children the intent of your program (Sebastian 1989) and allows it to flow smoothly—such as by keeping traffic areas free of congestion. Fourth, providing sufficient space avoids the unintentional collisions that can occur when children are in close proximity to each other, as well as avoiding 'deliberate' aggression and promoting cooperation (Lady Gowrie Child Centre Melbourne 1987).

Intervention. At any time throughout the day, children need private areas so that they can have some solitude (while still being visible to an adult). When their feelings are beginning to overwhelm them and they are displaying this through potentially harmful behaviour, the opportunity to withdraw from demands can be very beneficial. As I describe in coming chapters, a common behaviour management approach is to impose this solitude on disruptive children. This is called 'time-out'. However, I regard the loss of control of one's feelings to be a natural childhood event, and so I would make the solitary areas pleasant and calming places, rather than punitive and sterile settings. To punish children for becoming upset is to punish them for being children and, in my view, is entirely inappropriate.

The program or curriculum

The curriculum is 'all of the interactions, experiences and routines that are part of each child's day' (Department of Education and Children's Services [DECS] 1996, p. 16). It aims to promote learning, caring relationships between adults and children—and among the children—and to foster children's healthy self-esteem. To that end you will plan and take advantage of spontaneous experiences which give children opportunities to consolidate and extend their learning. Even routines which are aimed at helping the day run smoothly will ultimately promote the comfort, health and well-being of the children (DECS 1996).

Prevention. The centre's program or curriculum will need to encourage active participation, provide a variety of appropriate learning activities and build on and encourage individual children's physical, psychological, social, intellectual and academic accomplishments (Greenberg 1992). To be able to tailor activities to individual children's abilities and interests you will need procedures and the resources to assess their skills, both formally and informally. By being responsive in this way to the children's needs, your curriculum will not only be developmentally appropriate but also 'humanly, culturally and individually appropriate' (Stonehouse 1994a, p. 76). An appropriate curriculum ensures that the children do not become stressed by inappropriate expectations (Doherty-Derkowski 1995), resulting in possible disruptions and aggressive behaviour.

Intervention. It makes no sense to teach children to explore their world if, when their behaviour results in a disruption, you then insist that they do as they are told (McCaslin & Good 1992). If you teach children to be passive behaviourally, you will be teaching them to be passive about all areas of learning.

There are many excellent texts on programming for children in child care centres and I cannot even summarise the information here about how to encourage play, exploration and problem-solving skills. However, when applying the curricular guidelines to behaviour management, the most fundamental aspect of the curriculum is mediating children's learning so that they learn, first, how to plan their approach to solving problems and, second, to regulate their own behaviour. Self-management is the main cognitive task in the years prior to school.

Mediated learning—as distinct from direct learning through the senses—occurs when adults interpret the environment for children (Barclay & Benelli 1994; Klein 1992). Adults initially direct children's thinking processes towards a higher level than they can achieve alone, and then the children progressively learn to use new skills independently (Moss 1992). You can guide children's thinking skills through your comments and open-ended questions (Wallace 1983). When offering guidance you will incorporate five key strategies: focusing children's attention; attributing cognitive and emotional meaning to a stimulus; expanding children's awareness and thinking; offering feedback; and helping children to organise the task (Klein 1992).

By around four years of age, children developing normally will begin to learn how to talk to themselves in the same terms which you have been using in your talk with them. This is the beginning of self-control of their own learning. It is also the beginning of self-control of their own actions, which is fundamental to the behaviour management approaches which I describe in this book.

Child–child interaction

Prevention. The Australian accreditation guidelines do not include a statement on the importance of children's friendships, although the NAEYC (1983) recognises that this is a crucial aspect of the quality of early childhood programs. Friendships are fundamental to children's satisfaction with their care or preschool experience (Langsted 1994, in Pugh & Selleck 1996).

Friendships can be facilitated naturally in a supportive physical environment, in which the peer group is stable and the caregivers familiar (Lady Gowrie Child Centre Melbourne 1987). However, for some children, friendships might not necessarily develop naturally and so these isolated youngsters will need your help to find companionship. This will benefit the children socially, emotionally and developmentally as they are often more willing to learn from another child than they are from an adult; moreover, meeting children's social needs will prevent many behavioural disturbances.

Intervention. Having fostered cooperative behaviour between children, you will need to discourage hurtful comments and intimidation of others in the group. It is important that every child is protected from the behavioural excesses of other children.

It is also important that behaviour management methods do not scapegoat individual children. If you want the children to get along with each other, then your methods cannot teach onlooking children that a particular child is 'naughty' or not to be trusted. To me this is fundamental: the rewards and punishment type of approach might be successful with individuals (see chapter 2), but when you are responding to behaviours in a group setting you also have to consider the effects of your methods on the children who are observing them in action.

Staff–parent interaction

Prevention. Parents will need to know about your program and that their presence and contributions are welcome. To assist you in your task of caring for their child, you will need to use the parents' intimate knowledge of their child's abilities, preferences and interests. This will enable practices at the centre to support the routine at home. It will also help the children to understand what is expected of them, giving a better chance that they will be able to follow the routines which the centre observes. Children are more likely to settle in a centre when they know that their parents and care staff support and value each other's contributions. To that end the centre will need procedures for day-to-day communication with parents and for regular updates about a child's progress (NAEYC 1984). I discuss this issue again in chapter 26.

Intervention. When intervening with a child's repeatedly disruptive behaviour you can learn from what the parents tell you about possible triggers either at home or in the centre, and strategies which they find helpful at home. A respectful relationship between yourself and the parents will make the parents more responsive at those times when you have to convey sensitive information about their child.

Knowledgeable staff

Prevention. The accreditation guidelines address the importance of care-givers' and teachers' knowledge of child development, and how to meet children's needs in all aspects of a program. However, their silence on behaviour management practices and the lack of pre-service training in this field for teachers and caregivers unwittingly leaves children vulnerable to inappropriate management practices. In addition to all your other expertise, knowledge of the theories of behaviour management is fundamental because I believe that traditional behaviour management approaches can undo many of the gains made by a high-quality curriculum. When children are trained to do as they are told, they are less likely to explore even the most stimulating curricula. When behaviour management practices blame or shame children, even those who conform can feel intimidated and unsafe.

Intervention. Interceding when a child's behaviour has disrupted an activity, or upset another group member, requires moment-by-moment decisions. It is harder for these decisions to be wise when all you have to rely on is whatever 'seems like a good idea at the time'. Instead, if you can draw on a clear rationale for your practices, each decision will be more automatic. In turn, it is likely to be more effective, and less stressful for you.

Even with wide experience, extensive training and adequate support, no one knows everything about everything. So, when a child's behaviour is outside of your previous experience you must refer the child to a specialist (having first obtained parental consent). Referral to a specialist is not an admission of defeat—it would be negligent to continue to deal with something you knew little about. Your GP refers you to an oncologist if she or he suspects cancer; you would expect nothing less.

Naturally, referring children to consultants necessitates that you be aware of the pediatric specialists in a range of fields. Parents could be a useful fund of knowledge here. By asking your parents which practitioners they consult for their child and in which areas they specialise, you can build up a list of practitioners in various fields: paediatricians, podiatrists, physiotherapists, chiropractors, psychologists, pediatric dentists, speech pathologists, naturopaths, and so on—whose names you could give to parents when a need arises.

Staffing levels

Prevention. Staffing levels are among the most crucial factors in determining the quality of care—particularly of infants and toddlers—since high adult–child ratios permit close interactions between adults and children (Arthur et al. 1996; Phillips & Howes 1987).

There must be sufficient staff to allow for constant supervision of children and to replace an adult who takes a break or must respond to an emergency. Every attempt needs to be made to ensure continuity of adult care of each child (Elicker & Fortner-Wood 1995).

Intervention. Staff will need to work as a team, taking over from each other when one staff member is occupied dealing with a behavioural disruption. In chapter 3, I introduce the notion that behaviour management does not have to be consistent, as ordinarily thought, but instead needs to be responsive to the circumstances. This is aided when staff can be flexible about their roles, but also means that when staff simply are not available to deal at length with a disruption, a less labour-intensive approach could be used. I say more about this tension between consistency and flexibility later.

Nutrition

Prevention. Food is more than fuel for children's physical, social, emotional and cognitive development. It is an issue of human rights that children deserve food which meets their nutritional and cultural requirements and preferences. For certain children it will be necessary to accommodate very particular dietary requirements arising from food sensitivities or medical conditions. This will avoid medical complications and also erratic behaviour arising from a reaction to foods. In terms of behaviour management, hungry young children are less likely to cope with the demands of their day. Therefore, their meals need to give them enough fuel.

Mealtime needs to be a pleasant social experience for children. Although it could be tempting to set up an invariant routine to make it more orderly, mealtime can be educational in itself when you give children opportunities to make choices and exercise autonomy. Particularly older toddlers and preschoolers can decide where to sit, what and how much to eat, when to get themselves a drink, and so on.

Intervention. It has been a long-standing tradition to use food as a reward for appropriate behaviour, or even for eating a disliked food. However, using foods as rewards gives children an external reason to eat, rather than teaching them to eat to satisfy hunger—an internal need. Rewards also have the opposite effect to what we aim for—namely, they make the undesired food less attractive than it already seemed (Birch, Johnson & Fisher 1995). Therefore, food should never be part of a behaviour management reward system.

Health and safety procedures

Prevention. Your centre's health and safety procedures will be in place to safeguard both the children and the staff. When staff are not subjected to undue stress, nor exposed to avoidable illness, you will all be able to function better. Ultimately, this will prevent upsets in the children which can arise when staff are below par or taking leave through stress or illness with the result that the continuity of the children's care is disrupted.

Intervention. To promote children's physical and emotional safety, a member of staff will need to be present to supervise children at all times so that the children are not at physical risk of injury or abuse—including bullying from other children.

You will need to be aware of the signs of illness so that allowances can be made for unwell children. You will also need to be familiar with the signs of child abuse, since you are legally obliged to report any suspicious injuries to the child welfare authorities—see chapter 22.

Support for staff

Prevention. It will be difficult to provide high quality conditions for the children in your care, if your own working conditions are poor (Ebbeck 1991; Hilliard 1985). Your role is a demanding one, requiring clear thinking, quick responses and physical stamina. With this in mind, the centre will need to ensure that all staff take suitable breaks during the day, can receive ongoing training, and receive support from their colleagues.

Intervention. When a member of staff is confronting a particularly chronic or challenging behavioural difficulty with any of the children, other staff members need to give both practical and moral support, not as a favour but as a matter of course (Rogers 1994). This might even mean that staffing schedules will have to be adjusted until the child's behaviour settles and the extra demands have decreased.

Administrative systems

Systems need to be in place to ensure that the program runs efficiently and effectively so that it meets the needs and desires of children, parents and staff (Sebastian 1989; Simons 1986). To allow staff to plan for meeting these needs, they should be freed from child contact or be paid for time spent in planning. Having established written procedures and policies, these will be need to be reviewed regularly (NAEYC 1984).

Evaluation

Regular staff reviews, evaluation of the progress of each child and of the effectiveness of the program are necessary to ensure the program is effective in meeting its goals for children, parents and staff (NAEYC 1984). Appropriate programming will avoid many behavioural difficulties; ongoing evaluation of specific intervention programs which target a particular child or behaviour is essential for avoiding unwanted side-effects of the program.

Conclusion: quality guidelines

From research, three criteria of high-quality care have emerged as the most important. These are: adult–child ratios—especially for infants and toddlers; group size; and caregiver training (Butterworth 1991; Phillips & Howes 1987; Scarr, Eisenberg & Deater-Deckard 1994; Wangmann 1992). In turn, these characteristics are significant because they all have an impact on the closeness and quality of adult–child interactions.

Ethics

A second source of guidance to staff about behaviour management practices comes from the early childhood professionals' Code of Ethics (Australian Early Childhood Association 1991; National Association for the Education of Young Children 1989). Again, like the accreditation guidelines, the code does not specify what to do about behaviour management, although it too conveys caregivers' responsibilities to children, families, colleagues, the community and society, and to themselves as professionals. (The code is reproduced in Appendix A.)

Three features of professional child care make a code of ethics particularly crucial (Katz 1995). The first of these is the vulnerable age of the children in our care; the second is the fact that teachers and caregivers are responsible to two groups at once—parents and children—as well as having to serve society's interests in terms of how we care for and socialise children; and, third, a code of ethics is necessary when there is little evidence about which practices are best. When there is little evidence to prove that one way of working is better than another, workers can instead be guided by ethical statements.

All three features apply especially to behaviour management practices in early childhood centres. First, the children are young and so cannot protest about unfair disciplinary practices—and their reports might not be believed anyway (Katz 1995). Second, you might be pressured by parents to act towards the children in ways that would not be in the children's best interests. Third, you might have misgivings about certain behaviour management practices but have little evidence to back up your concerns. In such a case, you can refer back to your code of ethics.

Nevertheless, despite the measure of protection which codes of ethics are able to provide to the consumers of a service and to professionals themselves, they specify minimum standards of conduct only, rather than optimal standards (Corey 1996). Further, they can only ever provide broad principles for responsible practice and, therefore, cannot prescribe particular behaviour on the part of professionals.

The principles of codes of ethics

All codes have some underlying moral principles (Corey 1996), four of which have particular relevance to behaviour management. These are:

- *non-maleficence*—which means doing no harm;
- *justice*;
- *fidelity*—which refers to keeping commitments to others; and
- *autonomy*—which refers to the ultimate aim of empowering the people in our care—in our case, young children—to exercise control over their

own lives. This means guiding children to control their own behaviour instead of needing constant supervision.

Principle 1: Do no harm

A fundamental principle of the early childhood code of ethics is that as a caregiver or teacher you may not participate in practices which are disrespectful, degrading, intimidating, psychologically damaging, exploitative, or physically harmful to children (Australian Early Childhood Association 1991; National Association for the Education of Young Children 1989). The code recognises that young children are vulnerable, with little power over their own lives, and few skills with which to protect themselves. It asserts that, therefore, you must use your influence over children in their best interests.

Principle 2: Justice

The core values embodied in the early childhood code of ethics are: respect for the uniqueness of children, for their families and their cultural values; support of children and their families; open communication with children, parents and colleagues; responsiveness to children's needs; and professional integrity (Australian Early Childhood Association 1991; Department for Education and Children's Services 1995). These values define what is right, rather than what is expedient; what is good rather than what is simply practical (Katz 1995); and what is just rather than what is merely opportune.

The concept of justice refers to giving everyone with whom you work equal and fair treatment, both in the sense of not discriminating against children or their parents on the basis of their culture, gender, religion and so on, but also in the sense of balancing the rights and interests of the various groups to whom you are responsible—mainly the children and their parents.

Principle 3: Fidelity

Fidelity implies keeping personal commitments to the children and parents in your centre. One of these commitments is preserving children's and parents' privacy. The principle of privacy states that people have a right to choose who knows personal information about them, especially when that information could be used to discriminate against them (Coady 1994; Thompson & Rudolph 1996).

Confidentiality is a related principle which refers to your responsibility—as set down in your profession's code of ethics—to respect children's and parents' privacy and to limit who has access to personal information about them (Thompson & Rudolph 1996). Confidentiality is central to establishing a trusting and effective professional relationship between yourself and parents (Corey 1996).

In practice, this concept implies discussing a child's behavioural or other difficulties only with the staff who need to know about them, and never with other parents or visitors to your centre. It means gaining the parents' permission before you talk with consultants about their child.

A strong belief that I have which relates to the notions of confidentiality and fidelity is that teachers and caregivers need to avoid loose diagnostic terms when describing children's behaviour. Labels such as *attention-seeking, manipulative, aggressive* (when applied to a child, rather than a behaviour), and even more formal diagnoses, such as *behaviour disordered*, all convey disrespect for children, and imply that there is something wrong with them and that they can be blamed for their behaviour (which is not the same as giving them responsibility for it). The result can be that the emphasis is moved to a child's apparent deficits rather than on your staff team's responsibility to help the child to grow.

Principle 4: Autonomy

In a lecture I once gave on behaviour management, to a group of medical students, one objected to my approach on the grounds that you can train children just as you can train your pets—with rewards and punishment. My answer to this assertion is, yes, you *can*, but would you *want* to? Surely, the essence of our humanness is our ability to make decisions for ourselves, and the task of growing up is to enable us to take control of our own lives so that we do not have to rely on being supervised. We expect our pets to remain dependent on us; we expect our children to become self-reliant. As I see it, the methods you use to teach autonomy are—and should be—different from the methods to teach compliance.

Conclusion

The guidelines for high-quality care and the early childhood profession's code of ethics imply that behaviour management practices cannot be divorced from the quality of the overall program being delivered to the children. The curriculum's opportunities for growth and learning set the scene for children to learn to regulate their own behaviour for the good of themselves and others.

The next chapter describes some theories about behaviour management. An understanding of these theories will equip you with a rationale for your practices. The chapter will offer a critique of the various theories, as based on the accreditation guidelines and code of ethics which I have summarised here.

Suggestions for further reading

For information about the accreditation guidelines for child care centres:

Department for Education and Children's Services (1995), *Quality matters: A learning manual for quality assurance in early childhood services*, Department for Education and Children's Services, Adelaide.

National Childcare Accreditation Council (1993), *Putting children first: Quality improvement and accreditation system handbook*, National Childcare Accreditation Council, Sydney.

For a thorough review of the research into high-quality child care and its implications for practice:

Doherty-Derkowski, G. (1995). *Quality matters: Excellence in early childhood programs*, Don Mills, Addison-Wesley, Ontario.

Greenman, J. & Stonehouse, A. (1997), *Prime times: A handbook for excellence in infant and toddler programs*, Longman, South Melbourne.

Koralek, D. G., Colker, L. J., & Dodge, D.T. (1993), *The what, why, and how of high-quality early childhood education: A guide for on-site supervision*, National Association for the Education of Young Children, Washington, DC.

For curriculum ideas in all developmental domains:

Gestwicki, C. (1995), *Developmentally appropriate practice: Curriculum development in early education*, Delmar, Albany, NY.

Hohmann, M. & Weikart, D. P. (1995). *Educating young children*, High/Scope Press, Ypsilanti, Michigan.

For a detailed look at environmental planning to ensure children's needs are catered for:

Greenman, J. (1988), *Caring spaces; learning places: Children's environments that work*, Exchange Press, Redmond, WA.

For a discussion of the early childhood practitioners' code of ethics:

Stonehouse, A. (1991), *Our code of ethics at work*, Australian Early Childhood Association, Watson, ACT.

2

• • • • • • • • • •

Theories of behaviour management

Advice contained in the well-known saying 'If you want to get ahead, get a theory', is particularly apt for disciplining young children. Unless we understand why we do what we do, we cannot explain why we are successful in managing behaviour, nor why something we have tried hasn't worked. So, don't let a chapter on theory scare you off. Theories are nothing more than an orderly set of beliefs and principles. Because they are orderly they help us describe, explain and predict behaviour. They can organise our thoughts and give us a rationale for our practice.

This chapter will describe four key theories of behaviour management. Each one has influenced practices in early childhood centres, so even if you are not yet familiar with a particular theory by name, you might recognise its practices being used in your child care or preschool centre.

The four key theories

There are four key theories of behaviour management in common use with young children. They are applied behaviour analysis, cognitive-behaviourism, neo-Adlerian theory, and the democratic theories. I believe that the main difference between them is the amount of power they give to the adults, compared with the amount of autonomy they give to children. With this distinction in mind, I have arranged the theories along a continuum, shown in Figure 2.1. On the left are the authoritarian theories in which the adult has control over children. Applied behaviour analysis is the main authoritarian theory used in the early childhood years. At the other end of the continuum is the permissive or laissez-faire approach which grants children a free rein, with very few adult-imposed restrictions. This approach has no modern adherents. The middle ground is occupied by the authoritative theories—humanism and

17

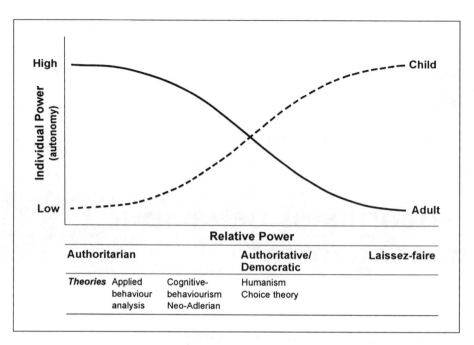

Figure 2.1: Theories of behaviour management in the early childhood years (adapted from Porter 1996, p. 10)

choice theory—that promote children's self-control. These are also referred to as the democratic theories, although adults and children do not share power equally: adults still act as leaders and, when necessary, make executive decisions on the children's behalf.

Applied behaviour analysis (ABA)

Applied behaviour analysis (ABA) is the new term for behaviour modification. According to this theory individuals acquire new behaviours through imitation and through a process called shaping, in which a complex skill is learned by mastering a series of small steps that together make up the total task. Once an individual has learned a behaviour, she will repeat it if it works or, in the language of ABA, it is 'reinforced'—that is, it earns her something she values, making it likely that she will repeat the behaviour.

Therefore, if you want a child to stop engaging in a particular behaviour, you have to prevent it from working—from receiving a positive response. To do this you increase the rewards you give to an alternative, more desirable behaviour so that, comparatively, the behaviour you are targeting no longer works for the child. The kinds of rewards used in early childhood include: social reinforcers such as praise, hugs, or a smile; the opportunity to do a favourite activity; a sticker or some other tangible reward that the child values for itself; and food rewards (although these are not recommended—see Birch et al. 1995).

If rewarding an alternative behaviour does not work, then the adult can punish the undesirable behaviour. According to ABA, the term *punishment* means to reduce the rate of a behaviour, and so anything that achieves a reduction in the behaviour is a punishment. There are two types of punishments: taking away something that the child wants, or administering something the child does not like. Taking away something the child likes includes withdrawing her privileges, and time-out—probably the most widely used punishment in early childhood centres. Time-out is based on the assumption that something in the environment is maintaining (reinforcing) the child's undesirable behaviour and so, if you remove the child from that environment and place her where she cannot receive any reinforcement, then the behaviour will stop. The second class of punishments—delivering something aversive or unpleasant—includes verbal aversives such as reprimands and physical aversives such as smacking. (Experts agree that physical aversives should never be used. Besides being ineffective in controlling behaviour, they prompt anger and resistance in children and can spiral into serious abuse.)

So far, two central themes of applied behaviour analysis have been introduced: first, that rewards will increase the rate of a child's desirable behaviours; second, that punishment will reduce the rate of a child's undesirable behaviours. The third key principle is that when using ABA it is absolutely crucial that you observe and record the circumstances that precede the behaviour (its antecedents) and what happens after the behaviour (the consequences). This allows you to choose an appropriate intervention. Careful recording of the behaviour rate before and during the selected intervention also allows you to evaluate whether the behaviour management program is working, and to change it immediately if it is not. Such observation guards against frustration which may cause you to feel mistakenly that the child's behaviour is not improving, and ensures that unwanted side-effects of punishment are detected early, so that the program can be changed if any side-effects occur.

Strengths and weaknesses of ABA

The great strength of ABA is its emphasis on unbiased observation of the child's behaviour and careful monitoring of the success of a management program. On the other hand, the detailed recording that ABA requires is difficult to do in addition to one's other tasks. A second strength claimed by proponents of this approach (for example, Alberto & Troutman 1995), is that it works efficiently. However, most ABA studies occur in tightly controlled conditions that cannot be duplicated in less structured settings. Another criticism is that the behavioural gains made by the ABA approach come at a high price. (Later chapters will enlarge on the costs to the individual child, to onlookers, and to the adults, when adults impose control on children instead of guiding the children to manage themselves.)

This leads to my assessment of ABA's weaknesses. Because ABA is highly technical—more technical than this brief summary suggests—it takes a great deal of skill and training to use it effectively. The first challenge is that while the use of rewards and punishments seems like common sense, it is fraught with pitfalls—which I detail in chapters 6 and 12.

Second, because adults are in charge they are doing all the work to decide how to manage a child's undesirable behaviour. The child is not engaged in this process. This means that adults fail to capitalise on children's inner resources for managing their own behaviour. This is both inefficient because it does not use the children's ideas about solving the problem, and also it does not motivate them to comply, since they did not contribute to the decisions about their behaviour.

Finally, the theory gives staff little guidance about how to prevent inappropriate behaviour and so avoid the need for a restrictive management program.

Although the theory is highly technical, it is actually the basis of most child-rearing. Most parents believe that they should reward a child's 'good' behaviour and punish the 'bad'. However, in chapter 3 I will be arguing that this concept is actually based on the idea that children are naturally naughty and need manipulating into doing the right thing—a belief that is not consistent with the child-centred focus of early childhood care and education.

Cognitive-behaviourism

A recent variation of ABA is cognitive-behaviourism, which aims to overcome these criticisms of ABA. I have placed cognitive-behaviourism between the authoritarian and authoritative positions on Figure 2.1 because the adult remains partly in control of the child, but at the same time involves the child somewhat in managing his own behaviour.

Cognitive-behaviourists believe that besides the consequences of behaviour, an individual's behavioural choices are affected by his planning skills, emotional state, developmental stage and the environment (Kendall 1991). When a child's behaviour appears to be inappropriate, cognitive-behaviourism attempts to identify and remediate deficiencies in any of these elements. In this way, it looks for possible causes of the behaviour both within the child and within his environment. The underlying belief is that it takes more than ability to complete a task successfully, and that how the child feels about doing the task can block his achievement of it.

This theory focuses on how the child feels about a task by:

- improving the child's *self-esteem*—mainly through praise;
- ensuring that he believes his actions can make a difference to the outcome—this is termed 'having an internal locus of control';
- teaching him to believe in his ability to organise and execute a chosen behaviour—this is *self-efficacy*;
- teaching him to apply to a new activity knowledge that he gained from a related activity—this is termed 'a *learning set*';
- improving *motivation* by ensuring that what he is being asked to do is relevant for the child and therefore has intrinsic or built-in natural rewards for him.

Cognitive training involves teaching children to manage themselves—either their task completion or their behaviour. The first aspect of self-management is teaching children to notice or *monitor* their own behaviour. They can monitor themselves formally—with a chart, for instance—but in the early childhood years it is more likely that at the time of a disruption an adult might simply ask the child something like, 'What are you doing? Is it a good idea?'.

Next, cognitive-behaviourism aims to teach children how to give themselves helpful *instructions* about their approach to tasks or their behaviour, rather than talking to themselves in ways that make success less likely. For instance, instead of the child telling himself, 'This is too hard. I can't do it', you might teach a child to say to himself, 'This is tricky, but if I think about what I want to do, I'll be all right'—or a simplified version of this for very young children.

Third, children are taught to *evaluate* whether their behaviour has met an agreed standard. When it has, the adult delivers a reward, then the adult and child together administer a reinforcer, and finally the child reinforces himself independently, although this last stage may be too ambitious for preschool-aged children.

These general approaches can be used to teach children specific behaviours such as how to adhere to routines, follow instructions, manage frustration, and so on. The methods focus on the children's thinking and planning processes and on teaching children that they can regulate their own behaviour. Children can also be taught directly how to solve problems, beginning with how to recognise when a problem exists, identifying their goals, getting in touch with their skills for solving the problem, generating some possible solutions, and selecting a response which they think is likely to work best.

Strengths and weaknesses of cognitive-behaviourism

The first strength of this theory is that it consults the child about how to address his problematic behaviour, and so he is more likely to be motivated to control his own behaviour than when the adult imposes control on him.

A second strength of this theory is that it can address three problems at once. A common pattern of difficulties for children is when they show demanding behaviour, learning problems, and low self-esteem all together. Cognitive-behaviourism can address all three aspects with the one self-management program by teaching self-monitoring to improve the child's awareness of his behaviour, self-instruction skills to remediate his learning difficulties, and self-evaluation to heighten his awareness of his abilities.

However, some criticise cognitive-behaviourism for being imprecise (Benson & Presbury 1989; Lee 1993); a criticism that is answered by the assertion that cognitive-behaviourism's imprecision means that its interventions can be more flexibly tailored to specific individuals (Dyck 1993; Dobson & Pusch 1993).

A second debate is whether the cognitive and linguistic demands of the cognitive-behavioural methods make them unsuitable for use with very young children. But with appropriate adjustments in language, even very young children can be taught to regulate their own behaviour. For instance, inductive discipline—which explains to children the direct consequences of their behaviour on others—will teach children as young as age two to consider the effect of their behaviour (Berk 1997). The fact that children do not completely master this by the time they begin school reflects the fact that learning to manage oneself takes all of childhood: it is not a fault of this theory, but is part and parcel of being a child.

Neo-Adlerian theory

A second theory that falls between the authoritarian and authoritative positions shown in Figure 2.1 is neo-Adlerian theory, so called because it represents modern writers' refinements of Alfred Adler's writings early in this century. Neo-Adlerian theory was originally popularised in the US by Don Dinkmeyer and his colleagues in the *Systematic training for effective parenting/teaching* packages (Dinkmeyer, McKay & Dinkmeyer 1980; Dinkmeyer & McKay 1989) and is advocated in Australia by Maurice Balson (1992, 1994) for school-aged children, and Jeannette Harrison (1996) in the early childhood age group.

Neo-Adlerian theory has two distinct parts: the prevention of behavioural disruptions, and methods for intervening when disruptions occur. Its preventive aspect focuses on creating warm relationships with children; listening to them; fostering cooperation and reducing competition between children; and encouraging rather than praising them. Of this list, most features have been borrowed from the democratic theories to be discussed in the next section, although the use of encouragement instead of praise is a unique contribution of this theory. (The distinctions between praise and encouragement are given in chapter 6, although I use the term *acknowledgment*.) Encouragement aims to overcome the disadvantages of praise that arise when children resist being manipulated into repeating behaviour of which the adult approves or when, conversely, they become compliant and submissive.

In contrast to its preventive component, the neo-Adlerian approach to intervention with difficult behaviour is largely under adult control. That is, the adult diagnoses children's motivation for their behaviour and subsequently chooses an intervention. Neo-Adlerians believe that all children are striving to belong and that when they cannot do so through prosocial behaviours, they resort to antisocial behaviour by seeking attention, power, revenge, or withdrawing from adult demands. Adults can diagnose which of these goals is motivating the child by noting their own feelings about the child's behaviour, how they normally discipline the child, and how the child responds to that discipline. Table 2.1 summarises these clues.

Having diagnosed the child's antisocial goal, the adult can then plan an intervention, which will differ for the various goals. The adult will ignore attention-seeking behaviour, or apply logical consequences

Table 2.1: Neo-Adlerian clues to the goals of inappropriate behaviour

If the adult feels	If the adult responds by	If the child's response to correction is	Then the child's goal is
annoyed	reminding, coaxing	to stop, but then repeat the behaviour	attention
angry	fighting or giving in	to confront or ignore authority	power
hurt	wanting to retaliate or get even	to become devious, violent or hostile	revenge
despairing or hopeless	agreeing with the child that nothing can be done	to refuse to participate or cooperate, is uninterested	withdrawal

(defined below) when ignoring is not possible. At the same time, the adult will give the child extra attention when she is behaving appropriately.

The adult should not fight with or resist the power-seeking child's need for power, but should give the child opportunities to exercise her power in constructive ways. Natural consequences (defined below) can be used when the child's power-seeking leads to inappropriate behaviour.

A child who is out for revenge needs acceptance, which is difficult when her behaviour is so hurtful. Nevertheless, the adult must build a trusting relationship and encourage the revenge-seeking child. Natural consequences can also be administered if necessary.

Last, if the child is trying to withdraw from demands, the adult can refuse to believe that the child is incapable and can try—through acceptance and encouragement—to show the child that she can be successful. The adult must refuse to give up on the child. Recognising the child's deep discouragement, the adult avoids all criticism, acknowledges all positive efforts, and refuses to pity the child since this would convey low expectations of her.

Instead of punishment used by ABA to reduce undesirable behaviour, neo-Adlerian theory employs natural or logical consequences. Natural consequences are those—as their title implies—that occur naturally, without adult manipulation. Logical consequences are arranged by the adult but unlike punishment, which can be arbitrary, logical consequences are related to the act. For instance, a natural consequence for a child who throws sand in the sandpit might be that she is asked to play somewhere else so that everyone can be safe; a logical consequence might be that she is banned from the sandpit for a specified time period; a punishment might be sending her to time-out to consider her actions.

Strengths and weaknesses of neo-Adlerian theory

Neo-Adlerian theory's strengths lie in its preventive aspects and its use of encouragement instead of praise. Although I prefer the term acknowledgment, I believe that replacing praise with encouragement or acknowledgment is a powerful and unique contribution to children's behaviour management.

However, I have two criticisms of its interventions. My first criticism is that the interventions are based on illogical assumptions that the child's behaviour *makes* the adult feel a certain way; and that how the adult feels is a reliable indicator of the child's motivation, when an adult can feel disturbed by a child's behaviour for reasons other than the actions themselves. The adult might be tired, or the particular behaviour might be the last of a series of disruptions, causing the adult to feel more irritated than if the behaviour were an isolated incident. A second criticism is that the neo-Adlerian interventions contradict the democratic flavour of the theory's preventive component because the interventions are determined by the adult. The children are likely to doubt that they are truly respected if, when they cannot behave appropriately, the adult steps in and imposes control on them.

The democratic theories: Humanism and control (choice) theory

The democratic writers include humanists Carl Rogers, a leader particularly in humanistic counselling for fifty years until his recent death; Thomas Gordon; Haim Ginott; Dan Gartrell, a writer in behaviour management in early childhood; and the person who first proclaimed choice theory, Bill Glasser. (In all his writings, Glasser has called his approach *control theory*, but he recently changed the title to *choice theory* in recognition that individuals' choices are central to how they behave.)

All these theories are categorised as democratic, although they are not founded on a belief that adults and children are the same. Children and adults have different roles and exercise different responsibilities, but they have equal rights to have their needs met. Under a democratic system the adult facilitates children's learning by acting as a leader rather than a boss (Glasser 1992). That is, the adult gains respect by being expert— by being authoritative—rather than by exercising power over children.

The democrats believe that most of children's difficult behaviour can be avoided by creating a child-centred program that meets children's needs. The adults guide and facilitate children's learning by creating the conditions in which children want to behave appropriately because they value the adults' warm regard, and because doing so meets their own learning needs plus the emotional needs for self-esteem, belonging, autonomy, and fun (Glasser 1986; Rogers & Freiberg 1994). (Note that this list of emotional needs is more comprehensive than the neo-Adlerians' single need to belong.) As can be seen from this description, early childhood care and education share many humanist principles.

To satisfy children's need for self-esteem, the democrats avoid praising children and instead teach them to evaluate their own actions. They also ensure that children are successful at learning skills that are relevant to them in the present or will be useful to them in the future. To satisfy children's need to belong, the adults create a warm relationship with each child; they ensure that the children can spend most of their time learning from each other; and they engage the children in cooperative activities and games. Children's need for autonomy is safeguarded by facilitating their self-control rather than imposing discipline on them. The last emotional need—for fun—is met indirectly by satisfying children's learning and emotional needs (Glasser 1986).

Before making a decision to intervene with disruptive behaviour, Thomas Gordon (1991) reminds us that we must understand children, so that we accept most of their behaviour as being normal for their stage of development. If we accept little of what they do, then our expectations are unrealistic. On the other hand, when a behaviour interferes with someone's rights, then that behaviour is unacceptable and it is crucial for everyone's happy adjustment that the adult intervenes to change it.

The person affected by disruptive behaviour might be the child himself, in which case the adult *listens* to the child and helps him find a way to meet his own needs without hurting himself or anyone else. Listening to a pre-verbal child may involve just observing what his behaviour is telling you. (Listening skills are described in chapter 5.)

At other times, a child's behaviour negatively affects other people. In this case, the adult must speak up, must state honestly and *assertively*— but not aggressively—what effect the behaviour has on other people. (Assertiveness is detailed in chapter 14.)

A third communication skill—*collaborative problem-solving*—is used when both the child and the adult are being affected by the child's behaviour (except if someone is in danger, in which case the adult takes charge unilaterally). Collaborative problem-solving involves both of the other skills—listening and assertiveness—for the adult to find out what the child needs, and to state the adult's own needs. Next, the adult and child together suggest some possible solutions that would meet their needs; choose one of these; enact it; and, later, check whether it worked. This process might result in a contract, or 'deal', with a child, but with the unique feature that the contract is reciprocal. A reciprocal contract not only specifies what standards the child must achieve, but also states how the adult will help the child to meet those expectations. The process might also result in the adult's demands being adjusted, instead of simply requiring the child to comply with what is being expected of him.

The democratic writers do not use praise, rewards, logical consequences or punishments. However, if a child breaks a reasonable agreement or cannot behave appropriately, then Glasser (1977) advises the adult to isolate the child until the adult and child can 'work it out' again. Unlike time-out, this 'time away' would be in pleasant surroundings where the child could occupy himself enjoyably, but he would not regain his freedom until he could find a way to behave appropriately.

Strengths and weaknesses of the democratic theories

By meeting children's developmental and emotional needs, the democratic-authoritative approaches aim to prevent most disruptive behaviour. The humanists argue that their theory's strength is that it does not provoke the child to rebel because his autonomy has been denied by an authoritarian adult. By refusing to punish or reward children, the humanists say they safeguard the adult–child relationship, increase a child's motivation to follow reasonable rules, and retain a child's self-responsibility. The rights of the miscreant, the victim of his behaviour, onlooking children and adults are all protected by a response that does not blame or shame anyone (Ginott 1972).

The strengths of this theory, however, are also its weaknesses. By rejecting all forms of punishment, the democrats have few interventions to use for disruptive behaviour. They do believe in natural consequences but, at very young ages, it can be unfair to let children suffer a natural consequence for their inadequate planning when poor planning is developmentally normal at their age. For example, when a child does not play in a friendly way, other children will dislike him. But instead of allowing him to become isolated as a natural consequence of his antisocial behaviour, it would be better to teach him how to behave prosocially.

Case application

To illustrate some of the differences between how each theory would be used in practice, let's apply them to a 2½ year old with normal language and other developmental skills who is biting other children.

Applied behaviour analysis would begin by observing how often the behaviour occurs, under what conditions, and with what result. This would show whether the behaviour was occurring often enough to be of concern. Considering it is causing injury, the behaviourist would intervene even with a low rate of biting, beginning by trying to change the conditions that appear to be giving rise to it. In examining the conditions, the behaviourist would focus on the events occurring immediately before the child bit another child, and would try to alter those specific circumstances. The behaviourist might, for instance, try to reduce crowding or give the children more toys so that there are fewer occasions for disputes to arise about sharing, if observation showed that these factors were giving rise to the biting. If the biting continued nevertheless, then the ABA practitioner would address the consequences of the behaviour— that is, in an attempt to alter the behaviour, the behaviourist would change the response it received. To do this, the behaviourist would either reinforce an alternative behaviour—such as asking for a disputed toy, instead of biting. The behaviourist would begin with the most natural reinforcer—namely, a social reinforcer—although a tangible reinforcer such as a stamp on the hand might be used if ongoing observation and recording showed that social reinforcers were not reducing the biting. If neither reinforcer caused an improvement in the biting, the behaviourist might put the child in time-out as a punishment. The effect of this would be monitored to ensure it was reducing the biting; if it was not, perhaps the behaviourist would remove the child's right to play alongside other children in the particular circumstances that appeared to lead to biting. This punishment is called a loss of privileges.

A cognitive-behaviourist would use the same first step as ABA, identifying possible environmental causes and trying to remove them, although the cognitive view of these would be broader than ABA's focus. The cognitivist would consider the child's emotional state, developmental status, and social context as well as the specific conditions existing just before a biting incident occurred. If changing the social conditions failed, the cognitivist might assume that the child lacked the appropriate social skill and would teach that, using reinforcement when the child exercised the new skill. If the child were older, the cognitive practitioner would encourage her to manage her own behaviour through self-monitoring, self-instruction and self-evaluation. But since the child is so young, only the last of these methods might be applied by highlighting when the child has been successful, so that she becomes more aware of her own successes. The cognitivist would also begin to give her guidance about other ways to solve a problem instead of biting another child.

The Neo-Adlerian theorist would reduce competition between the children, not only by ensuring they did not have to compete for equipment, but also that they did not have to compete for the approval of adults. Staff would encourage—rather than praise—all the children so that they all felt that they were valued and could be successful. If this did not eliminate the biting, the adult would examine how he or she feels and responds when the child bites. The adult might realise that he or she feels angry, and tries to stop the child from doing it again. It might be that the child simply ignores these attempts. These three clues tell the adult that the child is seeking power. With this knowledge, the adult would try to make the child feel powerful in other ways, maybe by letting her help to prepare the fruit or a meal. Following this, if the child bit again, the adult would apply the natural consequence of having the perpetrator nurse the victim's injuries.

Prior to intervening, the **democratic theorists** would ensure that the program was meeting the child's developmental and emotional needs so that the behaviour was not provoked by the child's social and physical surroundings. They would assume that the child's behaviour is communicating something about her emotional state. They would 'listen' to this message and, where possible, would change the program to suit her needs more closely. A key part of this would be ensuring that the child felt she belonged by establishing a warm and nurturing relationship between the caregivers and the child. For a short period one particular adult might be given sole responsibility for the care of the child, to ensure that the child had an emotionally secure base and that she learned to value the guidance of her caregiver. A second key aspect would be ensuring that the child felt physically comfortable and safe in the centre, and ensuring that her needs for self-esteem, freedom and fun were being met by the program. (Fun would be particularly important for the very young child.) If the child bit again, humanists would be aware that the child's needs are not being met, but also that the victim's needs are being violated, and so the adult must be assertive about that. Nevertheless, the adult might give an empathic assertive message such as, 'I know you're very cross, and it's all right to get cross. But it is not all right to bite someone, even when we are angry. What could you do instead?'. The adult would then guide the child to find better ways to manage her feelings. Or, if the child were capable verbally, the adult would guide her through the collaborative problem-solving steps of identifying how she feels and finding another way to vent her emotions. That is, the main humanist intervention method is communication: the adults would not punish the child for biting and neither would they reward alternative behaviours. Nevertheless, the humanist would apply the natural consequence of having the child nurse her victim's injuries.

Criteria for evaluating the theories

To guide your practice, you will need to evaluate these theories on some criteria. Your options include: blending attractive elements of each theory, choosing a theory with goals that match your own, examining the research evidence for the various approaches, or judging them according to ethical and other guidelines for early childhood care and education.

Eclecticism

When choosing a theory to guide your practice, it might be tempting to select elements of all the theories to arrive at an eclectic blend. To be eclectic means to select the best practices from various theories. This can occur in three ways (Young 1992). The highest form of eclecticism, *synthetic* eclecticism, is an attempt to synthesise or draw together compatible approaches, resulting in a more complex and comprehensive theory than any of the original theories alone. The second form, *technical* eclecticism, utilises one organising theory and borrows some approaches from other theories. The third form is *atheoretical* eclecticism, in which the practitioner lacks a theory base and so uses whatever methods 'seem like a good idea at the time'.

The theories of discipline which I have described in this chapter differ in their goals and in the resulting status of adults versus children. These differences make many of their practices incompatible with one another. This means that their practices cannot be blended into a coherent whole. Therefore, I recommend selecting only those methods which share the same philosophy or rationale and goals.

Goals of the theories

Rather than being eclectic then, you might choose a theory that shares your discipline goals. The various theories of behaviour management have different goals—one managerial and four educational goals. These goals are:

1 To create *order* so that the group can function effectively: so that adults can teach and children can learn. This is the managerial goal of discipline (Doyle 1986).
2 To teach children *self-discipline*: so that with support children learn to take responsibility for their actions, with the result that they can be trusted to make wise decisions about their behaviour, whether they are being supervised or not (Glasser 1986; W. Rogers 1991).
3 To teach children to *express their feelings appropriately*, without getting themselves distressed and without upsetting the other people around them (Gartrell 1994).
4 To teach children to *cooperate* with other people (Hill & Hill 1990; Johnson & Johnson 1991).
5 To teach children to have the confidence and *integrity* to make ethical choices and to exercise their social responsibilities as well as their rights (Gartrell 1994; Ginott 1972; Glasser 1986, 1992; Gordon, 1970, 1974, 1991; Greenberg 1992a, 1992b; Knight 1991; Porter 1996, 1997a; C. Rogers 1951, 1978; Rogers & Freiberg 1994). Although this is a long-term aim, it begins in early childhood when adults teach the moral principles behind children's decisions, and encourage children to empathise with other people.

Table 2.2 summarises the goals of each of the theories of behaviour management. It can be seen that the democratic theories have a more comprehensive range of goals than the authoritarian theories. This is clearly an advantage because discipline must do more than foster order alone, since order is necessary but not sufficient for learning to occur. Instead, discipline has to be educational as well. It must teach the same skills that are promoted by the wider curriculum—such as self-management, considerateness, problem-solving and communication

Table 2.2: Goals of each theory of discipline

Applied behaviour analysis	Compliance/order
Cognitive-behaviourism	Compliance/order Self-discipline Cooperation
Neo-Adlerian theory	Self-discipline Cooperation
Humanism/Control (choice) theory	Self-discipline Emotional expression Cooperation Integrity Order

skills—because children will not learn to take risks and explore their world if, when we manage their behaviour, we demand that they do as they are told and in the process cause them to feel badly about themselves and each other.

Research evidence

Another criterion that might inform your choice of a discipline theory is research evidence about the approaches. Recent research confirms earlier findings by Baumrind and colleagues (e.g. Baumrind 1967) that authoritative discipline produces children who are more self-controlled, self-confident, independent and social, both in preschool and in later years. It is more likely that children who are reared under an authoritative approach will accept demands that are fair and reasonable, rather than arbitrary, and so they will voluntarily observe fair standards that are expected of them. In contrast, authoritarian discipline that demands compliance produces withdrawn, anxious, unhappy children who become hostile when frustrated and are unwilling to persist at tasks (Berk 1997).

Ethics

When assessing which theory best fits within an early childhood program, the issue of justice or ethics is fundamental. In the previous chapter I concluded that behaviour management practices must comply with accreditation guidelines—both their spirit and their letter—and with the ethical principles of doing no harm, being just, preserving respect for children and promoting children's autonomy. I believe that the authoritative approach best satisfies these criteria.

Conclusion

This chapter has described how four theories would be applied to disruptive behaviour in early childhood settings. I have argued that the authoritative or democratic approaches offer more to staff and children in early childhood settings because they satisfy the quality and ethical guidelines introduced in chapter 1, they share the same educational goals that you promote in the wider care and education program, and they are known to produce happier, more responsible children. They teach appropriate behaviour while avoiding the risks of the authoritarian approaches.

Suggestions for further reading

For detailed descriptions of all the theories mentioned in this chapter, and some additional theories that apply to school-aged children, I recommend:

> Porter, L. (1996), *Student behaviour: Theory and practice for teachers*, Allen & Unwin, Sydney.

For further readings about the individual theories described in this chapter, my recommendations (in order of my preferences) follow.

Applied behaviour analysis

Alberto, P.A. & Troutman, A.C. (1995), *Applied behavior analysis for teachers*, 4th edn, Merrill, Columbus, Ohio.

Cognitive-behaviourism

Rogers, W.A. (1994), *Behaviour recovery*, ACER, Melbourne.
Wragg, J. (1989), *Talk sense to yourself*, ACER, Melbourne.

Neo-Adlerian theory

Harrison, J. (1996), *Understanding children: Towards responsive relationship*, 2nd edn, ACER, Melbourne.
Dinkmeyer, D., McKay, G. & Dinkmeyer, D. (1980), *Systematic training for effective teaching*, American Guidance Service, Minnesota.
Balson, M. (1992), *Understanding classroom behaviour*, 3rd edn, ACER, Melbourne.

Humanism

Gordon, T. (1991), *Teaching children self-discipline at home and at school*, Random House, Sydney.
Gartrell, D. (1994), *A guidance approach to discipline*, Delmar, Albany.
Gordon, T. (1974), *Teacher effectiveness training*, Peter H. Wyden, New York.
Rogers, C.R. & Freiberg, H. (1994), *Freedom to learn*, 3rd edn, Merrill, Columbus, Ohio.

Choice (control) theory

Glasser, W. (1993), *The quality school teacher*, Harper Perennial, New York.
Glasser, W. (1992), *The quality school*, 2nd edn, Harper and Row, New York.

3

· · · · · · · · · · ·

Teaching considerate behaviour

Everyone agrees about the *outcome* of discipline: we all want children to be well behaved. For a group to function effectively—that is, so that children can learn and you can teach and nurture the children—you need a certain amount of orderliness. But when this is *all* you want there are some risks. Not only is this outcome limited—it ignores the educational goals of discipline which I described in chapter 2—but the disciplinary methods you have to employ to bring about orderly or obedient behaviour carry their own risks to each child, to you, to your relationship with the children, and to the wider society.

Two types of discipline

In our society, we have a long tradition of adults being in control of children—so long, in fact, that we think that 'discipline' *means* 'control'. Most of us experienced this form of discipline when we were children. It is based on an idea that hardly anyone actually believes—which is, that children are naturally 'naughty'. The extension of this concept is that because children are naturally naughty, they need to be directed—virtually forced—to behave well. Even though few of us believe this idea, we *act as if we do*. We still praise or reward children when they behave well, as if we think that they won't behave well again unless we 'reinforce' their appropriate behaviour. Or we punish them when they behave in ways which we regard as inappropriate, as if we think they will behave badly again unless we come down hard on them now.

But no one truly believes that babies are naughty. That being so, then when do infants become naughty? And when do they stop? No one talks about naughty adults, and so at some age, children apparently 'grow out of it'.

So, maybe children actually aren't naughty. Maybe that is just a myth. If we reject this myth then we can reject the methods of discipline that were built on it. But—and it's a big but—we can only reject the controlling methods when we can replace them with something else.

The something else is called *guidance*. Unlike control, guidance aims to teach children all the skills I listed in chapter 2. That is, children are encouraged to become self-disciplined, express their feelings appropriately, cooperate with other people, develop integrity and empathy, and be orderly when being disorderly would interfere with other people in the group. Put together, these behaviours are considerate of others. Considerateness has two aspects: first, that children learn to think in advance about what effect their behaviour could have and, second, when told that their behaviour is harming someone else, they can consider this information and change what they are doing.

Therefore, the guidance approach to discipline aims to teach children to be considerate of the other people in their lives, rather than teaching children to do as they are told. Guidance helps children to make wise decisions about their own behaviour so that in the long run they can behave suitably whether or not an adult is there to supervise them.

Discipline skills to guide rather than control

The skills you would use to guide children can seem very similar to the controlling approaches, but the two methods are very different in their intent and flavour. Guiding discipline is built on respect for children as people, and aim to teach rather than control them. In this section, I describe a range of guidance skills, and I expand on them all in later sections of this book.

A developmental view of behaviour

The key to using guidance rather than control when disciplining is to realise that learning to behave is a developmental task like any other—although it is far more complex than any other skill a child will learn. Just as a child needs to learn how to walk, so too he needs to learn how to be considerate. And just as we wouldn't punish a toddler for falling over, so too we should not punish a child who makes a behavioural mistake. Mistakes are just an opportunity to teach a child more skilful behaviour.

Leadership

When you guide rather than control children you act as a *leader*, not a boss, of the group. This means you guide children to take charge of their own lives. Their decisions start out small—such as whether to choose a grape or a slice of apple from the plate of fruit—and become bigger as their problem-solving skills grow. With practice each child will come to know more about himself and his own needs than other people will know about them.

On the other hand, when you act as a leader you do not give up your responsibilities as an adult and a skilled professional. It is important that you lead the group of children, rather than having an 'anything goes' attitude. You will need to let the children know that they are expected to consider other people in the group and, while you will offer children some choice of how they learn, you will not be giving them the option of *whether* to learn. Because of your special expertise, you will make what I call 'executive decisions' for the children.

Honesty

When we have only negative and punitive ways of disciplining children, we put off using them. We delay using them because we're nice people, because we love children, and because our instincts—which are accurate—tell us that too much control will damage our relationship with the child. But delay means we are asking ourselves to tolerate the intolerable. We are having to be patient, when honesty would be more useful to the child and to everyone else. Because guiding methods are not negative, we can use them early, before the child's behaviour harms someone else and before our tolerance is pushed to its limits.

Flexibility

As adults we are often told to be consistent when we discipline. But in the real world things happen that get in the way of consistency, making it unwise or just impossible to stick to our usual discipline methods. At these times you are in a bind as a controlling adult because you cannot change your mind or 'give in' to a child—you believe that the child will have 'won' and you will have 'lost'. On the other hand, the 'leader' is concerned with getting everyone's needs met. When a child protests about your decision, you are willing to be flexible and to change your mind, as long as this will not interfere with your own rights.

Acknowledgment for considerate behaviour

In your training or when guided by more experienced colleagues, you were probably told to praise and reward children to encourage appropriate behaviour. But praise is secretly manipulative: it tries to make children do more of what we want them to do. Remember, the hidden belief is that children won't behave well naturally: they need to be forced to. But we don't reward our adult friends or tell them that they are good people when they help us out. All we do is thank them, so we can do the same for children. They are not good people when they please us and bad people when they displease us. It is not up to us to judge or label them, but we can say when we appreciate their considerate behaviour. This is a natural outcome (consequence) of their actions, not an attempt to bribe them into repeating the behaviour again. (In chapter 6, I discuss the differences between praise and acknowledgment.)

Natural consequences for considerate behaviour

Rewards are another of the controlling methods. Their aim is to bribe a child into repeating a desirable behaviour. Instead, you can let natural consequences take their course. When a child says, 'Thank you' for being given something, you don't have to tell him he's a 'good boy' for using his manners, but instead could say something like, 'You're welcome' or, 'It's a pleasure' or give him a warm hug. We all appreciate being thanked, and it's natural to show it.

Prevention of inconsiderate behaviour

Punishing children *after* they have harmed someone is like shutting the stable door after the horse has bolted. Instead, guidance methods allow you to have more influence over children because you can guide their behaviour *before* they get into unnecessary trouble, and before someone is hurt or inconvenienced. I list some ways to prevent disruptive behaviour in chapter 1.

Listening

Instead of telling a child what to do, when you act as a guide you will try to understand what his behaviour is telling you about what *he* needs. When his behaviour is telling you that he cannot cope, you can change what you expect of him, instead of forcing him to change how he is behaving. You can change your demands, not the child.

Assertiveness about inconsiderate behaviour

It is important for you to look after yourself. You have a right to have your needs met, and so you need to take responsibility for yourself, and for telling other people what you need. This is assertiveness. You can't expect other people to know what you need if you don't tell them.

Assertiveness means telling a child what effect his behaviour is having, without blaming or criticising him. The difference between assertiveness and aggression is that assertiveness tells the child about your needs—using the word 'I'—whereas aggression tells him about himself—using the word 'you'. Assertiveness is discussed in chapter 14.

It is easier to be assertive instead of aggressive if you can speak up early. But we often put off being assertive about inconsiderate behaviour—that is, we force ourselves to be too patient—because the only discipline methods that we know are punitive.

Conflict resolution

On hearing two people in conflict about their different needs, the boss is likely to leap into the middle of the confrontation and demand, 'Alright, who started it?'. The leader, though, looks for a solution, not a culprit. If two children are arguing the leader will guide them to solve the problem through collaboration and will avoid imposing his or her own solution. (This method is described in chapter 10.) As well as helping to sort out disputes among children, collaborative problem-solving can help find a solution to a conflict between you and a child or between colleagues.

Give choice

During the collaborative problem-solving process, or when you give an instruction, the leader does not tell a child what to do but instead offers him a choice. If you don't mind what the child decides, you can give him a choice of *whether* to do something; if you don't want to give him a choice about whether to do it, you can still ask *how* he would like to do it, or let him decide how he *feels* about it.

Natural consequences for inconsiderate behaviour

For centuries we have believed that punishment will force children to stop behaviour which we do not like. But even though punishment can appear to work at the time it has many negative effects—which are looked at in chapter 12. Also, punishment is arbitrary. For example, it makes no sense to a child that he is not allowed to go outside to play because he has not eaten his lunch. Instead of being arbitrary, natural consequences are directly related to the behaviour. If a child cannot be sociable, then he cannot have company. If he cannot share his toys, then his playmates will not want to play with him. This is life. (The exception is physical danger—you don't let a child run onto the road to teach him to take notice of you when you tell him not to.) More about natural consequences in chapter 15.

Teach new skills

Young children's disruptive behaviour usually comes about because they have not been alive long enough yet to learn more mature behaviour. Even if they know a more mature skill, their feelings can overwhelm them so that they are not able to use it. A controlling approach to discipline will punish them for not managing their feelings, which means that we punish them for being a child. Instead, the guidance approach will give them support to learn how to take charge of their feelings. Ways to do this are given in chapter 15.

Benefits of guidance instead of control

The guidance approach will teach children how to be considerate, rather than how to obey. This outcome is better for them, for us, and for the whole community. A guidance approach will also build a positive relationship between you and the children in your care, whereas a controlling approach is likely to harm that relationship.

Self-discipline

When you guide rather than control children they understand the reasons for considerate behaviour and so they develop a 'conscience', for want of a better word. They can be trusted to behave well, even when an adult is not there to control them; whereas, when bossed, children will behave well only when they are supervised and when they are afraid of being punished.

Increased independence

Guidance teaches children to be more independent about their behaviour, whereas with the controlling approach you can end up doing more and more work to control them. While this means that you are working harder and harder, it also means that the children will not feel good about themselves because they are not managing their own behaviour.

Promotes cooperation

When you guide children you demonstrate and teach the communication skills of listening to other people, being assertive, and solving problems collaboratively. They can then use these skills to cooperate with other people. Children who are controlled, on the other hand, often compete against, instead of cooperating with, each other.

Child safety

Guidance ensures that individual children are safe from abuse because they will not blindly do as they are told. Although their being headstrong can be inconvenient at times, they are not likely to be bullied or intimidated into taking part in behaviour which will hurt themselves or someone else.

Adults can safeguard their own rights

When you use controlling methods to discipline children your rights will be violated again and again because these methods are negative, and so you will put off using them. But while you delay taking action you are having to tolerate intolerable behaviour—you are being too patient. When you are assertive though, you can ensure that the children consider your needs as well as their own.

Prevents harm to others

You can deliver punishment only *after* someone has been harmed, which is too late. Instead, you can prevent someone being hurt or inconvenienced by giving children guidance *before* they get into trouble.

Guidance avoids teaching negative behaviours

When we use our power to make children conform we teach them to resist, rebel and retaliate (Gordon 1970). They learn how to be sneaky, how to outsmart us, and how to tell lies to get out of trouble. These are often the very behaviours which we are trying to discourage and which lead to more punishment.

Guidance, however, is fair and respects children. They have nothing to escape or withdraw from and no one to rebel against. They learn to

Table 3.1: Summary of discipline skills for controlling and for guidance

Discipline style	Control	Guidance
Aims	Obedience Compliance Order	Considerateness • Self-discipline • Handling feelings • Cooperation with others • Integrity • Order
View of disruptive behaviour	Naughty Inappropriate	Developmental Natural
Adult's status	Boss	Leader
Response to considerate behaviour	Praise Rewards	Acknowledgment Natural consequences
Response to inconsiderate behaviour	Intervention Change the child Aggressive Inappropriate patience Inflexible Identify a culprit Impose a solution Punishment	Prevention Change the demands Assertive Honest Responsive to circumstances Identify a solution Find a solution collaboratively Natural consequences Teach new skills

take responsibility for their own decisions, since they know that you will be reasonable with them if they make a mistake.

More influence over children

You will have more influence over children if you can lead rather than boss them. Children who are respected and treated considerately will learn to be considerate of other people and are more likely to respect you in return.

Benefits to society

Finally, society is safe from harm when individuals think of other people before they act and balance their own rights with the rights of other people. In contrast, people who are taught to do as they are told will hurt someone if they are ordered to, and then deny that they were responsible (Gordon 1991). History is full of people doing inhumane things because they were told to, so teaching individuals to do as they are told does not guarantee that they will behave acceptably.

Conclusion

Discipline will only ever safeguard individual children from abuse and protect society from the behavioural excesses of its members when individuals accept responsibility for themselves and can seek to satisfy their own needs without violating the needs of other people. In the early childhood years the goal of discipline, then, is to give children the confidence to take increasing responsibility for their own actions and for their effect on other people. To achieve this, you will need to guide rather than control children.

The guiding skills which I have introduced here—and which I enlarge on in coming chapters—can be very similar to their controlling counterparts. A natural positive consequence can seem virtually the same as a reward, but your intent is just to acknowledge children, not manipulate them into repeating a desirable behaviour. The difference has to do with flavour or style, with how you communicate your respect for children. Children can detect the difference between an attempt to guide or to control them. They can read your non-verbal behaviour, and will respond differently to the two methods, even though they can seem outwardly similar.

Because the methods are similar though, you do not have to learn a completely new set of skills, but can apply the skills you already have, merely with a change of purpose and 'flavour'.

Suggestions for further reading

If you would like to read more of the ideas which I cover in this chapter, then I recommend:

Gordon, T. (1991), *Teaching children self-discipline at home and at school*, Random House, Sydney.

Part two

• • • • • • • • • • •

Children's self-esteem

Young children begin at an early age to define what sort of person they are. In their early childhood years they become aware of their own physical appearance, physical abilities, intellectual abilities and interpersonal skills (Rodd 1996). Once they have an opinion about the sort of people they are, they behave like that sort of person. When they have a healthy self-esteem they are more likely to cooperate with other people and display considerate behaviour.

Individuals with a negative image of themselves cannot form healthy relationships because they think that they have nothing to offer and because they rely on other people so much that they stifle them. They cannot take risks and be creative because they are afraid of making mistakes. And they are not happy.

Part two defines what I mean by self-esteem and examines how you can foster a healthy self-esteem in the children in your centre, so that they learn to believe in themselves and feel secure in your care. My views are summarised eloquently by Lilian Katz (1995, p. 34):

> Self-esteem is most likely to be fostered when children are esteemed. Esteem is conveyed to them when significant adults and peers treat them respectfully, consult their views and preferences (even if they do not accede to them), and provide opportunities for real decisions and choices about events and things that matter to them.

I believe that we need to compensate for the extra pressures of children's modern life by increasing the amount of support we give them, so that they can continue to grow as people. It is harder now for children to grow up feeling confident about the many skills they are expected to master at such young ages (Curry & Johnson 1990).

Therefore, it is crucial for children's development and their social and emotional well-being that we show them how to have realistic and positive opinions of their abilities and their worth as individuals. The most important way to teach them to be considerate of us is for us to listen to them and their needs, and to refrain from judging them.

4

● ● ● ● ● ● ● ● ● ●

What is self-esteem?

> Self-esteem is not a trivial pursuit that can be built by pepping children up with empty praise, extra pats, and cheers of support. Such efforts are temporary at best, and deceptive at worst. Our children need coaches, not cheerleaders.
>
> Curry and Johnson (1990, p. 153)

There are two ways of looking at self-esteem. The first view is that our self-esteem acts as a filter through which we judge our performances. In this way it determines how we approach future tasks. A second way of looking at self-esteem is that it is a *result* of achievement of relevant and worthwhile activities. My conception is that it is both. Self-esteem is both an *effect* (of past experience) and a *cause* (of future learning).

This means then, that improving children's self-esteem will both help them to learn more and to feel good about themselves. It also means that children's self-esteem will be improved only when their achievements are worthwhile. Success—at something meaningful—breeds confidence.

Building a picture of self esteem

Children's self-esteem is largely set in place in their very early years. They learn about themselves from their parents' and other people's reactions to them. Then they build this information into a picture of the type of people they are. As time goes on, their earlier experiences then act as a filter which distorts the information they receive from other people (Adler, Rosenfeld & Towne 1995).

In their first two years or so, when young children are learning to trust their caregivers, their self-esteem relies almost entirely on whether they feel loved and *accepted*. After that age their self-esteem begins to be fed by how much *control* they can exercise over their lives: hence their

43

determined cries of, 'I do it by myself'. They use your reactions to their attempts at independence to feel pleased—that is, *morally virtuous*—or guilty about their efforts, and they begin to define themselves as *competent* or as failures (Curry & Johnson 1990).

So self-esteem is learned. Your reactions to children tell them about the type of people they are and also the type of people you want them to be. Then children judge how much they measure up to this ideal.

Self-esteem has three parts (Burns 1982; Pope, McHale & Craighead 1988): the self-concept, the ideal self, and self-esteem itself.

The self-concept

This is our picture or description of ourselves. (This aspect is also termed self-perception.) It comprises more elements as children grow older and learn more about themselves (Sekowski 1995; van Boxtel & Mönks 1992). Young children's self-concept describes how they look, what they wear, their state of health and their possessions. As they get older, they begin to describe themselves in terms of their relationships, abilities and talents at sport and academic work, temperament, religious ideas, and ability to manage their lives (Burns 1982). Their ancestors, family and cultural membership will also be part of children's self-concept.

Global self-concept is an amalgam of five facets: social, emotional, academic, family, and physical self-concept (Pope et al. 1988; van Boxtel & Mönks 1992). Each of these aspects is further divided into subfacets which are lower in the hierarchy and become less stable over time and more situation-specific (van Boxtel & Mönks 1992). I would equate these to 'self-confidence', which is very skill- and situation-specific.

The ideal self

This is our belief about how we 'should' be. This set of beliefs comes about from actual or implied critical judgments by significant people in our lives, or by a process called social comparison, in which we compare ourselves to other people and evaluate ourselves accordingly (Adler et al. 1995). It is clearly important to choose realistic models with whom to compare ourselves, lest we generate an unduly lax or harsh set of ideals. These ideals can be explicit—such as wanting only distinctions in one's study—or implicit, with standards that the individual hardly knows she or he is imposing and which therefore can be more difficult to identify and challenge (Pope et al. 1988).

Self-esteem

Not all the characteristics that we possess are equally important to us. Feedback from others allows us to rank our characteristics according to how important or valued they are to other people and we usually internalise those value systems. The self-esteem, then, reflects how much we value our characteristics: it is a judgment about whether our abilities and qualities meet or fall short of the standards we believe are ideal. For example, my swimming skills make me look like a frog in a blender when I'm in the water, but I come from a family that didn't mind if I swam

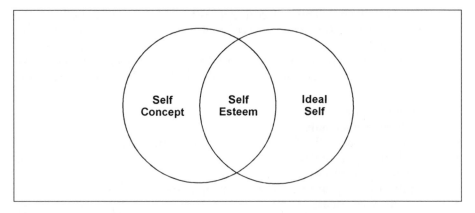

Figure 4.1: Self-esteem as the congruence between the self-concept and the ideal self

poorly and so my skills do not affect my overall self-esteem; if, however, I had come from a family of Olympic swimmers, then being able to swim well would have been central to my self-esteem.

Our self-esteem—the comparison of our performance with our ideals—has both an intellectual and an emotional component (Pope et al. 1988). That is to say, how we *think* about our achievements affects how we *feel* about them. If our thinking highlights our deficiencies and ignores our achievements, then our emotional reactions to our supposed deficiencies are likely to be unrealistic or 'over the top'.

Conclusion: The nature of self-esteem

It is clear that self-esteem is multi-dimensional. The self-concept contains many descriptors of ourselves, while the ideal self ranks these traits according to how highly we value each one. Our self-esteem is a measure of the extent to which our self-concept and ideal self overlap—see Figure 4.1.

An unhealthy or low self-esteem can come about in either of two ways. First, our beliefs about the type of person we are—that is, our self-concept—might not be accurate because we do not notice enough of our positive attributes. Second, our expectations of ourselves—our ideals—could be too high and, as a result, we believe that we have few of the characteristics we think we 'should' have.

Characteristics of children who have healthy self-esteem

A healthy self-esteem is one which 'realistically encompasses shortcomings but is not harshly critical of them' (Pope et al. 1988, p. 2). A person with a healthy self-esteem has a relatively balanced perception of her positive qualities and more realistic expectations of herself. As a result, she has a high degree of overlap between how she thinks she is and how she wants to be. (The self-concept and ideal self will never overlap entirely of course, otherwise individuals would have no ambitions or goals for which to strive.)

The following list describes the characteristics of individuals who have a healthy self-esteem (Adler et al. 1995; Clark 1997; Curry & Johnson 1990). They can:

- lead others spontaneously;
- make transitions easily;
- approach new and challenging tasks with confidence;
- set goals independently;
- have a strong internal locus of control;
- assert their own point of view when opposed;
- trust their own ideas;
- initiate activities confidently;
- cope with criticism and teasing;
- tolerate frustration caused by mistakes;
- describe themselves positively;
- make friends easily;
- accept the opinions of other people;
- cooperate and follow rules, remaining largely in control of their own behaviour;
- show pride in their work and accomplishments;
- make good eye contact (although this can vary across cultures).

Signs of low self-esteem in children

In contrast with this list, children who have low self-esteem can display a wide range of less adaptive behaviours. The signs of low self-esteem are different at different ages, and no single behaviour necessarily means that a child does not like himself. However, if a child in your centre is showing many of the following signs, then it might help if you can take some steps to improve his self-esteem.

Lacking an independent self-evaluation

If a child does not have a good opinion of himself—and if as well he believes that he has to earn adults' approval—then he might be overly helpful, or might constantly ask for your praise or for declarations that you love him. But the more you reassure him, the more reassurance he needs. His need for reassurance also shows when he gets hysterical if you tell him off. He over-reacts because it is too important that you approve of him, since he does not approve of himself.

The child who hasn't noticed his own qualities will not be able to list any positive things about himself, and might frequently say negative things about himself or his abilities, such as, 'I'm hopeless' or, 'I can't'.

Abused children believe they are unlovable and they frequently display self-destructive, risky, or self-mutilating behaviours, including suicide or having suicidal fantasies, even in their preschool years.

Social difficulties

A child with low self-esteem might not be able to have any fun, might be withdrawn, and might not be able to enter a group without becoming either too self-conscious ('shy') or too boisterous. Finding and keeping friends can be a problem, and negotiating conflict can be difficult because he does not have enough confidence to stick up for himself. He might be bullied on the one hand, or easily led on the other.

When a child expects too much of himself, he is often hard on other people as well. He might tell tales on his friends because he cannot break rules himself and believes no one else should. Potential friends can be put off by his competitiveness and their rejection feeds his low self-esteem.

A child with low self-esteem might rely so much on adults that he cannot separate from his parents at an appropriate age and so does not develop independent play and self-care skills at the usual age. He can also have strange fears—see chapter 17.

Approach to learning

A child who has doubts about his abilities will avoid trying something new, will refuse to take risks or be adventurous, or might give up easily. Instead, he might play the same game over and over—such as playing only in the sandpit—because he is afraid that he would fail at everything else. Or, he might not work without instructions in case he makes a mistake. He can get very frustrated with his mistakes and might prefer to avoid doing something than do it wrongly. He will lack initiative and will be uncertain about making decisions.

How children develop low self-esteem

By watching how you react to them, children learn what you expect of them, and they judge whether they generally meet your expectations. As well as receiving your feedback, they also watch how you feel about yourself and in doing so they learn from you how to react to their mistakes.

Imitation

Children copy how adults handle their achievements and failures. Every perfectionist child I have ever met has at least one parent who is a perfectionist, and who has shown the child how to demand perfect performances of herself. As an early childhood professional there is a lot you can do to undo perfectionist messages that a child has inadvertently received from home. Acknowledgment (see chapter 6) is the most important; other ways to improve children's self-esteem—as discussed in chapter 8—are especially valuable for the perfectionist child. Above all, you need to forgive yourself your own mistakes because children are not convinced by what you say about their mistakes: they copy what you do about your own.

Negative labels

We often talk about children in ways that put them down, even when we don't mean to. These negative labels can become self-fulfilling. Tasmanian family therapist and author, Steve Biddulph (1993), says they are like seeds in a child's mind, which grow into a negative self-concept.

An important group of negative labels are put-downs that we use when disciplining children. Instead of giving a simple command, we might put children down with a comment such as: 'Give that back. Don't be selfish'. Pet names that are put-downs, or using sarcasm to put children 'in their place', also convey to children that they are a disappointment to us or are incompetent. We might talk about their shortcomings in front of them, or we might praise them for overly mature behaviour that they can't possibly sustain.

Last, using emotional blackmail to get children to behave will lower their self-esteem. The first form of this is using guilt to control children: 'How could you behave like this, after all the fun we've been having?'.

These many negative messages are reinforced by ridicule if the child challenges the opinion of her that our statement implies: 'You can't take a joke, can you?', 'Don't be silly. I didn't mean it.', 'Grow up, don't be a baby'. In fact, children *never* have a sense of humour about being put down, because it isn't funny.

Comparison and competition

Children will develop low self-esteem if we compare them to someone who is more capable than them. This will teach them to apply unrealistic standards to themselves. Having standards and ideals is fine, as long as they are realistic, and help us to be happy. But when they make us a slave to standards that are not relevant to us we will lose confidence in ourselves.

Creating dependence

Children will develop low self-esteem when we repeatedly solve their problems for them. This tells them that we believe they do not know how to solve problems for themselves. Likewise, protecting children from making mistakes can make them dependent on us and unwilling to take risks.

Conclusion

A healthy self-esteem will arise when children have a realistic picture of their capabilities as well as reasonable ideals or self-expectations. This understanding has set the foundation for our discussion of how to enhance children's self-esteem. The first skill is to listen to children and accept their experiences. This is described in the next chapter. The next most crucial approach is to stop praising children for meeting our standards, and instead acknowledge or celebrate with them when they have achieved their own goals. This is called acknowledgment and is discussed in contrast with praise in chapter 6. Some specific approaches for boosting children's self-esteem are then discussed in chapter 7.

Suggestions for further reading

If you would like to read more about self-esteem in young children, I recommend:

Biddulph, S. (1993), *The secret of happy children*, rev. edn, Bay Books, Sydney.

5

• • • • • • • • • • • •

Listening to children

> Many of us find it difficult to handle other people's strong
> emotions. We've been taught to conceal our own anger, fear,
> and hurt, and we're uneasy when we see such emotions
> expressed. Even outbursts of joy can be unsettling to us when
> the time isn't 'right'.
>
> Dinkmeyer et al. (1980, p. 72)

While it is probably true that all of us could be better at listening, I have observed that early childhood professionals are actually very skilled at listening to children. We can recognise a baby's cry of pain, and distinguish it from a hungry cry or a lonely cry or a frightened cry. We understand that a young child is upset, even if we don't understand why. We can hug and soothe children even when we as adults would not feel what they are feeling. When toddlers tell us something, we often repeat back what they have said, either to show them how to pronounce their words or to check that we have understood what they are saying. This is the very same skill which you can use for older children when you want to reflect their feelings or what they are telling you.

When you listen to children and can accept their experience of the world, they will know that you accept them for who they are. They will develop a healthy self-esteem and will learn how to handle their feelings, listen to other people, and solve their own problems.

Listening skills

Listening involves giving children attention, being willing to listen rather than trying to impose your own ideas on them, noticing their feelings as well as their words, and actively reflecting what they are saying. To do all this well, you will need to abandon the idea that adults are responsible for a child's feelings. You don't have to give in to a child 'to keep her happy' since no one is responsible for another person's feelings. You also need to want to help by listening, rather than trying a 'quick-fix' solution of your own.

Attention

You have a lot to do, and often you find yourself doing two (or more) things at once. However, when you want to tell a child that you are interested in what she is saying, then you will need to stop and make genuine contact with her, giving her real attention. You need to be willing to focus on the child alone, engaging in what Stonehouse (1988) calls 'child time' rather than an adult's busy version of time.

Listening to babies and infants who aren't talking yet involves mainly paying attention to the cues they give out—where they are looking, how they are looking, their gestures and sounds—to establish what they need. It is vitally important that you respond to their cues, so that they develop trust that you will look after them and so they can begin to control their interactions.

Invitation to talk

An invitation to talk involves five skills:

- *Listening with your eyes.* You can notice when a child is sending non-verbal signals that something is wrong. Most of our communication is sent non-verbally when we're emotional, so noting a child's body language can invite her to talk about it. In this way you don't have to wait until the child approaches you: you can give a description of her body language, such as: 'What's up?', 'You look a bit sad', 'You look excited'.
- *Invitation to talk.* You can simply ask, 'Do you want to tell me about it?'
- *Attentive silence.* The adult gives the child time to decide whether she wants to talk, and how to say it. Robert Benchley (in Bolton, 1987, p. 48) says:
  Drawing on my fine command of language, I said nothing.
  While a preverbal child will not be able to talk about her feelings, you can offer her a cuddle and some time to sort out her feelings.
- *Giving minimal encouragers.* The listener says very little (maybe only 'mm hmm', 'oh', or 'really?') or repeats back the last few words the child said, to encourage her to continue talking.
- *Asking infrequent questions.* Questions help the child to clarify her feelings, but it pays to ask very few questions so that you follow rather than direct the child's conversation and don't make the child feel she is being subjected to an inquisition.

Listen for feelings

It can be difficult for adults to handle children's strong feelings, even the positive ones like joy or excitement. It can be especially difficult to accept when a child is angry at us. Some people just don't let children express anger at adults, but if you don't want to use a controlling approach, instead it can help to remember that anger is only ever the second thing that we feel: it follows fear or hurt. This means that instead of getting upset about a child being angry with you, you can notice the feeling that caused it: 'I can see that you're hurt that I wouldn't help you when you wanted me to'.

Identifying young children's feelings can be difficult because they don't have very many words to describe how they feel. So you will have to teach infants words to describe their feelings.

Reflection

Now that you have listened to a child's feelings, it can be helpful to reflect these back to her. For example, you could say to an angry child, 'Sounds like that hurt your feelings'. You can reflect the content, the feeling, or the meaning behind what the child is telling you. You can do this by paraphrasing or summarising what she is saying. Bolton (1987, p. 51) describes paraphrasing as:

- a *concise* response
- stating the *essence*
- of the *content*
- in the listener's *own words*.

Listening

When a child has hurt herself, she cries to communicate her pain. Because adults feel distressed to see a child in pain, they often scold her: 'I told you to be careful'. This ignores the fact that accidents can happen even when we are careful, and criticises rather than comforts the hurt child.

Or, we tell children that they aren't allowed to show hurt: 'Ssh, don't cry'. This can prolong the tears until the child gets you to offer the comfort she needs, or until she gives up, learning that you won't help her.

Instead, you can:

- Acknowledge that it hurts: say so.
- Tell her it will hurt for a while. Because she knows this, she will believe the next thing you say.
- Point out how strong and healthy she is, or how she has 'good, red blood' and that she will heal quickly and the pain will go.

If you can accept her experience and her right to express what she feels, then she will feel safe, will know that she can trust you to be there for her and, with your support, she will have learned that in future she can recover from pain.

At first, reflecting back what someone is saying can seem very false—silly, almost. It sounds as if you will be saying the obvious. Or you might worry about getting it wrong. But children won't mind that—let's face it, they're often misunderstood—and they will probably be more patient with trying to make you understand than you are. And as to saying the obvious, well, reflection can teach children new words for their feelings and you can both become clearer about what they are saying. Try it: it works.

Roadblocks to communication

Instead of genuine listening, we can easily fall into the trap of saying things that discourage other people from talking to us. Gordon (1970) described twelve common conversation habits that we think are genuine listening but which instead stop the conversation. He called these habits 'roadblocks to communication'. The following list of roadblocks includes examples of responses to a child's statement that he doesn't want to have a nap today:

Judging

It is important that you accept children's feelings, even when they are different from yours. This means not judging a child for feeling something ('Don't be silly; it's not that bad'). The judging roadblocks include:

- *criticising or blaming*: 'You never want to do anything. You should know that you need to have a rest'. The child will see this as unfair, will retort with something negative about you, or will believe what you say about him, which will lower his self-esteem.
- *praising*, in a effort to talk the child out of his feelings: 'You're such a good boy, I know you will do what's right and have a nap.' (In the next chapter I describe some of the many negative effects of praising.)
- *name-calling*, which is very similar to, and has the same effects as, criticising and blaming a child.
- *diagnosing or interpreting* what the child is feeling, which is an attempt to tell the child what his 'real' problem is: 'At your age, you don't know when you're getting tired and need a sleep. I think you're tired enough to need a rest'.

Sending solutions

Sometimes, instead of listening, we are quick to tell a child what we think he should do about his problem. Giving our own solutions can take five forms:

- *Directing* the child to stop what he is feeling: 'I don't care what you want: you're going to have a rest.' This tells the child that his needs aren't important: he must do what you want, not what he wants.
- *Threatening* imposes your solution on the child: 'If you don't get ready to sleep *right now* then I'll sit you on the time-out chair until you have

thought about it'. Threats make a child fearful, resentful, and liable to test you to see if you'll carry out the threat.

- *Preaching* explains to the child why he should feel differently: 'You should have a nap or you will be too tired to play this afternoon'. Preaching is patronising because it treats the child as if he didn't know this already.
- *Interrogating* asks a series of questions to get to the bottom of the problem: 'Don't you feel tired? Is it too noisy in the sleeping room with the other children?' Probing suggests that you are about to find a solution for the child instead of trusting him to find his own.
- *Advising* is an attempt to impose a positive solution: 'Perhaps you can bring your teddy in from home tomorrow, and that will help you to get to sleep'. Although the solution is meant to be positive, it still tells the child to get over his feelings before he is ready to.

Giving advice is probably the most common of the roadblocks because adults want to help children to feel better. But giving advice has many disadvantages. It tells the child that you won't listen to him because you did not wait to hear about his real concerns: if the answer were that obvious, he would have thought of it already. Giving advice tells him that you do not think he is able to find his own solution and it does not give him any practice at solving his own problems. And at the same time, giving advice makes it less likely that he will do what you suggest because it wasn't his idea. As a result you will have to stand over him to make him do as you say and he will feel resentful. All this makes your job harder than it needs to be.

Avoiding the other person's feelings

A third group of roadblocks tries to take the heat out of the child's feelings, usually because they upset us. This class of roadblocks includes:

- *distracting* the child from his problem, without letting him resolve his feelings first: 'Why don't you have a little nap now and then we can do something exciting after you wake up?'. If you ignore children's feelings they will learn that they can't come to you for comfort, which will leave them without supports at too young an age.
- *logical argument*, which sends the message: Don't feel: Think: 'You know you need to have a rest each day. Now climb under your blanket'.
- *reassuring*, which tries to change how the child is feeling and tells him that he isn't allowed to feel badly because it upsets you: 'Don't get upset about having a nap. You'll feel a lot better when you wake up'. Reassurance ignores the depth of the child's feelings, telling him you don't understand him.

The thirteenth roadblock

Robert Bolton (1987), who wrote a handy book on communication skills, adds a thirteenth communication roadblock to Gordon's 'dirty dozen'.

He says that accusing other people (blaming them) or feeling guilty ourselves for using the communication roadblocks, is itself a communication stopper.

If you've had an attack of the guilts while reading this chapter, take heart. It's never too late to bone up on your listening skills. One way to start is to notice the roadblock that you use most, and work on stopping that. Then work on your others in turn. And remember to be kind to yourself and to notice when you've genuinely listened at a time when in the past you would have used a roadblock.

Another useful exercise is to take a blank sheet of paper and divide it vertically down the middle. On the left-hand side, write down the reasons you want to make a change in your life that you've been thinking about for a while, but haven't been able to begin. It could be that you want to exercise more, eat less of particular foods, or change jobs—whatever. As you write, be aware of what you've been saying to yourself about yourself and about not managing to make a start. Write these comments down on the right-hand side of your sheet of paper. My bet is that you'll find that you use Gordon's roadblocks on yourself, and that they are causing you to be so critical of yourself that they paralyse you and keep you from getting started on your new goal. Now that you are aware of this, you can practise more genuine listening—both to your own needs and to other people.

Non-verbal messages

Listening tells children that you accept them. Your own non-verbal behaviours can let them know this too, when you maintain good eye contact while they are talking with you, use a courteous tone of voice with even the youngest of children, and make sure that you chat about things that interest them, instead of talking only when you want to give an instruction.

A final non-verbal message that tells children that you accept them is when you don't interfere with what they are doing. Letting them do it their way tells them that you believe in their abilities. Children will learn more when they discover information for themselves than when you teach it to them. This means that you have to become comfortable with children making mistakes, and with not being needed.

Conclusion

Taking the time to listen to children and accepting what they feel—even when you don't understand why—tells them that you accept them for who they are. This can involve listening both to what they say and how they say it. It can also mean watching their behaviour for signs that they aren't coping with your demands. When you listen to children, they learn how to listen to other people, and so listening is a basic building block for teaching children how to be considerate.

Suggestion for further reading

If you would like more information on communication skills, my favourite handbook is:

Bolton, R. (1987), *People skills*, Simon and Schuster, Sydney.

6

· · · · · · · · · · ·

Acknowledgment

If you want children to develop a healthy self-esteem, stop praising them.

I believe that the single most powerful way that you can help children develop a healthy self-esteem is to acknowledge and celebrate their successes, without praising these. To justify the idea of stopping praise, in this chapter I will describe why I believe praise is risky, and how praise differs from acknowledgment.

The costs of praise

Although we probably don't intend it, praise is an attempt to manipulate children into repeating a behaviour that we like. Because we decide what standards to enforce, and are in charge of giving or withholding praise, we are the boss. This makes praise a power-based or controlling discipline approach. Although clearly praise does less harm than punishments, it still has many disadvantages, mostly for the child's self-esteem.

Effect of praise on children's self-esteem

Praise tells children that we approve of them when they meet our standards. It doesn't take much for them to realise, therefore, that they are 'bad' people when they disappoint us. They know we don't accept them, and so they don't accept themselves.

Praise fills children's ideal self with adult standards that they can't possibly live up to. They can become very anxious about not being able to live up to our expectations. Even a positive label (such as, 'You're a good girl') can set up an unrealistic expectation that the child should be good all the time.

57

Another important effect of praise is that it teaches children that other people's opinions of them are more important than their own judgment. They do not learn to notice and appreciate themselves and their achievements, and so they do not feed their self-esteem with realistic impressions of their own abilities.

Of course, you can still tell a child she's terrific, although not for doing something that pleases you, but simply because she is. The reason you tell her that she's terrific is to let her know you like her. Praise, on the other hand, tries to make her be a particular kind of person.

Interference with learning

When children are more interested in your opinion of their efforts than their own, they try to 'read' you for signs that you approve. This 'adult watching' can take valuable energy away from what they are doing, and because they focus only on the rewards they get at the end, they lose sight of the joy of doing the task.

Praise doesn't tell a child specifically enough about her achievements. If, say, you tell her that her painting is 'beautiful', how does she know how to do another 'beautiful' painting? She'll probably repeat something very similar, and so she will avoid being creative or adventurous. At the same time, she might avoid other, difficult or unknown tasks in case she fails at them. This can limit her learning.

Ineffectiveness of praise

Because we are busy, we often praise children in an automatic, meaningless way. We might tell a child that her painting is beautiful, but in the same breath tell her to hang it up to dry. And our pat phrases and contradictory non-verbal messages often rob our praise of its credibility (Hitz & Driscoll, 1988). For example, we might tell a child that her drawing is a beautiful house, when she actually drew a rocket, or we might praise an excellent effort when the child knows she did a half-hearted job: in either case, she will learn to ignore our praise because she does not believe it.

Praise is unfair

We need to be very expert to use praise well, because we have to know when and how much praise the child deserves. Some children become very good at 'pulling' praise from adults by beaming proudly and showing off their work, and so we might praise this sort of child a lot. But other children who don't come to us for our comments receive less praise than they deserve.

Finally, praise increases competition between children, who can become resentful or jealous if another child receives praise and they don't. As well as resenting each other, they can also resent us for trying to manipulate them.

Acknowledgment

For all of these reasons, it is less risky if we stop praising children and instead show them how to acknowledge their own successes. Admittedly, this assertion has little research evidence (see Slaby et al. 1995). That is why I say 'less risky' rather than making stronger claims about the superiority of acknowledgment over praise.

Acknowledgment is different from praise in the following ways:

1 Acknowledgment teaches a child to *evaluate his own efforts*: 'What do you think of *that*?', 'Was that fun?', 'Are you pleased with yourself?', 'You seem pleased that you did that so well'. In comparison, praise approves of work that meets *adult* standards.
2 Unlike praise, acknowledgment *does not judge* the child or his work, although we still might choose to tell him what we think or feel about the work. For example, 'I like the colours you used', replaces the statement that a painting is 'beautiful'.
3 Acknowledgment focuses on the *process* rather than the outcome. You can comment on his effort, rather than on the end product: 'Looks like you're having fun over there', or when a child has written his name well on his work: 'I see you're enjoying writing your name'.
4 Acknowledgment is a *private* event which does not show children up in public or compare children with each other. Unlike praise, acknowledgment does not try to manipulate other children into copying a child who has been praised. Acknowledgment simply describes—in private—what you appreciated: 'Thanks for being quiet while I found a book to read you', or, 'I appreciate that you put your toys away'. The private nature of acknowledgment helps children to appreciate that they are special, but not *more* special than anyone else. In this way it helps children to cooperate with rather than compete against each other.

The examples in Table 6.1 illustrate the distinction between praise and acknowledgment.

Lilian Katz (1995) reminds us that we do not want children to become preoccupied with themselves and with how other people see them. That is narcissism, not self-esteem. We want children to develop a deep and meaningful sense of self-confidence and self-worth. Acknowledgment aims to achieve this by helping children to become aware of their very real achievements, rather than giving them empty flattery. Real achievements are those which help children to understand things which are worthy of their attention, says Katz.

Conclusion

Young babies get very excited when they walk for the first time, which shows that they already know how to notice when they are successful. At the other end of the age range we adults need to evaluate our own efforts, because none of us would want to be holding our breath waiting

Table 6.1: Examples of praise and acknowledgment

Praise	*Acknowledgment*
You're a good helper.	Thanks for your help. I appreciate your help. Thanks: that's made my job easier.
I'm proud of you for writing your name so well.	Congratulations. I'm proud for you. Looks like you're enjoying writing. What do you think of that?
You're a good girl.	I love/like you. You're terrific! Thanks for your help.
That's a beautiful painting.	I like the colours you've used. Do you like your painting? Are you pleased with yourself? Looks like that was fun.
Your drawing is excellent.	I like your drawing very much.

for someone else to tell us we're wonderful. But in between we train children out of noticing when they do well.

Self-esteem is literally that: *self*-evaluation. Children might doubt other people's opinions of them, but they will believe their own. Therefore, we need to teach children how to assess their own actions, and how to set realistic standards for themselves. Being able to do this will directly help their self-esteem both as children and as adults. When they make a mistake, they do not have to become discouraged because they notice their achievements as well as their failures, and this awareness will give them a balanced view of their abilities.

As well as these benefits to their self-esteem, children who can monitor their successes have learned how to be aware of their behaviour and so can notice when their actions might hurt someone else. This is the basis of learning how to behave considerately.

7

• • • • • • • • • • •

More ways to improve children's self-esteem

So far in this section of the book I have said that listening to children tells them that they matter to you. Next, acknowledging considerate behaviour and celebrating their successes will teach children to notice their own achievements. Both will enhance their self-esteem. This chapter gives some additional ideas which can help children to view themselves constructively, have realistic standards for themselves, develop competence in skills which they value, and respond to negative feedback about themselves in a way that helps them to develop new skills.

Promote a constructive self-concept

Some children's perception—or view—of themselves can be dysfunctional and unduly negative. These youngsters are probably the ones we are referring to when we talk about children who have low self-esteem. Following are some suggestions for helping these children.

Accept yourself

Children will watch how you react to your own successes and mistakes. If you accept yourself—even your own imperfections—then children will learn from you how to be gentle with their failures too. If you acknowledge your successes, they will learn that it's okay to notice their own. So, instead of only ever saying negative things about yourself, try saying some positive things, like: 'I've been really organised today' or, 'I'm a star!' or, 'One thing I like about me is . . .' or, 'I'm really good at . . .'. When you do this, the children will copy your positive attitude to self.

Accept children

Their behaviour. When children make a mistake, you can accept the person without having to accept his behaviour (Rodd 1996). I believe that this notion can be too complex to explain to young children directly, but you can convey the attitude powerfully enough in the way you respond to mistakes.

Their feelings. It is crucial that you accept children's feelings, even when they are different from how you would feel. Fields and Boesser (1997) make the point that some adults believe that 'little people have little feelings' which is clearly not so. Children's feelings are as meaningful to them as ours are to us, and it is important that you accept what they are feeling, even if you don't understand why they feel that way. (See chapter 5 for more discussion on how to listen to feelings.)

Their backgrounds. Another part of accepting children is acknowledging their cultural backgrounds. You will need to do more than give children information about the exotic customs and dress of other cultures; you will need to demonstrate acceptance of children's diverse backgrounds in your day-to-day interactions with all the children. By accepting diversity of all kinds, you make it possible for the children to accept each other.

Create a supportive environment

Adults can choose to take part in activities and to associate with people who bolster our self-esteem, but children are at the mercy of the contexts in which we place them (Katz 1995). This means that they rely on you to create an accepting environment in which they can feel emotionally safe and confident about their ability to meet the demands being placed on them.

Talk with children respectfully

To let children know that you value and respect them, you will need to talk with them courteously, regardless of their age or ability levels. It is also important to talk with children about things which interest them and to gain information that you don't already know, rather than just giving instructions or asking instructional questions such as, 'What colour is that?'. With very young infants, there is no need to use baby talk or an upward intonation at the end of your statements, but instead use your normal tone of voice, while perhaps speaking more slowly and with simpler words.

Respond to babies

Babies and infants love playing reciprocal games: they bang their hand on the table, and so you do it too. They make gurgling sounds and you copy. With this sort of play, they get practice at taking turns, which is the basis of making conversation. They also know that you are responding to them and so reciprocal games let them know that you value them.

Toys cannot replace social interaction, but when it is time for some quiet object play, make sure that young children have something to do, rather than being passive observers of toys such as mobiles. Manipulation of toys teaches them that they have some control. The information which the toy itself teaches—such as colours and shapes—is less important to children than learning that they can act on their intentions: when they turn the toy over, they make something happen. So, you can help children to feel powerful and foster their self-esteem by having toys which they can manipulate rather than just look at. And when children drop a toy, instead of handing it back to them you can place it nearby where they can reach for it, again to show them that they can act on their intentions.

Listen

When children are disappointed in their performance it is tempting to reassure them. But instead of reassurance, reflective listening can show them that you understand and that you know that they can cope with feeling disappointed. You might say something like, 'I can see that you're disappointed in your model', perhaps followed by a question, such as 'Do you want to do anything to make it better, or leave it as it is?'.

Permission to be yourself: Five freedoms

The freedom to see and hear what is here
Instead of what should be, was, or will be.

The freedom to say what one feels and thinks
Instead of what one should.

The freedom to feel what one feels
Instead of what one ought.

The freedom to ask for what one wants
Instead of always waiting for permission.

The freedom to take risks on one's own behalf
Instead of choosing only to be 'secure' and not rocking the boat.

Satir, V. (1976) *Making Contact*. Celestial Arts, Millbrae, CA.
Reprinted with permission

Foster belonging

Because children need to feel connected to others, your relationship with the children in your care is important to their self-esteem. Your relationship needs to involve acceptance, attention, appreciation, affirmation and affection (Albert 1989, in Rodd 1996).

Children also need to feel connected to each other. Their friendships matter as much to them as adults' friendships matter to us. Friendships not only meet their social needs but also feed their self-esteem and protect children from stress.

Encourage autonomy (independence)

We all need to feel that we have some degree of control over our lives (Rodd 1996). Yet sometimes our good intentions to help children mean that we do something for them which they could do for themselves (Brown 1986) and, in doing so, take away their chance for self-control. Children will feel best about themselves and their abilities when they are meeting meaningful challenges and putting in some real effort (Katz 1995). They need opportunities to exercise choices, initiative and autonomy. Therefore it is important to provide some structure for children and also to give them some freedom to make choices within that structure (Hay 1993). Children need to know that the amount of effort which they put in to a task makes a difference to the outcome, and so your feedback linking their effort with the finished product will teach them that they are in control of their own achievements.

There are three levels of choices which we can offer children. When the activity has to be done—such as washing hands before a snack—we cannot give a choice of *whether* to do it, but we can give a second level of choice about *how* to do it (using the hand drier or paper towels, going with a friend, or whatever). At the third level, if there is no choice about how the task has to be done, then we can give children a choice about *how to feel* about it. For instance: 'It is time for your nap. You can get upset about that, or you can lie down quietly and think about happy things. It's up to you'.

It will also be useful for you to involve the children in making decisions about aspects of the program and rules which affect them. Asking for their suggestions and listening to their ideas tell them that you value them and believe in their abilities to have a say about things which affect them.

Give specific feedback

Especially when children are becoming discouraged about their performances, you will need to acknowledge and support their efforts. However, Jones and Jones (1995) report that adults' feedback is often too vague and does not specify success or failure accurately. Instead they advise that adults should give feedback which specifies exactly what the child has achieved. Children might also need help to notice positive feedback and not to take negative feedback too much to heart.

Not only does feedback have to be specific, but it also needs to be *authentic* (Curry & Johnson 1990). For this reason, I advocate using acknowledgment rather than praise (see chapter 6).

Activities to help children to notice their qualities

It is important for children to have a realistic picture of themselves. Partly because of their age, but sometimes also because of a pessimistic outlook, many young children see themselves in black-and-white terms: either they are completely hopeless, or totally wonderful. These children need help to appreciate their qualities in a more balanced way.

If children are perfectionists or are not noticing their own qualities sufficiently, you can help them to make a list of things they can do. You can begin with a heading: 'Jake can . . .' and then make a list of all of the child's thinking, physical, social, play, self-care, speech and caring-for-others skills. Some of the items on the list could be, for instance: 'Jake can run, listen, answer the telephone, help set the table, wash his own hands, feed the cat, smile, make friends, be happy, pick up toys, feel angry' . . . and probably a hundred other, very specific skills.

List *anything* that he has ever done: a single instance is enough to tell you that he can do it, even if he does not do it all the time. And don't qualify these statements with 'sometimes' or 'when he tries', or with descriptions of how well he does the activity. But if he insists that you write down that, for example, he can run fast, then you make that two items: 'Jake can run' and, 'Jake can run fast'. Remember also that the skills which you list must be appropriate for the child's age: he can feed a pet, but he cannot be responsible for its total care; he can give his Mum a cuddle when she is upset, but he cannot be responsible for looking after her.

Other similar activities include the *'All about me'* books in which children draw themselves and write down their favourite things. These activities are intended to expand children's self-*concept*—that is, to broaden their description of themselves. But such activities will not improve their self-*esteem* if the children do not value the skills which these activities help them to recognise. Therefore, Katz (1995) advises focusing on enduring skills and traits, such as being able to try when a task gets difficult or being a considerate friend, rather than skills such as being able to ride a bike, which virtually every child can do. Similarly, if you acknowledge a child's inherited characteristics, then his self-esteem will not improve, because he had no control over those characteristics and cannot take the credit for them. So instead, you will need to acknowledge *effort* rather than cleverness, *personality* rather than appearance, learning *style* rather than the outcome (Katz 1995).

Promote realistic ideals

Children's self-esteem is likely to be high when their ideals are realistic. Therefore, as well as helping children to be more aware of their own skills—that is, you have helped to expand their self-concept—you can also help them to set realistic expectations of themselves.

Self-expectations

Self-esteem is the measure of how well we achieve the standards we expect of ourselves. Part of having realistic ideals is having a valid reference group to whom we can compare our own performances (Adler et al. 1995). If we compare ourselves to people who are very different from us, then we will have unrealistically deflated or inflated views of ourselves. (Ways to respond when children are disappointed in their achievements are discussed later in this chapter.)

Expectations from others

It is important for adults to convey realistic expectations of children. On the other hand, all people will perform down to low expectations, and so you must communicate your faith in every child's ability to be successful (Jones & Jones 1995).

Allow mistakes

Children will get discouraged if we expect them to get things right every time or to 'do their best' always. Likewise, when we point out their errors, we imply that making a mistake is wrong, when instead mistakes mean that they are learning and so they are a necessary part of becoming competent. (If you are not making mistakes, then you already know how to do the task—in which case you are practising, not learning.) Balson (1992) notes that our focus on children's mistakes is due to our erroneous belief that this is how to help them to learn. Instead, it discourages effort and contributes to continued failure by focusing on children's deficiencies and not highlighting their strengths. Mistakes indicate a lack of skill and skill is acquired only through practice, but a discouraged child refuses to practise and so does not learn.

Most children realise that making mistakes is a part of learning, in the same way that falling over was a part of learning how to walk. Adults, on the other hand, are often more uncomfortable about watching children struggle than the children are themselves. So, let children experiment with doing things their way, even if you know in advance that what they are doing cannot work out.

When a child has not been as successful as you would have expected, it is still important to comment on what she *did* achieve. For example, instead of asking what went wrong when she wrote her name backwards, you can congratulate her for beginning to understand how to write her own name.

I believe it is helpful to teach ourselves and others to live by the rules:

> Strive for excellence, not perfection.
> Have the courage to be imperfect.
> On worthwhile tasks, strive to do your best, but not to *be* the best.

As well as accepting natural mistakes, you can actively teach children how to make deliberate mistakes by doing something together and failing at it badly, as long as no one gets hurt. You might try to lose at a game. It will also help when you make light of your own mistakes so that children learn that errors are okay—they can even be funny.

Promote competence

Children will feel good about their achievements only if the activity is challenging and meaningful to them. If they find a task easy or trivial, their achievement of it will not make any difference to their self-esteem. This makes developmentally appropriate programming an important part of promoting children's healthy self-esteem.

To encourage children to achieve to their maximum, you will need to teach them how to apply themselves, to achieve age-appropriate independence, to explore and solve problems, and to enjoy learning and achieving (Curry & Johnson 1990; B. Knight 1995; Yong 1994). At the same time you will need to ensure that the children have a sufficient history of success so that they are willing to attempt a task which carries a risk of failure (Whitmore 1980). Some guidelines for appropriate curricula were discussed in chapter 1.

If children lack confidence because they are being unsuccessful in important ways, you do not want to boost their self-esteem artificially, but instead build their skills (Curry & Johnson 1990). Their low self-esteem is both valid and functional, because it might motivate them to achieve.

You cannot fool children by making tasks too easy. If an activity is easy or trivial, achievement of it will not make any difference to their self-esteem (Bandura 1986). It might actually do harm by teaching them *help-lessness*—that is, that no matter what they do they will always get it right because the task has been made so easy (Seligman 1975). Instead, children need tasks which increase their opinion of their abilities (Seligman 1975).

Establish priorities

If a child is rightly dissatisfied with his present skills, then you can help him to decide on skills which he would like to learn. Next, with your help, he can set priorities for himself and plan each step. It is obvious that self-esteem will be most directly enhanced if children are able to achieve in skills which are useful and of interest to themselves.

Record improvement

Sometimes it can help for children to have a visual record of their progress. However, as I mention in chapter 12, it is not wise to reward improvements since outside reinforcers can reduce children's natural motivation to learn. Therefore, you can use a star chart or some similar method as visible evidence of a child's progress—as long as the stars are not seen to be external rewards either in themselves or to be traded in for a special privilege.

Place realistic limits on children's behaviour

Children need to know that you notice them, and so it is important that you respond to instances of inconsiderate behaviour, rather than ignoring them. When children know your limits, they are more likely to be able to behave within them—which helps everyone—and they realise that you care enough about them to respond to their behaviour.

Children will feel proud of themselves when they know that they can control themselves (Pope et al. 1988). When they can behave within fair limits they will be accepted by other people. And when they can manage their own emotions they will feel safer.

This does not mean imposing controls on children, however. The type of discipline you use will need to appeal to children's pride, competence and concern for others (Clarke-Stewart & Friedman 1987, in Curry & Johnson 1990)—that is, it needs to foster considerate rather than compliant behaviour.

Teach children to cope with negative feedback

At times everyone will fail at something or will be snubbed or rejected by other people. It is important that children notice this sort of negative feedback about themselves, especially when it is valid. But it is also important that they do not let a single failure define themselves as failures as people, or take other people's opinions of them more seriously than they take our own (Katz 1995).

So, your first response when a child is disappointed in himself, is to listen and accept what he feels. He will think that you do not understand if you insist on reassuring him that things aren't that bad or if you tell him to cheer up. (You might remember from chapter 5 that reassuring someone blocks communication.)

On the other hand, if a child is reacting to an invalid criticism or is expecting unrealistically high performances from himself, you might gently ask him whether he is being realistic, without giving advice or telling him off for feeling what he feels. You could, for example, ask gently, 'You seem disappointed that you can't do that well. But do you think you're as good at it as a four-year-old? Isn't that all you can expect when you are four?'. I sometimes tell children that they will be able to do an advanced skill only when they are x years old and that, 'It's not your turn to be that old yet. It's your turn to be four'.

If the child is accurate in assessing that he is not as capable as other children of his age, then you could say that he is right to think that he is not especially good at that particular activity but that, with practice, he will be able to improve.

But also realise that children's self-esteem will fluctuate from time to time and across different areas of their skills. An occasional low period is not a cause for alarm.

Conclusion

Children's self-esteem is both a *result* of past experiences and a *cause* of their future approaches to challenges. This means that we need to help children to acknowledge their achievements so that they are willing to apply themselves in future. It also means that we have to help them to be successful at worthwhile tasks and not placate them with platitudes to help them feel better about unsatisfactory performances (Seligman 1995). Self-esteem comes about from being successful at worthwhile activities, not from false flattery.

Suggestions for further reading

Berne, P. H. & Savary, L. M. (1996), *Building self-esteem in children*, exp. edn, Crossroad Publishing, New York.

Curry, N. E. & Johnson, C. N. (1990), *Beyond self-esteem: Developing a genuine sense of human value*, National Association for the Education of Young Children, Washington, DC.

Also, many children's books have themes about self-esteem. Some titles are listed in Appendix E.

Part three

· · · · · · · · · · ·

Children's social needs

Once children believe that they have something to contribute to other people and they trust that other people accept and value them, they are willing to relate to other people. So, after self-esteem, our second most important emotional need is for friendships. By accepting children you set the scene for them to be able to form close and healthy relationships with others.

You can encourage children's acceptance of each other through an anti-bias curriculum, through structuring cooperative projects and other activities, and by leading cooperative games. These will give children experience of playing with other children.

Nevertheless, social skills don't always come naturally to some children. Sometimes, they feel different from other people and find it difficult to mix socially; sometimes they simply don't get enough practice at relating with other children; or maybe they haven't yet learned a particular skill—say, how to be assertive.

In that case, it can help to teach children the particular skill or set of skills they need to know. The chapters in this section describe how children can ask to join in the other children's play and how to cooperate once they are part of a game.

On the other hand, having few friends might not necessarily be a sign that a child has social skill deficits. It might be that the child enjoys a great deal of solitude but that, when interested, she or he can join in other children's play. Or, it could be that an aggressive child uses antisocial behaviour—such as snatching another child's toy—simply because that behaviour works. You will need to assess whether the aggressive child lacks social skills—or knows which skill is appropriate but is choosing not to use it. If the latter is the case, the child will not need coaching in social skills as such but will need help to gain control of his or her impulses. By managing the child's behaviour, you offer him or her the best chance both of developing friendships and of learning considerate behaviour.

8

• • • • • • • • • • •

Encouraging children's friendships

Young children are attracted to each other and are interested in one another from a very young age. While the text books often tell us that young children lack social skills until the emergence of cooperative play at around four years of age, those of us who work with young children know that even young babies want to explore each other and that they enjoy the company of other children. Even at this very young age, babies will often get upset when another child is sad, which is the beginning of their ability to understand others.

Benefits of friendships

Since parents who have young children are increasingly involved in the paid work force, children are now spending more time in the company of their peers. This will probably change our understanding of their social development, since extra contact with other children is likely to advance their social skills beyond what we currently expect of children of their age. It will also advance other areas of development, because peers can make unique contributions to children's development in many domains.

Social learning

Having friends teaches children about intimacy, managing their feelings, cooperating with other people, negotiating conflict, adopting another person's perspective and having fun (Hartup 1979). Children's friendships give them the opportunity to learn humour (engage in pranks), and to engage in imaginary play (Asher & Parker 1989; Asher & Renshaw 1981).

Cognitive (thinking) skill development

During play children teach each other facts and attitudes which they would not learn from adults (Johnson & Johnson 1991), while the negotiation and problem-solving practice that they get with friends teaches them how to reason (Perry & Bussey 1984). This information, plus thinking skills, helps children interact with others in increasingly sophisticated ways and, in turn, improve all areas of their development, including language skills (Kohler & Strain 1993). Whereas adults guess the meaning of a child's incomplete utterances, other children require her to complete the thought, giving her practice at using language (Rubin 1980).

Self-esteem

Other children's acceptance feeds a child's self-image as a competent person (Asher & Parker 1989). By comparing themselves with their playmates children can develop a realistic view of themselves. They can appreciate personal qualities which otherwise they might have taken for granted, and can acknowledge when their own behaviour does not match up with their peers'.

Emotional support

Friends reassure each other when they feel stressed and give each other the confidence to take risks which will advance their development. For instance, children will engage in less stereotyped and more extended play with friends than they will alone (Asher & Renshaw 1981). Friendships also allow children to express their emotions in a safe and playful context. From this they become familiar with their feelings and learn how to handle them and so find them less threatening.

Supplementing home experiences

Peers and family members teach children different sets of skills which complement each other. Parents offer security and conversation, whereas other children offer partners in play (Rubin 1980). Each type of learning supports the other: security frees the child to enjoy play; fun enhances the parent–child relationship.

Peers can also teach particular skills—such as dealing with conflict—which a child's parents might lack (Hartup 1979). Friends can give children love and support which they might not receive at home—say, in a violent household. Finally, the group play which peers provide and which is seldom available at home allows children to experience multiple and changing roles (Rubin 1980). This is good training for adopting various roles during adult life.

Benefits of cross-sex play

Children are often teased about having a friend of the other sex, which can discourage these friendships and make the child self-conscious about them. This is a pity because children gain a lot from their friendships with children of the other sex. They learn a wider range of play styles and activities, and being able to choose either boys or girls as friends expands a child's pool of potential friends. Also, cross-sex play makes children aware of the qualities which both sexes share, rather than concentrating on their apparent differences. And if they have friends of both sexes as children, then they might find it easier to get along with members of the other sex when they are adults.

Benefits of cross-age play

Children usually choose friends whose development is at a similar level to their own. This has implications for groupings in centres: there must be enough children of similar abilities for every child—even those with atypical development—to have a big enough pool of potential friends; on the other hand, a large group with many older children can be threatening to a younger child.

During this century we began to group together children of the same age. But restricting children to same-age playmates deprives them of the benefits of cross-age play, which include:

- If children can look for friends from among older and younger children they are more likely to find children who have similar abilities to themselves and with whom, therefore, friendships are more likely.
- Younger children are more likely to copy an older child than an adult, and so they learn more from older playmates. For instance, young children's language skills improve when they are playing with older children (Katz, Evangelou & Hartman 1990). Also, older playmates can stimulate young children to deal with cognitive challenges earlier than they might otherwise. For instance, they can create complex play for the younger ones who can then participate but would not have been able to initiate that level of play for themselves (Katz et al. 1990).
- Younger children spend less time in parallel play and need less adult direction when they are in a mixed-age group (Katz et al. 1990).
- Older children are able to empathise with young children and are willing to understand things from their perspective. For example, they will use less sophisticated speech to help younger children to understand them. Boys might especially gain from learning to nurture younger children, since usually they are encouraged to be competitive instead (Rubin 1980).
- Older children can enjoy being admired by younger children, and do not have to compete with them because they already have higher status because of their age and superior abilities. Playing with younger children also gives them the opportunity to consolidate their skills before moving on to the next stage of development (Theilheimer 1993).
- Children whose development does not fit in with their same-aged peers can feel less pressure to conform in mixed-age groupings. A wider range of behaviour is likely to be accepted and tolerated in a group which has a wide age range. The result is less competitive pressure on children to 'fit the mould'.

- When they have the choice, children who are the eldest at home frequently choose to play with a child who is older than themselves; children who are youngest in the family often choose to play with a child who is younger than themselves. This gives them the chance to practise roles which they do not have at home (Theilheimer 1993).
- When the group comprises children of mixed ages, brothers and sisters can be in the same group, offering each other support.
- Mixed age and ability groups will require different play materials and levels of adult attention. Therefore, there can be less conflict in groups of different aged children than when they are all of the same age and are competing for the same materials and types of adult attention.

The presence of children of various ages within the group necessitates a wide range of activities which are targeted at varying levels of skill. This allows not only for differences in skill levels between children, but also allows for individual children's uneven development across the various developmental domains (Katz et al. 1990).

Having children with a range of ages in one group allows you to observe the stages of development (Theilheimer 1993). This will help you to identify children whose development is either advanced or delayed, and to appreciate and acknowledge when an individual child has made developmental progress.

Mixed age grouping resembles the natural world of families and the community. Indeed, one study found that when children are free to select friends, they choose mixed-age peer groups more than half the time and same-aged peers only 6 per cent of the time (Ellis, Rogoff & Cromer 1981, in Katz et al. 1990).

As Katz and her co-writers argue, children aren't born in litters and yet we insist that they be educated in them, even though grouping children of the same age together does not produce a group with the same teaching and learning needs. And, because families are smaller these days, many children will have no experience of playing with children of different ages at home, making it doubly important for their social development that they gain some of this experience in early childhood centres.

Early childhood centres are ideally suited to mixed-age groupings since their curriculum is informal enough that individual children's skill development will not be jeopardised by the presence of younger, less mature children (Katz et al. 1990). Nevertheless, simply placing children of different ages together will not be enough to ensure that they benefit from the experience. Only when you can plan the curriculum to suit each child will the children all benefit from the opportunity to play together. To individualise the curriculum you need to know three things: each child's interests, experience and abilities; how each child learns; and with whom each child plays (Theilheimer 1993). Equipped with this knowledge, you can then consciously stimulate cross-age play by creating opportunities for the children to work and play together (Theilheimer 1993).

Problems with developing friendships

Most children will experience temporary isolation at one time or another. Being isolated can come about when children are new to a group or when they have just lost their favourite friend.

For other children, their isolation is long-lasting. Isolated children usually want to make and sustain friendships, but do not know how. Sometimes these children don't have enough social experience to learn social skills: their parents might be shy or unassertive and so they do not learn assertiveness skills from home. Or, some children have learning difficulties which make it hard for them to know the right way to behave socially or to play the same games as the other children. Or, they can feel alone because other children do not have the same interests as them. (This can happen to gifted children—see chapter 25.)

Other children have problems making friends because they are involved in adult issues and so they feel different from other children, whom they might think are immature and silly. These youngsters might be worried about a parent or about their parents' marriage, or they might have been abused. Or some have just had more adult company at home and so they are not as confident about relating to children as they are to adults.

A child with low self-esteem might look for adult company because adults are more likely than other children to tolerate him, especially if he does not have enough skills to be socially rewarding to other children.

Still other children might be withdrawn, although withdrawal can be the result rather than a cause of rejection (Coie et al. 1989) and so does not necessarily mean that they lack appropriate social skills.

Regardless of the cause, it is helpful if you can intervene with isolated children at an early stage for a number of reasons: first, being isolated causes children pain (Schneider 1989); second, children who are isolated miss out on the important benefits which friendships offer; third, isolated children lack the social opportunities to practise their social skills; fourth, isolated children will have fewer supports for coping with the daily stresses of life, and less confidence in and experience at eliciting support from others. These difficulties can carry over into their adult life (Asher & Parker 1989).

Ways to promote social skills

At young ages, children's isolation can be helped by giving them lots of social opportunities to practise social skills in a safe setting, so that they know that it's okay to make mistakes.

Democratic discipline

When you guide rather than control children, you build a close relationship with them and they learn that you accept them as they are. Your acceptance gives them the confidence to make friends independently of you. It also avoids scapegoating those children whose behaviour gets them into frequent trouble: when you deal fairly with these children, their peers are less likely to regard them as 'naughty' and avoid them as a result.

Example

The communication skills which you model within a democratic discipline approach—listening, assertiveness, collaborative problem-solving, understanding another person's point of view, and recognising other people's qualities—teach children the skills which they need to relate to other people. A guidance approach to discipline also teaches children personal attributes which other children value—such as self-reliance, self-control, exploration, leadership, and the ability to solve problems.

Provide social opportunities

Children need lots of chances to play with each other, and enough freedom to sort out disputes, as long as these do not become violent. It can help if you avoid competitive games, so that the children can play with each other without having to win or lose. Competitive games are more likely to make children argumentative and less willing to share (Bay-Hinitz, Peterson & Quilitch 1994). They include (Orlick 1982; Sapon-Shevin 1986):

- *Taunting or teasing* games in which children chant or call other children names, as in 'I'm the king of the castle; you're the dirty rascal'.
- *Grabbing or snatching* at scarce play equipment, for example musical chairs.
- *Excluding other children* as in circle games where one child has to break into the circle, or piggy-in-the-middle in which some players monopolise the ball.
- *Physical force* games in which children push each other, or hit each other with a ball—for example, rope wrestling or ball tag.

The alternative to these competitive games is planned cooperative activities.

Cooperative activities

Cooperative games aim to involve isolated children and to pair up children who ordinarily do not play with each other. In this way they expand the pool of each child's potential friends. Cooperative games help children to form a cohesive group; teach cooperation skills, turn taking and sharing; decrease aggressiveness; and provide a non-threatening context for modelling and rehearsing social skills (Bay-Hinitz et al. 1994; Hill & Reed 1989; Orlick 1982; Sapon-Shevin 1986; Slaby et al. 1995; Swetnam, Peterson & Clark 1983). Earlier beliefs that young children are too egocentric to play cooperatively have been supplanted by the awareness that our understanding of children's egocentrism might be due to how we rear children in Western societies (Slaby et al. 1995). Therefore, we can anticipate increased cooperation skills if we actively encourage their development.

Cooperative activities require coordinated effort by all members of the group for them all to achieve success. You might facilitate cooperative endeavours by providing props to encourage open-ended cooperative activities in a home corner (Slaby et al. 1995); setting up group art or construction projects which begin with adult suggestion and instruction but which are subsequently left to the children to complete—such as having many children painting a mural cooperatively. Or, you could lead the children in cooperative games. Examples of the latter include non-elimination musical chairs which involves removing a chair—not a player—whenever the music stops, so that all the children end up having to fit on the one remaining chair. (For further examples of cooperative games, see Appendix B.)

It can be difficult at first to engage children in cooperative games (Hill & Reed 1989). Some children prefer competitive games to cooperative ones, and are reluctant at first to participate in cooperative activities or to touch other children if that is part of the game (Bay-Hinitz et al. 1994; Hill & Reed 1989). Nevertheless, children still benefit from even low participation rates (Bay-Hinitz et al. 1994), and can be encouraged to participate when you use gentle persuasion and when they can see that the other children are enjoying themselves (Hill & Reed 1989).

Another difficulty is that simply playing cooperative games will not necessarily ensure that the children will generalise their skills to other activities. Therefore, you will need to supplement cooperative games with teaching the children how to be cooperative in their natural play (Sapon-Shevin 1986).

Teach group entry skills

To enter a group a child needs to recognise when is a good time to ask to enter. A socially capable child typically follows a series of steps: first, she approaches some other children and quietly observes their game. Next, she waits for a natural break to occur, and then she begins to do what the other children are doing. That is, she imitates their play. (Adults do the same thing at parties: we shoulder in to a small group of people who look as if they might not reject our advances, wait quietly until there's a suitable break in the conversation, and then say something about their topic of conversation.)

In contrast, when less competent children try to enter a group they disrupt the group's play by calling attention to themselves, asking questions, criticising the way the other children are playing, or introducing new topics of conversation or new games. The group members will usually reject these disruptive attempts to become part of the group, and so the less competent child learns yet again that other children do not like her.

If the other children tell her that she cannot join them, a competent child will have the confidence to try again, whereas less adept children appear to need to save face but, in their attempts to do so, behave in ways which are likely to lead to repeated rejection (Putallaz & Wasserman 1990).

Making new friends

Socially competent children are graceful when they make friendly over-tures. They use greetings more often, ask about the other child (for example, 'What do you like to play?'), give more information about themselves ('I like climbing'), and more often try to include the other child in their games. If children have trouble knowing how to initiate friendships, then you can teach them these simple ice-breakers.

Non-verbal messages

Non-verbal behaviour is complex: it is often unclear, and the non-verbal message can contradict what people are saying. Children need to be socially perceptive to be able to read other people's non-verbal behaviour accurately. The socially competent child can use and understand non-verbal behaviour—such as eye contact, facial expressions, and body posture—to send and receive social messages. For example, she can assess good and bad times for trying to join a group. She can interpret the meaning behind a verbal message ('Okay, then, you can play—if you really want to'), and the non-verbal message which might contradict the words. She can also smile, make eye contact, and send out messages with her posture to indicate that she is willing to cooperate.

In contrast, the boisterous child might be rejected simply because her activity level (her non-verbal behaviour) is out of step with the group's. Aggressive children are also likely to be rejected. This comes about because they often misinterpret other people's behaviour. For example, if someone trips them up, they assume it was deliberate, when in fact it might have been an accident. They become aggressive in return, and other children will reject them as a result.

Teach skills for maintaining friendships

Now that the child has become part of the group, she needs to be able to maintain the relationship. This requires her to use a number of skills.

Supportive actions

Once she is part of the group, a child needs to know how to be supportive of her peers. A competent child is skilled at complimenting, smiling at, complying with, imitating, and sharing—both toys and her feelings—with her playmates. This tells them that she is keen to cooperate and can be trusted. In contrast, unskilled children not only support their peers less, but they also have unusual ideas about what is friendly behaviour. For example, they might punch another child to say hello, and will not stop even when they have been asked to, because they think that is how to be friendly.

Awareness of others

The socially competent child is sensitive to other children's needs and wants. She can be tactful. She will moderate her behaviour to suit her playmate, such as modifying her displays of affection when she realises that they are annoying or embarrassing her friend. She will also notice when another child is trying to make friends with her, and is less likely to turn her down.

Conflict management

When children are faced with a conflict, they need choices about how to respond. They need to be able to submit, be assertive, or—in extreme cases—act aggressively, and need to know the best time to use each of these options. Finally, they need to be confident enough to use their chosen option.

Competent children can use persuasiveness and assertiveness rather than bossiness when they make suggestions about the group's play. They can obey social rules such as taking turns as group leader and about sharing, for example. They can solve disputes by citing a general rule of acceptable behaviour, and can offer alternative suggestions to a child whose actions have been disputed, so that the conflict is resolved peaceably.

Language skills

Children will need to be competent at talking so that they can ask for what they want—such as asking to join the group—and so that they can sustain and elaborate on the group's play. Competent children will monitor their speech so that their playmates understand them, will express their rights, are able to suggest and accept compromises, can ask questions of their friends, talk about their feelings and clarify misunderstandings. They are also able to listen.

Moral understanding

Socially competent children have a sophisticated understanding of right and wrong. They are more likely to judge an action according to its effect on other people rather than whether it is rewarded or punished—especially as they grow older. Other children are likely to find socially competent children more amiable as a result of their interest in justice.

Conclusion: Social skills

When children are feeling isolated and are having difficulty starting or sustaining friendships, you can teach them these general skills. If, however, they have a more specific skill deficit, then they might benefit from coaching in particular social skills, which I describe in chapter 9. On the other hand, some children know which skill to use but are not using it. In this case the problem is a behavioural—not a social—one and will need handling in one of the ways I discuss in chapter 15.

Check the child's development

To be able to play the same games as others, children will need similar developmental skills to their peers. For example, if a child is not coordinated enough to play the other children's games, it can be a good idea to suggest to his parents that they have his eyesight checked in case poor vision is interfering with his eye-hand coordination. If his eyesight is okay, then a physiotherapist could check his physical development and coordination. I also believe that food sensitivities can make children uncoordinated, so these might need investigation too, especially if the child has a family history of allergies and if he has some health complaints—such as eczema or asthma—as well. (It is worth saying here, however, that evidence about food sensitivities is in its infancy only and that unorthodox approaches such as dietary management are not yet scientifically proven, might not fit with parents' beliefs, and might not have more benefits than disadvantages for the child, and so each case will have to be weighed up individually.)

Help the lonely child to fit in (within reason)

Children like other children who behave similarly to them. It probably has to do with being able to predict their behaviour. Although not everyone can or wants to be the same as everyone else, you might be able to help a child who feels left out and lonely to fit in. It could be that he has an unusual appearance, which can be helped if he dresses a little more like the other children; or the children have trouble remembering a child's very unusual name, in which case an abbreviation or nickname could help. You can also make sure that he behaves considerately so that other children will enjoy playing with him.

At the same time, it will be important that your centre include community volunteers, staff and children from a range of cultures and backgrounds, so that the children can experience difference as interesting rather than as something to be feared or shunned.

Respond to inappropriate behaviour

The most common reason for children to be rejected is aggression, especially after the ages of seven or eight (Coie et al. 1989). To prevent later problems, therefore, you will need to respond to a child's aggressive and other antisocial behaviours, first to protect the other children and, second, to protect the aggressor from being shunned by her peers. Rejection by them can in turn exacerbate the inappropriate behaviour, which cements their rejection . . . and so on. Responses to aggression and other difficult behaviour are suggested in chapters 15 and 18.

Conclusion

It is important that you do not make a child feel guilty if she does not have a lot of friends, because she can become obsessed with doing so to please you (Rubin 1980). Also, having just one or two friends is normal for both children and adults. As long as a child can balance the need to be alone with the need for company and—mostly—meet her needs for both, then she will appreciate and enjoy both her own company and other people's friendship.

9

• • • • • • • • • • •

Coaching social skills

Positive peer relationships are important to parents, to caregivers and teachers, and to the children themselves. Taking each of these individuals in turn, one of the main reasons *parents* choose centre-based child care and almost all choose to enrol their children in preschools, is that they want their children to socialise with other youngsters. Next, *teachers and caregivers* need the children in a centre to have appropriate social skills because a disruptive or isolated child can negatively affect the atmosphere in the centre, provoke discipline issues, and limit the activities that can be offered (Mize 1995). Last, *children* need social skills so that they feel part of the group and can develop friendships. If young children lack social skills it is likely that they will continue to do so into their school years. The result is that they will be unpopular with their peers, might have emotional difficulties throughout childhood and into adulthood and do less well academically than popular children (Mize 1995).

Early childhood is an ideal time to intervene if young children are having difficulty with learning social skills naturally. Because they are so motivated to play socially, they are willing to be guided by adults, and there are many natural opportunities every day when they can be taught social skills. Intervention during the preschool years avoids their social difficulties becoming entrenched. If we leave social skills training until school age, an unskilled child will have developed a reputation with his peers, which is harder to undo as he gets older. Also, while the years have been passing the unskilled child has not had the positive peer relationships which competent children have enjoyed, and so he has not had the opportunity to learn more subtle and sophisticated social skills. That is, an initial skill deficit gets progressively worse the longer it is not addressed.

Social skill and social competence

Children need both the skills to behave prosocially and the ability to use those skills at the right time and place. It is not enough to be pleasant: children need to be sensitive to the context and to their playmates so that they respond appropriately in the circumstances.

To play cooperatively and competently together young children need to be able to:

- communicate their feelings;
- give information;
- ask for information or help;
- manage their own feelings;
- negotiate differences in opinion with their friends;
- deal with conflict constructively;
- achieve what they want without hurting anyone else;
- respond to provocation such as teasing or bullying;
- evoke favourable responses from other people;
- deal with people in authority.

In short, young children need the skills for dealing with the impact of the world on themselves and for influencing that world. They will need to use these skills when establishing, maintaining and elaborating play.

Identifying socially at-risk children

You might be concerned about certain children's social skills for any number of reasons, including the fact that they play alone a good deal of the time; they engage in repetitive simple play past the age when they ought to be able to play in more sophisticated ways; or you notice that they are particularly aggressive, impulsive or withdrawn.

Isolated children

Not every child who plays alone is socially at risk. Some children like a great deal of solitary time but are very competent and agreeable when they are with other children (Perry & Bussey 1984). But you could become concerned if a solitary child seeks some company but cannot find a way to enter a group.

Not all solitary play is identical. There are three types of solitary play: passive solitary play, active solitary play, and reticent behaviour. All three types can look like social withdrawal, although they don't all mean that a child lacks social skills. The three types are:

- *passive solitary play*. This form of play is appropriate and benign during early childhood: it would become a problem only if the child were to continue with it as his main form of play into middle childhood.
- *active solitary play*, which often disrupts other children's play and can be very impulsive, and so indicates some potential or actual social difficulties.
- *reticence*, which involves looking on and not being engaged in other

children's play. Reticence in early childhood is not necessarily caused by social anxiety or shyness, but it could mean that the child needs some help to enter a group.

This list implies that the amount of time children spend on their own is not necessarily a sign that they are having social difficulties. As Perry and Bussey (1984, p. 305) note:

> If children are wasting their time while alone—if they are unoccupied or are doing something that is better done in a group—then high rates of solitary play may be detrimental for the children's development. But if children are spending their time alone wisely, then solitary play may be beneficial.

Type of children's play

Young children engage in functional repetitive play, and as they reach 3–4 years of age their play becomes more constructive. In the ages between two and seven years comes dramatic or pretend play that symbolises real events; and finally, games with rules begin appearing in the 4–5 year age range and continue until adolescence (Perry & Bussey 1984). These are not stages, but instead can be regarded as layers, like the layers of an onion. The first stage appears as the inner layer, and does not get displaced but merely overlain by subsequent layers. This means that older children have access to all four forms of play and might not necessarily use their most sophisticated form of play most often. A child who, however, relies on simpler forms of play despite being of an age to have mastered more sophisticated play, may have social difficulties (Frosh 1983).

Apparent skill deficits

You can observe the type of social behaviours which particular children display, and identify those children who experience repeated difficulties. These difficulties might be *ineffective* social actions—they do not result in the child receiving what he needs; or the child's social behaviours could be *unacceptable*—they might work but are undesirable (Slaby et al. 1995).

Social skilfulness means that a child's behaviour is appropriate for the context. Direct observation lets you appreciate the conditions that gave rise to a child's social behaviour and so to change features of the environment which could avoid a recurrence, rather than focusing attention on the child's skills only.

As well as possessing prosocial skills, competent children generally lack irritating behaviours which lead to rejection by other children—such as interrupting an ongoing activity, disrupting games, being aggressive or abusive, arguing, making contentious statements, displaying impulsive and unpredictable behaviour, having tantrums, and monopolising equipment. These behaviours are irrelevant, inappropriate to the context and out of tune with the other children and their play. As a result, they frequently disrupt the other children's activities and so are often ignored or rebuffed (Mize 1995).

I described the particular social skills for entering a group and for maintaining friendships in chapter 8. If a child is not responding to the general methods for improving these skills which I mentioned in the earlier chapter, then planned social skills coaching might be useful.

Social skills coaching

Social skills are usually—but not always—learned naturally. Children learn new information every time they interact socially and they receive repetitive guidance from adults. This will be enough for most young children to acquire and practise appropriate social skills. However, social skill deficits—and aggression in particular—are unlikely to disappear spontaneously (Schneider 1989). Therefore, individual children who have social skill deficits will need additional coaching.

Improving high-risk children's social skills allows them to form friendships within which they can practise their skills. Problems which can have begun merely because the child lacked the opportunity to play socially or because he had a mild delay in learning social skills can become a significant problem for the child, unless he is given both the opportunity and the guidance to practise appropriate social skills.

A second reason to coach social skills is when you have children with intellectual disabilities in your centre. The most important skill which helps them to be included in the regular setting is not their intellectual level as might be expected, but rather their social skills (MacMullin 1988; Salend & Lutz 1984, in Cole & Chan 1990).

Training methods generally comprise teaching children about social goals—such as having fun together (Mize 1995); giving them opportunities to practise new social skills; and supplying feedback (Ladd & Mize 1983; Mize 1995; Rose 1983). For instance, Mize used hand puppets, asking children for their ideas about how to teach the puppets to have fun together. The children then acted out their ideas—with the puppets, then with other toys, and finally in the early childhood setting.

During training, a coach must be careful to avoid making a target child feel that he is being singled out or that his unsuccessful behaviour is being focused on (Mize 1995). During training sessions the coach will begin where the child is presently functioning and will provide support so that he can perform at a slightly higher level than he could independently. The coach's support might involve whispering prompts to the child.

A suggested social skills program

An example of a social skills training program for early childhood is provided by Mize (1995). She withdrew a pair of children—one a target child who had social skills deficits and the other a popular child. She began the first coaching session by using a hand puppet to ask the children if they could help it to teach two other puppets how to have fun when they played together.

After the coach had worked the two puppets and asked the children for their suggestions to help the puppets have fun together, the children would rehearse their suggestions by working the puppets themselves. Next, the coach and children would together look at pictures of play equipment typically found in child care or preschool centres and the coach would ask the children to think of ways to use their ideas to have fun with other children who were playing with the toys in the picture.

Then the coach asked the children to try out their ideas by playing together with toys during the session. During their play the coach would use the first puppet to offer suggestions, encouragement and feedback to the children. By doing this the coach would not judge the children's attempts but instead would engage with them as equal participant/teachers to the puppets.

At the beginning of each new session the coach would ask the children to recall what they had learned in previous sessions about what made playing fun. Over the course of the training—of around ten sessions—rehearsals became more realistic and addressed the specific skill deficits of the targeted child. Finally, once targeted children could display the skills confidently and with poise in the coaching session, they needed support to use them in the natural play sessions (Mize 1995). Adult prompts were used to guide the child to select the appropriate skill to use at any given time.

Mize's program focused on three key components of social competence: knowledge, skills, and self-assessment.

Component 1: Knowledge

Children need to know about culturally-approved social goals—such as maintaining friendships and ensuring that all players have fun (Mize 1995). In contrast, if a child wants to win at all costs, to direct all the play or to monopolise play equipment, then he is likely to be rejected by other children.

The social skills coach can teach prosocial concepts by focusing on ways children can have fun playing together, rather than trying to teach abstract concepts such as cooperating or being 'nice' (Mize 1995). At the same time, the coach will teach the children to notice the negative effects of inappropriate behaviour by enacting scenarios with the puppets in which low-key aggressive behaviour makes the other puppet feel sad. (Mize warns that if you depict aggression with puppets in an animated way, the children will copy that with great gusto, instead of focusing on its negative effects.)

Component 2: Skills

Although social skills differ at various ages and for various ethnic and cultural groups, there are some skills which are universal (Mize 1995). The first universal skill is being positive and agreeable—that is, having goodwill towards other children (Mize 1995). The second is being able to use relevant contextual and social cues to guide one's own behaviour. Third, children need to be sensitive and responsive to the interests and behaviour of their playmates.

As well as having positive goals, children need four specific skills for achieving their goals (Mize 1995). First, they need to be able to *lead*—that is, make positive play suggestions. Although these suggestions can be quite directive, they must not be bossy or delivered in an aggressive tone of voice. A lead might enlist another child in the pursuit of a common goal or play theme.

The second social skill is *asking questions* to seek help or information from one's playmate. Sometimes, leads are framed as questions so that they seem less directive; some questions are tagged on to the end of a statement—for example, 'We're doing this together, aren't we?'—as a way to establish common ground with one's playmate and to elicit a response from him.

The third social skill is *commenting on play*. These statements describe what is happening and so they seem obvious or unsophisticated to adults, but for young children the statements serve to remind each other of their play theme, establish common ground, and help the children to function cohesively (Mize 1995). To be effective and well received, however, these comments have to be relevant and in tune with the other children.

The fourth social skill is *supporting* playmates. Children need to be able to compliment or help their friends, suggest play options to sustain or elaborate play, offer compromises and negotiate conflict.

Component 3: Self-monitoring and self-evaluation

Children need to be able to notice important aspects of the social environment and observe the behaviour of their playmates so that they can judge whether their own actions are suitable. Some common mistakes of interpretation which children make include:

- some do not pay enough attention to relevant social cues;
- some notice only particular types of cues—for instance, aggressive children often assume that another child intended to be hostile, even when the other child's behaviour was accidental;
- some children are not aware that their behaviour will influence how other people respond to them;
- some misinterpret another child's reactions. For example, less competent children will blame rejection on their own inability to make friends and will withdraw as a result; or they will believe that the other child does not know how to be friendly.

In contrast, competent children are more likely to think that another child has rejected them because of differences in their personality, the bad mood of the other child, or a misunderstanding (Mize 1995). Because of these positive interpretations, competent children are more likely to try again and not feel insulted by rejection.

Therefore, the third part of social skills training involves coaching children to notice other people's reactions to their behaviour and to interpret their reactions constructively. For instance Mize (1995) describes a rehearsal session in which one child continued to throw toys at his playmate even when she had asked him to stop. The coach showed the children a videotape of that interaction and asked the aggressor to notice what his playmate was saying and how she looked; and asked the playmate to say what she had meant by her requests for him to stop.

Conclusion

Although young children can learn social skills quickly from coaching sessions and can learn to enact those skills in natural settings, it can take some time for the other children to respond more positively to them (Mize 1995). In the meantime you will need to continue to offer encouragement and to structure the group—through cooperative play and the other interventions already mentioned—so that the atmosphere in the group is one of acceptance and inclusion. This will give all children—but particularly previously rejected children—the confidence to re-enter the group and will provide a safe context for making the occasional social mistake.

Social skills coaching might not be appropriate for aggressive children who know how to behave prosocially, but who use their aggression strategically and with great success, since they will not be motivated to change. Therefore, some aggressive children might need some behaviour management to gain control of their impulses, following which they might be able to acquire the normal social skills naturally, without structured coaching.

10

Settling disputes

Whenever people are in groups, disputes between them are inevitable. There will always be times when what one person wants is at odds with what someone else wants. Although most of us see this as a negative feature of life, conflict can teach us how to deal with high emotion, so that as children we do not learn that feelings are frightening or that to feel something strongly makes us a bad person. When given suitable guidance, conflict teaches children constructive ways for handling their feelings. It allows them to get to know their own needs and gives them practice at being sensitive and responsive to other people's needs.

Collaborative problem-solving

Whether dealing with disputes among children, between yourself and a child, or between staff members, your aim will be to find a solution—not a culprit. Each person needs to find a way to meet her needs without interfering with the other person's needs. The way to do this is through collaborative problem-solving, which involves six steps:

1 The people concerned agree to talk it over.
2 Each person listens to what the other person needs and then says what she needs assertively—but not aggressively. This might tell you both where your differences lie.
3 Together, you come up with ideas of what you *could* do, so that both of you would get your needs met. At this stage, you do not evaluate how practical the suggestions are, just brainstorm all possibilities, even silly ones. If it helps, write them down.
4 Next, you decide which of the options you *will* do. Don't choose a compromise which does not meet anyone's needs, but instead persist until you can find a solution which meets both your needs.
5 Next, decide when and how to carry out your chosen solution.
6 Finally, once it is in place, check whether the solution is working.

Benefits of negotiation

When negotiating between an adult and child, finding a solution with which you both agree means that the child is motivated to carry out the decision because she participated in making it and you are not imposing it on her. Therefore, you don't have to enforce the solution, and you and the child can work with—not struggle against—each other. Also, helping to decide what should be done develops a child's thinking skills.

Listening to the other person—be it a child, a parent, or a colleague—means that you do not have to guess what she needs and you don't have to come up with a solution by yourself. This means that you have more chance of finding a high quality solution, because two heads are always better than one, and it reduces your workload by having someone else with whom to share the decision-making.

Finally, negotiation tells the other person that you think her needs are worth listening to.

Limitations of negotiation

Collaborative problem-solving will not work when a child is in danger, or when there is true time pressure to get something done. In these cases you will need to take charge without consulting the child, although you might explain your reasons later.

Collaboration works best when you can deal with each source of irritation when it comes up, rather than leaving your grievances to mount up, in which case hurt feelings will turn to anger.

Negotiation will not teach children to be considerate. If children have not learned the value of considering other people, then debating it with them will not lead to considerate behaviour. You will need to teach them that you expect to be taken seriously when you insist on considerate behaviour. Part four discusses ways you could achieve this.

Children's disputes

As I have said, we often assume that conflict between children is negative, but their disputes can be developmentally normal. Learning to handle conflict is an important task which needs repeated practice throughout a person's life. Before a conflict escalates, however, you can guide the children through the collaborative problem-solving steps which I listed above.

If a dispute has already resulted in some physical aggression, then withdraw the involved children and soothe the victim. You might empathise, saying something such as, 'That hurt you, didn't it? . . . Yes, Alex might be feeling frustrated or angry, do you think? But he forgot to use words'. Nurse any injuries, perhaps inviting the child who inflicted them to assist in this process.

When the incident has involved verbal aggression you can use the same approach, perhaps beginning your comfort to the aggrieved child with, 'That hurt your feelings, didn't it? . . . That was not a kind thing for Alex to say.'

In my observations, it is most effective if you can address the recipient, not the perpetrator, of aggressive behaviour. However, if the perpetrator is calm, you might choose to speak with him directly about his aggression. If you decide to do this, then make sure that:

- the discussion does not degenerate into a lecture
- you do not humiliate the perpetrator
- the discussion is brief.

Overall, it is important to realise that you cannot reason with a child while he is being unreasonable. Any discussions with the perpetrator will have to wait until he is calm and receptive. When the aggressive behaviour is habitual, the perpetrator has already heard it all before and will tune you out. Instead, regard habitual aggressive behaviour as a sign that a child cannot exercise control over his feelings, and help him to calm down. This approach is outlined in more detail in chapter 15.

Part four

• • • • • • • • • • •

Difficult behaviour

In Part four I recommend some ways for dealing democratically with children's inconsiderate behaviour. The democratic methods, based on guidance, accept that children have rights but that other people do not have to suffer a child's inconsiderate behaviour.

The first chapter describes difficult behaviour as any act which interferes with someone's rights. However, this broad definition needs some further refinement. Disruptive or difficult behaviour can be thought of as coming in two forms: the original incident—which Bill Rogers (1998) calls the primary behaviour—and the child's reaction to being corrected—which is the secondary behaviour.

I have observed that young children often display a sequence of wrong-doings—maybe three behaviours in a row. I used to think that this was because they were on the wind-up and that they were getting out of control of themselves. I still believe that this is true to some extent, but I now think that the 'wind-up' can sometimes come about not so much because the child's feelings are getting out of control, but because of how the first incident was handled. If the child feels shamed or upset by the adult's reaction to the first incident, then in my observations he or she is much more likely to repeat another disruptive behaviour.

This means that how we respond to the first behaviour is crucial. It makes sense to respond compassionately when a child behaves inconsiderately—if for no other reason than you do not want to make your life any harder by provoking other incidents to which you have to respond.

We cannot expect children who are four years old to behave as if they are twenty—nor even to behave like they are five. The intention of the guidance approach to discipline is to teach children a more mature skill, rather than to punish them for behaving immaturely—that is, for behaving like children.

11

• • • • • • • • • •

What is difficult behaviour?

Like many things in life, children's behaviour falls along a continuum. At one end is acceptable, considerate behaviour which you appreciate and can acknowledge. Even children who are referred to specialists for behavioural difficulties show acceptable behaviour almost half of the time. This section, however, is about those times when the child's behaviour is not acceptable.

Types of difficult behaviour

Difficult or disruptive behaviour is any act which interrupts the group and prevents group members from functioning—which means it prevents you from teaching and guiding the children or interferes with their activities. It can take one of three forms:

- a normal behaviour which occurs excessively—that is, it occurs too often or beyond the age at which the child could be expected to have learned more appropriate behaviour (Herbert 1987);
- a constellation of normal behaviours which by themselves would not make management difficult but in combination present some management problems (Herbert 1987);
- an appropriate behaviour that is mistimed. For example, dancing and walking around are appropriate acts but they become disruptive during group story time.

These sorts of behaviours might include unsafe behaviour, misuse of equipment, aggression, interference with another child's play, or breaking a behavioural agreement. They are unacceptable because they *violate your rights* or the rights of other children in your care. They violate your rights if they hurt you or interfere with meeting your needs—or do the same for another child. They can even harm the child himself—for example, when he behaves so poorly that no one wants to be around him.

Once you have told a child that his behaviour is having a negative effect on someone else, then continuing with it is inconsiderate. You have a right to act on inconsiderate behaviour. Nevertheless, how you deal with it will depend on whether you think that the behaviour is normal, that it comes about because the child does not know how to act any more skilfully, or it is a sign that the child is getting out of control of himself.

Type 1: Irritating behaviour

Many behaviours of young children can be inconvenient and irritating to adults, but are normal nevertheless. For three months a two-year-old will throw tantrums when she has been disappointed. For weeks, she will refuse to stop playing with the water in the bathroom. Then she'll refuse to wear socks in winter and will want to eat nothing but sausage rolls for six months. All these behaviours are trying to busy adults, but are normal for children. No one's rights suffer much, but they are irritating.

To deal with this type of behaviour, you need to understand that it is normal for young children to behave like this. When the behaviour starts to inconvenience you, though, then you can be assertive about it, saying what effect it is having and helping the child to find an alternative.

Type 2: A skill deficit

Most young children behave as they do because they have not yet learned more mature behaviour. You will need to teach them the appropriate way to act and explain how that skill will benefit them and other people. For example, you will explain to a toddler how to share, and that if he cannot learn to share, other children will not want to play with him and will not want to share with him when he wants something they are using.

The reason that we seldom report behaviour problems with under-two-year olds is that we realise they do not have the skills to behave any better. After that age, though, we start to expect more mature behaviour. However, slightly older children cannot behave maturely all the time because they get easily overwhelmed by their feelings. This leads to the third type of behavioural difficulty, and probably the one that is the most challenging for parents and early childhood professionals alike.

Type 3: Disorganisation

As you know, young children can become disorganised very easily. If they are tired, hungry, or stressed by our demands, they get overwhelmed and cannot organise themselves to use a skill which they can display at other times. Even when they know what to do, they can't do it. Their feelings get out of control and they lose the plot. For example, they might not use words to ask a playmate for a toy, but will snatch it because they want it *now*.

Remember from chapter 3 that learning to handle feelings was one of the components of considerate behaviour. When their feelings are overwhelming them, children need help to get calm again, before they will be able to use their more mature skills. But there is no point in punishing them for being overwhelmed, because in effect you would be punishing them for *being* children.

There are two reasons why it is normal and quite common for young children's feelings to get out of balance. First, babies have to act on every feeling and communicate what they need so that they can receive the care they need to stay alive. But adults have learned that there are times and places where acting on our feelings is not suitable. It takes us the sixteen or so years of childhood to move from our baby state to our adult state, and so we cannot expect a four-year-old to have mastered his feelings already.

Second, it is understandable that at times children cannot use speech rather than actions to communicate what they want, given that they have so recently learned to talk. None of us can use new skills when we are stressed.

I have observed four patterns of disorganised behaviour. I call these patterns *tantrums*, for want of a better word, although in a way it is an unfortunate term because it implies that the child is being deliberately obstructive. But I use it only as a shorthand way of saying that the child is overwhelmed by his feelings and so cannot get on with the job at hand.

Types of disorganised behaviours ('tantrums')

I believe that growing up is a process whereby, although we are allowed to feel the full range of emotions, we need to learn to express our feelings in ways which do not make us more distressed and don't bother other people. When a child cannot act on his feelings without disturbing other people, he could be said to be having a *tantrum*. His feelings have got out of his control.

Children's tantrums can be very active, which makes it fairly obvious to you that the child is upset. But sometimes the tantrum is passive, and that can be harder to identify and to know what to do about it.

Active tantrums

The first active tantrum is the *protesting* tantrum that we've all seen—or experienced—in a shopping centre when a child is angry about not getting what he wants. This type of tantrum involves crying, screaming, hitting or kicking, and is very active. However, it is not very common after the age of three or so because adults recognise it for what it is and generally deal with it.

The protesting tantrum is different from a pre-verbal child's attempt to communicate that he is disappointed. *That* is not a tantrum: it is legitimate communication. A tantrum is where a child can usually say what he needs, but has got so worked up that he cannot use words at the time.

A second active tantrum is a *social* tantrum. This involves verbal abuse, refusing to share or take turns, bullying, and generally not being friendly. Sometimes during play, two or more children have lost control of their feelings in this way, and so they all can be said to be having a social tantrum.

Passive tantrums

The active, protesting tantrum is sometimes replaced with a more passive version, which can go on for years, largely because adults don't recognise it for what it is. The passive form of the protesting tantrum is *whingeing* or sulking. Whingeing tells us that a child feels dissatisfied with something, and cannot get past that feeling.

The fourth and last pattern of behaviour which signals that a child is not managing to overcome his feelings is *uncooperative* behaviour. The child cannot do as he is asked, because he does not want to and he cannot overcome his feelings about having to do it.

In my experience, being uncooperative is the most common tantrum type. I have also noticed that when a child has active tantrums—the protesting or social types—then he almost always has one of the passive types—whingeing or uncooperativeness—first. This means that you can often avoid the more active tantrums by helping the child to calm down earlier.

Secondary behavioural difficulties

Bill Rogers (1998), who is a teacher and writer about school behavioural problems, says that there is also a second class of disruptive behaviours, which he calls secondary acts. These are the child's reactions to being 'corrected'. This category of difficulty can include resistance, rebellion, aggression directed at you, verbal abuse, defensiveness, and refusal to cooperate. The child can also become hysterical out of embarrassment about making a mistake—or about being found out! These behaviours can be more disruptive than the original inconsiderate act. They can often—but not always—be avoided when you let the child save face (see chapter 13) by handling behavioural mistakes as you would any other error—that is, as a chance for the child to learn a new skill, not as an occasion for punishment.

These secondary behaviours are common reactions to an assertive message. However, once the child has become upset you do not need to be assertive any more but should revert to listening, because the *child* now has the problem. You will need to reflect back her feelings—using the active listening skills which I described in chapter 5. Then, when she is calm enough to listen, you can repeat your assertive message. If this combination of listening and assertiveness does not work, you might have to treat the reaction in the same way you would if the child were out of control of her feelings. See chapter 15 for ways to respond to tantrums.

Adults' responses to the behaviour types

Table 11.1 summarises the key responses to all four behaviour types. You can see from the Table that you would acknowledge considerate behav-

Table 11.1: Adults' responses to children's behaviours

Behaviour type	Adults' responses
Considerate	Accept Acknowledge
Irritating	Understand Be assertive
Skill deficit	Teach the skill Explain how the skill is useful
Disorganised/overwhelmed (The child has the skill but cannot use it)	Help the child to calm down If s/he cannot calm down, change your demands
Secondary behaviours	Prevention Reflective listening Repeat your assertive message If necessary, help the child to calm down

iour; understand irritating behaviour and be assertive about it once it begins to interfere with having your needs met; and, for immature behaviour, you can guide children to use more mature skills as they become ready to learn them.

The fourth class of behaviour is disorganised behaviour (tantrums). You can respond similarly to all four forms of tantrums. Your first option is to help the child to calm down so that he is able once again to use his more mature skills. This is the 'change the child' option. It might involve something as basic as putting a tired child to bed or giving a hungry child a snack.

If that fails, then you will have to change your demands because the child clearly cannot cope with what he is being asked to do. This is the 'change the demands' option.

The attention-seeking myth

You might have been told that disruptive behaviour is 'attention-seeking' and that you should try to ignore it. But if you do ignore it, you create two problems. The first is that you end up having to pay attention to the behaviour anyway because it becomes so dangerous, disruptive or intrusive that you cannot ignore it any more. By waiting, you teach the child to persist with inconsiderate behaviour, and so you've done the wrong thing. But you are not supposed to pay attention to it when it starts, either—so whatever you do is wrong.

The second problem is that the child thinks you are doing nothing—or that you don't know what to do—and so he learns not to take you seriously when you give directions about his behaviour. Instead of seeking attention, I think that it is more likely that the child knows that you are busy and that you cannot do two things at once: you cannot finish what you are doing, and manage his behaviour at the same time. So, seeing you talking with a visitor is the child's cue that you won't stop him from throwing sand at other children in the sandpit.

If it is a matter of not being clear that you will still insist on considerate behaviour—even when you are busy—then, the way to respond is to stop what you are doing, correct the behaviour, and then go back to your activity. Ignoring inconsiderate behaviour will not work. Many of us don't think to surrender what we are doing because we think it means the child has 'won' and has gained the attention which we assume he was looking for. However, when you do interrupt what you were doing and clarify what you expect of the child, then his behaviour improves. He didn't need your attention: he just wasn't clear that you would insist on considerate behaviour even when you were busy.

Dealing with your own emotions

Inconsiderate behaviour can make us feel exasperated, frustrated and angry at times. Usually though, we are more angry at ourselves for not knowing how to handle the behaviour, and so expressing anger toward a child will not help. The problem is our lost confidence, not her behaviour as such.

Some people lose confidence in their skills when a child behaves poorly for them but well for other people. If this sounds like you and you think that it means that you are doing something wrong, then think again. It might simply be that the child trusts you and knows that you will still care for her even when she's being a ratbag. The fact that she can behave for someone else also tells you that she knows how to behave considerately. Now all you have to do is impress on her that you are serious about being considered too. The next few chapters discuss why punishment will not work to teach a child this, and what you can use instead.

12

• • • • • • • • • •

Shortcomings of the controlling discipline approaches

Punishment is for criminals;
Guidance is for children.

Raines (1995)

The traditional controlling methods of discipline are built on a view which very few people actually believe—namely, that children are basically 'naughty' and will try to get away with inappropriate behaviour unless we come down hard on them. However, throughout this book I have said that learning how to behave considerately is a pure developmental task, just like learning to ride a bike or learning to read. We don't punish children for the mistakes they make when they are learning to ride a bike—we know that that would be very foolish because they would decide that they did not want to learn anything, if learning meant being punished.

You can tell when you are trying to control children because that word *if* appears: 'If you do that again, I'll . . .'; 'If you eat your lunch, you can . . .'. These statements—which are little more than threats and bribes—involve using one of the five common controlling discipline methods, which are: praising or rewarding children when they behave as we would like them to; ignoring inappropriate behaviour; taking away a child's privileges; putting the child in time-out; and smacking.

Each of these methods has its own disadvantages, plus some which are shared with all the controlling methods. I will talk now about the specific disadvantages of each method and then discuss the shortcomings of punishments in general.

The common rewards

It is obvious that rewards are less harmful to children than punishments. But the fundamental harm comes from trying to control children even when the methods which you use appear to be positive. Bossing children—instead of leading them—will damage your relationship with them, regardless of which methods you use.

Praise

I said in chapter 6 that praise tells children that they are good people—but only if they do things which please you. For this reason praise undermines children's confidence that they can meet your standards and so it lowers their self-esteem. It also encourages children to compete with each other for your approval. These and other disadvantages of praise and other rewards are listed in Table 12.1.

Reward systems (star charts)

The problem with star charts and other reward systems is that once you put one behaviour on a reward system, the child refuses to do other behaviours unless they too are rewarded, and so the program is contagious. At the same time as spreading to more and more of her behaviours, it also spreads to other children in the group. They see the child with the poorest behaviour receiving the most rewards, and so they get in on the act too. Soon, you have star charts going for every conceivable behaviour for a number of children, when the problem started out as one behaviour of one child.

Within a very short time you end up doing more work to control the children's behaviour than they do, and so the star system appears to be even more necessary than it was at the outset. In the meantime, the children involved can sit back and watch it all happening, taking very little responsibility for themselves.

Star charts *can* work when you aim only to 'punctuate' or draw the child's attention to something which she has achieved, such as keeping dry at the beginning of toilet learning. However, star systems do not work when you take the responsibility for that achievement from the child and instead become responsible for withholding or delivering the reward. This is a difficult distinction for a child to make and runs the risk of being seen by the child as a blatant attempt to control or reward her—in which case the star system will not work. Therefore, even when your intent is to punctuate or celebrate a success rather than to reward it, the risk that the child will misunderstand your intent causes me to be cautious about using reward systems at all.

The common punishments

The use of punishment is based on the belief that if we hurt a child by not giving him what he wants—such as not giving him attention when his behaviour is 'attention-seeking'—or by giving him something which

Table 12.1: Summary of disadvantages of rewards

Effects on children's self-esteem
- Praise implies the adult's superior position as possessor of all knowledge.
- Children will not feel accepted when they know they are being judged.
- Rewarded children might expect themselves to 'be good' all the time, lowering their self-esteem when this is impossible.
- Praise teaches children that other people's opinions of them are more important than their own. This can stifle their self-reliance.

Interference with learning
- Rewarded children may engage in 'adult watching' to assess which behaviours the adults will approve. This distracts children from their own developmental tasks.
- Rewards cause children to focus on external rather intrinsic rewards. It decreases self-motivation.
- Praise can interrupt children's concentration.
- Rewarded children may strive to please and may fear making mistakes, and so may avoid being creative and adventurous.

Rewards can provoke disruptive behaviour
- Discouragement that they are unable to meet unrealistic expectations may cause some children to behave disruptively.
- Praise can convey the adult's surprise at the positive behaviour, provoking negative behaviour in line with the inferred expectation.
- Rewards do not teach children to monitor their own successes and so do not give them the skills to regulate their inappropriate actions either.

Ineffectiveness of rewards
- Praise can be automatic for the adult and therefore delivered in a meaningless way.
- Adults and their rewards will lose credibility if children's evaluation of their work does not match the adults'.

Rewards can be unfair
- Adults need a high level of technical expertise to use rewards well.
- While some children can 'pull' praise from adults, other children cannot and receive less praise than they deserve.
- Rewards increase competition between children.
- Their experience that rewards are unfair can cause children to reject the adults who administer it.
- Many children come to resent being manipulated by rewards.

Source: Porter 1996.

he dislikes—such as time-out—we can force him to change his behaviour. The guidance approach to discipline, on the other hand, believes that no one can *make* anyone else do anything, and that using force will harm your relationship with that person.

Ignoring

Based on the idea that a child is misbehaving to gain attention, the refusal to pay attention to him is supposed to make the behaviour stop. But if the behaviour is a habit, the child can usually persist with it longer than you are able to ignore it, and paying attention to it eventually only teaches him to be persistent. As I said in chapter 11, it is more useful to see the behaviour as a sign that the child is not clear that when you are busy you will still insist that he behave considerately.

Ignoring a habit never works. On the other hand, if the child is doing something mildly annoying only, or if the behaviour is a new one, then you might tell him that you are ignoring him. For instance, you could say: 'Sam, I will ignore you until you ask again in a happy voice'. If this does not work then ignoring will not work.

Loss of privileges

With this method, you take away something that the child enjoys when he behaves unsuitably. You might not let him ride one of the bikes for a day or not let him play in the sandpit. The trouble with these sorts of punishments is that in the heat of the moment you might deprive the child of an activity for so long that in the course of the punishment both you and the child forget why it was imposed in the first place. Or a punishment can seem so harsh to the child that he gets into more trouble out of discouragement. Also, policing a harsh punishment can be harder for you than tolerating the original behaviour. And the punishment itself can be more inconvenient for you than it is for the child.

Time-out

Time-out usually means sending a child to an area which is isolated from the other children. The formal reason to use time-out is to send a child to somewhere unpleasant where he cannot get any rewards for his inappropriate behaviour, so that the behaviour will stop. But many people use time-out simply to get the child out of their face before they lose their cool altogether.

The trouble with time-out is that a distressed child might damage the area where he is forced to go. Or he might make so much noise that you cannot stand it, or it is difficult to get on with the regular activities over the noise he is making. Or the child might not stay there, meaning you have to keep putting him back in the time-out area. The resulting battle can be more disruptive than the original behaviour. On the other hand, you might forget about him and leave him there too long. (Those who favour the use of time-out believe that a child should be in time-out for one minute for each year of his age—so a four-year-old should be in time-out for no more than four minutes. If the time-out doesn't work within this time frame, then it isn't going to.)

These general disadvantages aside, I think the most important disadvantage of isolating a child in time-out is that it is asking a lot to expect a very upset young child to get back in control of himself by himself. It's a big task and one that is difficult even for adults. A young child's feelings can frighten him and make him hysterical, in which case I believe that it is cruel to leave him alone.

Finally, you cannot teach a child a more skilful behaviour when he is in one part of the centre and you are in another. You need—at least—to be in the same place if you are going to teach him how to behave more considerately and to manage his own feelings.

No child has time for time-out.

Raines (1995)

Smacking

Smacking is illegal in professional child care. Therefore, a book on discipline such as this could safely leave it out. However, I have no doubt that many of you will be approached at times by parents who invite you to use it for their son or daughter. In case you are stuck for a response to justify a non-violent policy, the following are my reasons for not smacking children.

The fundamental reason why professionals do not smack children is because it does not work. It doesn't work for many reasons:

1 Smacking does not help to calm a child down because it is fast and loud. It actually makes matters worse, and will make both the child and the adult more stressed than they were already.
2 It tells the child that you are out of control—or that he is controlling you. This will not help to teach him to take notice of you in future.
3 Because none of us likes to smack, adults often threaten it but do not carry it out. This actively teaches a child to ignore us. He doesn't have to take us seriously. Better instead not to threaten, but to use some other discipline method with which we *can* feel comfortable.
4 Smacking is usually our last resort. We use it only after a child's behaviour has been difficult for a long time. This means that by the time we do use it, he can have lost the plot entirely, and smacking certainly won't calm him down again.
5 Emotionally tender children become distraught if they are smacked— or if they see another child being smacked. Less powerful discipline methods would work for these children.
6 Other, more emotionally robust children treat smacking as water off a duck's back, in which case it will not work anyway.
7 It is foolish to use smacking—to be aggressive to a child—to teach him not to be aggressive. All it would teach him is that *he* cannot hit other people, but that *you* can. He might learn that he only has to get stronger, bigger, and better at getting away with it.
8 Another disadvantage is that you have to hit harder and harder, and more and more often, for a child to notice it. Smacking becomes a habit. It can escalate until it finally injures the child.
9 Many people have told me over the years that they were smacked as children and that it did them no harm. On the other hand, some of you

might have had the unfortunate experience of being intimidated at school by a violent teacher. This tells you that violence can harm children. It might not—but it *can*. And even if it doesn't harm children, I am certain that aggression damages *relationships*. Young children cannot escape violent teachers or caregivers, but they can learn to hate them and later to hate school and learning in general. They certainly will not be able to achieve as well in a violent setting as they could in an environment where they can trust the adults to protect and care for them.

If smacking does appear to work, then clearly the child can be controlled, and so a less violent method would also work without the risks of a smack. If smacking makes no difference, then why use something that doesn't work?

Disadvantages of punishments

A fundamental shortcoming of all these types of punishments is that you can use them only *after* the child's behaviour has inconvenienced or hurt someone. And because we put off punishing children, it is often the case that someone is inconvenienced over and over again before we do anything about it. This means that the victim has been hurt unnecessarily, that the perpetrator has been allowed to develop an antisocial habit, and that your tolerance has been pushed to its limits.

Punishments teach children to behave well, not because it is the right way to act, but simply to avoid being punished, and so they do not *learn* standards for their actions. Because of this someone must supervise them all the time. It is impossible, however, to see every incident and to know all the circumstances surrounding them. This means that there is a high risk of being unfair because you might:

- misinterpret the circumstances and punish the wrong person;
- not realise that the child did not intend the consequences of her actions;
- fail to appreciate that the outcome has already frightened (punished) the child;
- not understand the child's perception of events and what she regards as a fair punishment.

Even if you could detect misdeeds every time they occurred and could administer punishments perfectly and fairly, punishment will still work only temporarily. The result is that punishment regimes tend to go on for a long time because even effective punishments can only ever suppress an inappropriate behaviour. They cannot replace a disruptive behaviour with a more appropriate one.

Ineffectiveness of punishments

Children who are punished will repeat the same act but will try to avoid being caught the next time. They will calculate the risks or might decide ahead of time that the pleasure the behaviour will bring is worth being punished for it (Kamii 1985). This means that punishment does not actually make children behave well. And even if it did, it can only ever teach them what *not* to do. It will not teach them what *to* do. Children who have been punished are also likely to act up if no one is there to supervise them. They have no 'conscience'.

Effects on children

Punishment produces unwanted emotional side-effects. Thomas Gordon called these reactions 'the three Rs': resistance, rebellion and retaliation. Another negative effect of punishments is telling lies (denying responsibility for a misdeed) to avoid being punished. None of these behaviours is attractive in children, and they tend to bring on more punishment.

An opposite way in which children avoid punishments is to become submissive, compliant, and a 'goodie-goodie'. During the school years, these children become 'the teacher's pet', but they dislike themselves and their classmates despise them. When children conform, they do not have to make decisions or plan their own behaviour—all they have to do is obey. And so they don't learn to think.

Another important emotional side-effect is on children's self-esteem. Feeling that they have failed will lower their self-esteem and might make their behaviour worse because they feel discouraged.

The anxiety and distress which children feel under a punishment regime can interfere with learning (Clewett 1988). The affected children might never receive punishment themselves but by observing other children being punished they become intimidated.

Children who are punished might be seen by the other children as 'naughty'. Young children think something is right if it is rewarded, and wrong if it is punished. This reasoning can extend from the behaviour to the person. When you want the children in your centre to get along well together, stigmatising any of them as 'naughty' will not help.

Also, even very young children feel wounded when they lose face. They can feel humiliated and rejected when they are punished, and they can be mystified and hurt when they are punished for a behaviour which does not cause a problem at home (Clewett 1988). As a result, they might learn to conform to all adult demands, fair or not, rather than to adopt the particular behaviour being taught.

Finally, children might not want to take risks because they cannot judge whether a mistake will lead to punishment. Being unadventurous will limit their learning. For instance, Thomas Gordon (1991) reported a study which found that punishing babies who touched restricted objects had three effects: it *increased* the likelihood that they would touch those objects, it *reduced* the likelihood that they would obey restrictions, and it *lowered* their developmental skills, because they stopped exploring their environment altogether.

Effects on the adult and society

In the short term you are harmed because punishment becomes addictive, which means that you might injure a child in an attempt to discipline her. This clearly hurts her—but it also gets you into a pile of trouble.

Or, because you don't want to hurt a child but have run out of other discipline methods, you can threaten to punish her and never carry it out. This teaches her that she can ignore you, with the result that her unacceptable behaviour continues.

In the long run punishment will harm your relationship with children. There is another 'R' which can be added to Thomas Gordon's three Rs— revolt. Some children, after years of doing as they are told and pleasing other people, will revolt and turn against authoritarian adults. The resulting behaviour *looks* as if the person is making decisions for herself, but in reality all she is doing is the opposite of what other people tell her to

Table 12.2: Summary of the disadvantages of punishments

Limited effectiveness
- The child must infringe someone's rights before action is taken.
- Children learn to behave well only to avoid punishment, rather than developing a 'conscience'.
- Adults must be constantly vigilant to detect misbehaviour, which is impossible. Failure to identify the full circumstances leads to error in administering punishment.
- The effects of punishment are not permanent.
- Punishment may not replace an inappropriate behaviour with a more desirable one.
- Punishment only works for those who do not need it.

Effects on the children
- Punishment can produce negative emotional side-effects, including low self-esteem.
- It can teach children to imitate the punitive adult.
- Children may avoid punishing situations either by withdrawing or by becoming submissive.
- Punishment may provoke inappropriate behaviours which in turn attract more punishment.
- Punishment can intimidate onlooking children, even though they themselves may never be punished.
- Punishment can cause onlookers to define a punished child as 'naughty' and, as a result, might exclude her from their friendship group.

Effects on the adult and society
- Punishment can become addictive and can escalate into abuse.
- It can teach children to ignore adults who threaten but do not deliver punishment.
- Children might push adults who threaten punishment, to see how far they will go, or to force them to back down from an empty threat.
- Violence harms relationships.
- Violence in homes, schools and early childhood settings leads to a violent society.

---

do. She is being controlled, just as she was when she was being obedient (Kamii 1985).

Finally, we cannot have a peaceful society if our homes and schools—and the early childhood centres which supplement and precede them—are violent.

These many disadvantages of punishment are summarised in Table 12.2.

Conclusion

In chapter 3 I said that the methods for teaching children to behave considerately were similar to, but still different in flavour from, the skills which are used to teach them to do as they are told. In this chapter I have described what I believe to be the disadvantages of the controlling discipline methods. In the following chapters some more positive options will be explored.

13

• • • • • • • • • • • •

Principles for responding to inconsiderate behaviour

Managing children's behaviour is not only a question of *what* to do: it is also a question of *how*. So in this chapter I describe what might be termed a discipline style, while in the next two chapters I suggest some specific responses to inconsiderate behaviour.

Setting an example

Let's begin with the obvious: there is no way that children will control their feelings unless you do too. If you have tantrums yourself, you cannot expect children not to. That is to say, children will copy your example and will learn to manage their feelings if you show them how.

You are in charge

A disruptive child is boss of you and your whole centre. You have a good day if he behaves well; you have a bad day if he acts up. His moods determine yours. That is too big a job for a child, and so it is important that you can be a leader in the centre—but not its boss. Being the leader means not exerting power over the children, but guiding them.

It also means that you deal with adult business, so that the children are free to develop and grow without worrying about adults' problems. It means being in control of yourself, insisting that your rights are respected, and teaching the children to be in charge of their own feelings. This makes sure that their feelings do not upset other people, and it also protects the children from being disliked for behaving inconsiderately.

Be clear

Be clear about your limits. When you are debating whether to respond to a particular behaviour, ask yourself whether anyone is being inconvenienced by it. If your rights or the rights of another child in the group are being violated, you have a right and a responsibility to take action to stop the behaviour.

Once you have checked in your mind that it is right to act, talk in a tone of voice which tells the child that you expect to be taken seriously. Also, make sure that your tone of voice and your words send the same message. Sometimes we 'flirt' with a mischievous child, sending two messages: that what he is doing is amusing, but also that he should stop. This confuses the child and so he might think you're not serious when you really do want him to stop.

Be clear when you have achieved the behaviour you asked for, and let the matter drop. For example, don't demand that the child apologise because that will shame him and it might provoke another episode. Use the fact that his behaviour has improved as your proof that he is back on track.

Finally, be clear about what you are prepared to do when one of the children violates your rights or the rights of another child. You must be comfortable with the action you plan to take, otherwise you will threaten something which you don't carry out, and so teach the children not to take you seriously.

Give positive instructions

I said at the beginning of chapter 12 that using the word *if* is a sign that you are trying to control a child: '*If* you do that, then . . .'. To illustrate alternate ways of giving instructions, let's say that a child has asked if he can go outside. You could say, 'No, not until you've put away the toys' or, 'You can go outside *if* you clean up these toys'. But a more positive way of giving the same information is to reply, 'Yes, when you've put away these toys'.

Also, if you do not want a child to do something, you will need to tell her what to do instead, rather than saying what she should *not* do. If she is walking on the bathroom tiles with wet feet, a negative instruction would tell her not to run. But because of the way in which the human brain works, she will remember the word 'run' and forget the words 'do not', with the result that she is likely to do the very thing which you asked her not to. Instead, a positive instruction might be, 'Take small steps'. This will be easier for her to translate into appropriate action.

Don't tolerate intolerable behaviour:
Be assertive

Patience in adults is a curse. It violates your rights because you do not say what you need early enough. The result is that a small misdeed can grow into a really serious breach of your rights; you feel badly about yourself because you find yourself feeling impatient and frustrated more than seems reasonable; and it is dishonest when you will not own up to your feelings about inconsiderate behaviour. The child gets into unnecessary trouble and you get stressed. Therefore, I suggest that you assert your rights as soon as you can. No one has to tolerate intolerable behaviour—which is any behaviour that upsets or harms someone.

Consistency versus flexibility

In chapter 3, I said that we are often told that we have to be consistent, but in the real world no one ever is, and children can still tell the difference between each adult in their life. I also said that it was foolish to stick rigidly to a rule or routine when circumstances have changed. I think that it is more important to make intelligent decisions than it is to 'stick to your guns, no matter what'. Children will respect intelligence more than they will respect stubbornness.

It is true that you need to be consistent about looking after yourself and all the children in the group, and about being assertive when someone is being harmed. But one behaviour can bother you today when it didn't yesterday. Today you could be tired, or you could be involved with a visitor to the centre and so cannot respond in your usual way. That's fine. All you have to do when you change how you normally respond to a child is to explain why you have changed your approach.

If you have refused a child something and he protests about that, the principle of flexibility means that you can change your mind if, on balance, you decide that it would not interfere with your rights to grant his request. This is not the same thing as spoiling or giving in to a child. Spoiling means that you give in when you do not want to, just to keep the peace. Being flexible is simply taking into account the new information that what he has asked for means so much to him. You might say something like, 'I didn't realise it meant that much to you. I can see you're very upset that I've said 'no'. So I am thinking about changing my mind. But I can't think with all that noise going on, so once you've calmed down, we will talk about it'. This teaches him that you are willing to listen to what he wants, shows him that he can ask in a more reasonable way, and gives him the chance to calm himself down: all very valuable skills.

Of course, if you really do not want to give him what he asks for, then don't. The benefit of listening, though, is that he will know that on this occasion, you have a good reason for refusing—you don't just do it to 'teach him a lesson'.

Work together

You and your colleagues will not find the same behaviours irritating. You don't have to be consistent about what you find acceptable, as long as you each protect your own rights—assertively but not aggressively.

When the difference of opinion is important, however, it can be best if you can find a way to agree on a single course of action, even though one of you might doubt whether it will work. You might have to agree to disagree on ideology or philosophy. You can work as a team without being identical. On the other hand, a member of staff cannot be expected to use a management approach that violates his or her principles. (Chapter 27 deals in more detail with staff issues and chapter 28 discusses how to formulate a centre discipline policy.)

Another way of working together as a team is for the caregiver or teacher who begins a directive with the child to be the one to end it. Otherwise it looks as if one adult has had to rescue the colleague who couldn't get the child to do as she was asked. Again, at times, this isn't possible. You might have to leave work or you might have an appointment with a parent and so you have to leave a child in the middle of a tantrum. This is okay, as long as you pass responsibility for handling the child over to another staff member rather than looking as if you could not cope.

If a child has long-term behavioural difficulties, it will be particularly important for all the staff to pull together and unite to help the child overcome the habit. No matter how determined or skilled any one of you is, no individual can change habitual behaviour alone.

Don't reason while they're being unreasonable

When children are out of control of their feelings, their behaviour is a sign that they are already too stressed to listen to us. At times like this it will only make matters worse if you try to reason with them. Wait until they are calm, and talk then. Usually though, you don't have to explain later, because the child knew all along—she just couldn't act on the information—and now that she has overcome her feelings she doesn't need you to preach at her. In chapter 15, I describe some ways to help children get back in control, without too much talk.

Children will give off signs when you are talking too much. One is when they roll their eyes up, or they get That Look that makes you want to demand in exasperation: 'And you can get that look off your face as well!'. Another is what Steve Biddulph (1993) calls the Mona Lisa smile, and I've seen some youngsters smirk with a 'Go your hardest' type swagger. When they do this, stop talking: start acting.

Pace

When children get out of control we often copy their pace and get out of control ourselves. If you want a child to calm down you will need to stay in charge of your own pace. When you are slow, you can guide her to slow down too.

If they are worked up, children cannot get on with what they have to do. So one of the ideas which I have found useful for helping children to keep calm, is to ask them to do something *now* rather than *quickly*. Another way is to tell them that you will *wait* until they get started, instead of giving the same instruction over and over again. This implies that they will do it: it's just a question of when, and it gives them time to get back in control of themselves, rather than having to 'hurry up'.

It will be easier for you and the children to keep calm if you can notice when a child's behaviour is about to get out of hand. If you use controlling methods, you cannot do anything about escalating behaviour until the child has actually done something wrong; if you use the more positive guiding methods—which I describe in chapter 15—then you can stop the behaviour before it gets out of control.

Accept no excuses

You cannot let a child's difficulties scare you off from trying to teach him how to behave considerately, even when he has a known condition such as an intellectual disability or attention-deficit hyperactivity disorder (ADHD). A diagnosis lets you know how difficult it might be for him to learn how to behave considerately, but if you let that condition excuse inconsiderate behaviour, you are letting the child down and being unfair to yourself and to the children who might become victims of his outbursts. Let the diagnosis help you to understand him, but not excuse him from learning considerate behaviour.

Start with an easy behaviour

When a child has many difficult behaviours common sense would suggest that you start by trying to change the one which is most troublesome to you. But I suggest instead that you start with the easier behaviour, get some success with that, and then deal with the next—if it's still a problem. Sometimes, by dealing with the first behaviour, the child learns what you expect and the other problems go away. But even if the most difficult behaviour does not go away by itself and you have to attend to it after all, at least you already have some confidence and the child has been successful about changing a less difficult behaviour. One example is to start with uncooperative behaviour during normal session times rather than trying to deal with tantrums at nap time, when the other children are being kept awake by the child's protests.

Give advance warning

If you are planning to change how you respond to a child's behaviour, tell him what you'll be doing from now on. Knowing that you have a plan can be enough to convince him to change his behaviour without your having to use it. But if it doesn't, and you are forced to use your plan, telling him about it beforehand will avoid his testing you to figure out the new rules.

Routines

Because they cannot tell the time, routines help young children to know what will happen next. The children learn what they have to do, and so they do not need you to supervise them as much. Therefore, routines both help you and give the children a sense of control. On the other hand, as I've already said, if circumstances change then feel free to change the routine. There is no point in sticking to a routine slavishly if it is not useful.

14

. . . .

Assertiveness

When a child's behaviour is telling you that she is distressed, then you will need to *listen* (see chapter 5). On the other hand, if a child's behaviour is interfering with what you or another child needs, then you need to be *assertive* about that. You will have to tell the child about the effects her behaviour is having. Respecting children's rights does *not* mean that you therefore have no rights. So, to teach children to consider you, you need to say what you require—firmly but without hostility. You cannot expect other people to know what you need unless you tell them.

Assertiveness versus aggression

When a child is violating your rights, you have two options: you can tell the child about herself, or you can tell her about what you need.

Labelling the child

You could tell a child about herself ('you're naughty') or about her behaviour: 'That was very naughty'. Either one of these statements, however, reduces the child's self-esteem by blaming and criticising her, and it damages your relationship because the child knows that you are judging her. Also, it is not usually what you mean to say. These 'you' messages are what people mean when they call a statement aggressive.

Labelling your own reaction

Your alternative to labelling the child or her behaviour is to tell her about yourself and your own needs. This type of message begins with that word 'I': 'I am worried that you are climbing too high . . .', 'I need some quiet while I read you the story'.

The 'I' message does not blame someone else for how you feel: you are responsible for your feelings. If you send your 'I' message with the intent of accusing the child or making her feel guilty, then it is aggressive not assertive.

Advantages of assertion

After listening, being assertive is the second foundation stone for teaching children to consider other people. Once they can be considerate you benefit, and you can be more effective in your job because your tolerance is not being stretched unreasonably. And the children benefit because they can understand what is expected of them. They can take responsibility for themselves, without worrying about you. Your relationship with the children grows stronger because it is based on honesty.

In summary, assertiveness avoids the disadvantages of non-assertion—which include a lack of respect from others, loss of self-respect, and feeling walked over. On the other hand, it avoids the costs of aggression which are: being unable to control emotional outbursts which arise when you have been too tolerant, being avoided by others, feeling lonely, provoking retaliation, fear, becoming ill, and being overwhelmed by being responsible for so much.

Five types of assertive messages

Many of us have never been taught how to construct an assertive message. There are five ways we can do so (Jakubowski & Lange, 1978).

'I want' statements

Other people sometimes misinterpret a statement about what you want. They sometimes think it is a demand instead of a request. So, it can help to qualify your statement in some way. One way to do this is to ask how willing or able the other person is to do as you ask. For instance: 'I would like a few minutes to push Jarrod on the swing. Can you wait for a little while until I can join you in the sandpit?'.

A second way to qualify a request is to rate how strongly you would like it: 'I want you to wait for your turn on the swing. It's Jarrod's turn just now. This is a number eight want' (on a scale of 0 to 10). If the child is too young to understand numbers, you could use gaps between the fingers ('this much') or between outstretched arms ('thi . . i . . is much') to show how strongly you need something.

A third approach is to state what your request means and doesn't mean: 'I would like some time to speak with this visitor. You can come and talk to me when the big hand is on the three' (letting the child know how long she has to wait).

'I feel' statements

These are in the form of:

> When you (*do such and such*)
> I feel (*x*)
> Because (*my rights are being violated in this way*)

Your assertive statement does not have to be this formal, although usually it will contain each element, for example: 'I get tired when you don't wash your hands when I ask and I have to remind you' which in its formal version can be seen to contain the elements: 'When you *won't wash your hands when I ask*, I feel *tired* because *I have to say it again*'.

Mixed feeling statements

In this assertion method, you name more than one feeling and explain why you feel each. For example:

'I appreciate that you washed your hands before lunch. I'm disappointed now, though, that you have sprayed all this water on the floor, because that makes the floor slippery and dangerous to walk on.'

Empathic assertion

This assertive message conveys that you understand the other person, but still expresses your own needs. For instance:

'I know that you're enjoying yourself, and that it's fun to run and make noise with your friends. But it isn't safe to run inside and you are scaring the toddlers.'

I find empathic assertion to be the most useful of all the assertive messages. Because you are willing to understand and listen to their needs, the children are more willing to do likewise for you.

Confrontive assertion

A confronting message is useful when an older child has broken an agreement about her behaviour. The confrontive assertive message has three parts:

1 You describe in a non-judgmental way what the two of you agreed to.
2 You describe what the child did.
3 Next, you say what you want to do about that.

For example:

'We agreed that you would not throw sand in the sandpit. I see that you've thrown it and hurt Sarah's eyes. Now, I would like you to play somewhere else so that everyone can be safe.'

Limitations of assertiveness

Even when you send an accurate assertive message, the problem still might not be solved. This can happen when the child's needs are not being met either. When you both have a problem, then you need a way to settle your dispute. Collaborative problem-solving (which was described in chapter 10) is the approach to use in this case.

Guidelines for sending assertive messages

Assertive messages will work best when you can observe the following simple guidelines.

Explain the reason

Although our reason can seem obvious to us, children often won't be able to guess why we feel as we do about their behaviour and its effects. Therefore, remember to tell a child what concrete effect the behaviour has on you. If he is too young to understand what you are telling him, he will nevertheless realise that you do have a reason and you are treating him with respect. That can be enough to satisfy him.

Be accurate about your feelings

It is important to be accurate about the strength of your feelings. Rather than saying, 'I worry when you hit a baby', you will need to say something like, 'I get worried sick when I see you hitting Amy like that. I was terrified you'd split her little head right open. And I get angry to see a big person hurt someone so small'. It can pay not to qualify your message with words such as 'really' 'pretty' or 'a bit' since they water down the feeling word. On the other hand, don't overstate how you feel: children will learn to ignore you if you exaggerate.

It is also important to name your feeling accurately. For instance, don't express anger alone, because that is not the first, nor the most important, thing that you feel. We usually become angry after being hurt or frightened. Saying that you were scared or hurt will be more accurate and more effective than just telling a child that you are angry at him.

Don't suggest solutions

The 'I' message tells a child how you feel about something. It doesn't, however, tell him what to do about that, since he can figure that out for himself (although a younger child might need some suggestions or a limited choice about his options).

Listen to the child's reactions

After you have said what you need, the child might become emotional, aggressive or defensive. He might cry, withdraw or sulk. Or, he might debate the issue with you.

These reactions tell you that *he* now has the problem. You will need to give him some time to digest what you have said and how he feels about it. Then use listening and reflect back his feelings. For example: 'You think it's not fair that I want you to help pack up the equipment'. Or, with tears: 'It seems that you're too upset now to talk about it. We'll speak again later' or, 'What I've said has made you unhappy'. With sulking: 'You're not saying anything, so I'll take that to mean you're thinking about what I've said. I'll speak with you again later to check what we'll do about it'. With very young children, you might be better saying very little and instead giving them a cuddle until they feel better about having to cooperate.

Finally, repeat your assertive statement. It can take from three to ten assertive messages before another person will change his behaviour, so you will need to persist. And of course notice even a hint that the child is willing to do as you ask. If he seems willing, reflect this back as you would with any other reaction: 'Sounds like you'll be happy to help pack up. Thanks: that'll be a big help'.

15

• • • • • • • • • • •

Positive responses to inconsiderate behaviour

From time to time, children can behave inconsiderately because they are tired, hungry, unwell, or temporarily upset. Even children who usually behave considerately can become overwhelmed by their feelings every now and then, and so cannot consider other people's needs for a time. While annoying, these interruptions are not a big problem. But if a child's feelings often overwhelm him, his behaviour will be making life unpleasant for everyone around him.

The ideas in this chapter start from the most simple and work through to the more involved ways for you to respond. It is a good idea to use the easiest methods first, and graduate to the more complex ones only if you need to.

Prevention

Preventing a child from becoming upset is more fair to the child himself and to everyone else in the group. The information in the previous chapters will help to meet everyone's needs and avoid provoking difficult behaviour. I refer you to these chapters if you haven't already had a glance through them.

Catch the child 'being good'

When a child's behaviour has been difficult for a long time, it is easy to notice when she behaves inappropriately. But sometimes children act up because they feel discouraged, and so it's important to remind yourself to notice when she *does* behave considerately, and to tell her that you appreciate what she has done. Although it can be time consuming, writing down observations of her behaviour can help you to notice the occasions when she does behave considerately.

Be assertive

Without hostility you will need to say when a child's behaviour interferes with your needs or the rights of other children in your care. (See chapter 14 for a discussion of assertiveness.) If, after being told what effect her behaviour is having, the child cannot overcome her feelings and act on what you have said, then she is having a tantrum. See the section later in this chapter about tantrums.

Let the child save face

Don't set up a battle of wills: you will not have the stamina or the time for repeated struggles with a child. It can help if you give him a way out, rather than confronting or shaming him with a mistake, perhaps by saying things like:

- 'Sometimes people forget the rules. You'll probably remember next time. What do you think?'
- 'Looks like that was an accident. What could you do to make sure it doesn't happen again?'
- 'That was a mistake. I'm sure you wouldn't have done it if you had known that. Now that you know, I reckon you won't do it again.'

Because children don't always anticipate the effect of what they do, the result can startle them enough to teach them not to do it again, and you'll only humiliate them if you preach about something which they have already realised.

Listen

Sometimes it is enough just to tell a child that you understand that he is disappointed or unhappy. Once he knows that you have understood, he might stop trying to tell you how he feels. A hug works wonders. You might add that he can choose to keep feeling badly, or to find a way to feel better. Allow him time to feel better and, if he cannot, then give him some help.

Redirect

When a child has become upset during an activity, you can suggest something else for her to do. Or, if she appears not to be coping, you might invite her to do something with you. If you believe in the controlling discipline methods, you might think that this is giving her attention for poor behaviour; but if you believe in guidance, you will be happy to change what you expect of a stressed child, until she can cope again. (This is the 'change the demands' option, instead of trying to 'change the child'.) If a child cannot select a new activity or be distracted by your suggestions, then her feelings are still overwhelming her and she needs more time or guidance to overcome them.

Offer choice

It is important for children to have choices over the few things about which they are able to make decisions, particularly about their behaviour. However, you can offer a child a choice of *whether* to do something only if you don't mind which choice he makes. If you do mind, then don't ask, because you will have to ignore his choice and he will rightly feel annoyed at having a choice taken away from him. When something is compulsory though, you can still give the child a choice of *how* to do it. For example, having said that it is time to wash his hands before lunch, you could ask: 'Shall we hop into the bathroom or moon walk?'. Or, you can give the child a choice of how to *feel* about it. For example, 'It's time to wash hands before lunch. You can get upset about that if you want to, but it won't change it', or 'You can wash your hands happily or while you are crying. It's up to you'.

Collaborative problem-solving

When a child does not want to do something you ask, it could be that he has his reasons. The collaborative problem-solving steps which I described in chapter 10 might help to find a solution.

Relaxation

It can help to cuddle a child who is worked up, or to give him a large soft toy to squeeze, until his body feels more relaxed. With a calm body, he will be more able to overcome a distressed frame of mind.

Natural consequences

Instead of punishing a child for inappropriate behaviour, you can let him experience the natural outcomes of his actions. For example, if he refuses to wear a sunhat, he will have to play inside.

However, at very young ages it is often unfair to let children suffer natural consequences. Young children are still too young to plan ahead accurately, and so are too young to pay the price for poor planning. The obvious example is when they would be in physical danger. But other natural consequences can be inappropriate as well. For instance, you would not allow a child to continue to behave aggressively and suffer the natural consequence of having no one to play with. Instead, you would want to teach him the skills to play in a friendly way and to manage his feelings so that he could get along with the other children.

Give permission for the behaviour

The more you try to talk a child out of a behaviour the more she might want to keep it up. So, rather than trying to make her stop, you can give her permission to carry on with it. You might move a tantruming child to a more comfortable spot, or just tell her that since she is sad, you think it's a good idea to cry until all her tears have gone. (You have to be sincere with this approach—it won't work if you are sarcastic.)

At a theoretical level, this suggestion is built on the notion that people behave as they do because it *works* for them. Their behaviour might have negative consequences but, at the same time, it must work; otherwise they would stop it. Giving permission for a behaviour acknowledges that the child obviously needs the behaviour, even if you don't understand why.

Nevertheless, you might have to insist on a minor change in the behaviour to make sure that, legitimate though it is, the behaviour still does not interfere with everyone else. You could change its location—say, by telling the child that it's okay to cry but that she needs to go somewhere else so that the other children can have a quiet room. You could change the sequence in which the behaviour occurs. For instance, a child might usually get upset at nap time. So, half an hour before nap time, you could suggest that she get upset now, so that when nap time comes, she doesn't have to do two things at once.

Time away

As I discussed in chapter 12, time-out has many disadvantages: it isolates an hysterical child; he might damage the time-out area; he can create a lot of noise that does not give you the break you need; he might forget that he is being punished; and you cannot teach him more suitable behaviour when you and he are separated. In any of these cases, time-out will not work to discourage inconsiderate behaviour.

However, at times everyone needs a breather when a child has lost the plot. So you can use time away instead. Time away accepts that everyone needs solitude sometimes. So, when a child's behaviour tells you that he cannot cope, you can suggest that he go off by himself until he feels happier. This is not a punishment: he should find his solitude enjoyable and refreshing. If you use it as a punishment—like time-out—it will not work.

The time-away area could be a window seat looking out onto a play area or the street, or a comfortable armchair, with books and some quiet toys within easy reach. It can be reserved for just one child at a time, with children withdrawing to it voluntarily when they want some peace and quiet, or they might go at the invitation of an adult. There could be a rule that no other children can go into the quiet area if someone is already using it, and so they might have to ask an adult for help to negotiate with a present occupant when they could use it. For instance, there could be a waiting list outside the area, on which children could write their names or attach their name card.

Time away is important for you too in times of stress. Your centre needs a policy that when any adult is overwhelmed they can withdraw for five or ten minutes to recover their composure, while another member of staff watches the group. Not only does time away help the adult, but also it shows the children that everyone gets upset at times and that being by yourself is a good way to calm down.

Reciprocal contracts

Most contracts, agreements or deals with children specify what the children must do to meet your needs. But a reciprocal contract also specifies what you can do to help him achieve that. Being willing to meet children half-way treats them with respect, generates goodwill, and increases the chances that they will abide by their agreements.

Explain growing up

Growing up is a process of learning how to be boss of our feelings. Adults (mostly) have learned that we can't act on every impulse. In contrast, young children believe that if they feel something, then it's okay to act on it. This is part of normal development. However, as they are approaching school age, they need to be beginning the life-long process of learning how to be in charge of what they do about their feelings.

So, I explain to a child that while his body—his outside—is getting taller, bigger, stronger, and so on, his insides might have forgotten to grow up. His feelings boss him around, and get him into trouble—or get him upset, as the case may be. Since he is growing up to be a kindy or school person shortly—or will be *this* old at his next birthday—now is the right time to start *thinking* about growing up on the inside as well.

You cannot talk a child into growing up, or he will not want to do it. Also, you cannot give him ideas of how he can achieve it. All you can do is say that it will take him a lot of time to think about growing up, and that you are sure that part of him knows how to do it.

While he is thinking about how to teach his feelings to grow up, you will help him when they get out of his control. This will mean using one of the next methods.

Guided relaxation

Children who cannot consider you after you have told them what you need, are clearly out of control of their feelings. They are too stressed to listen. Often they cannot calm down without your help. For this reason it can work very well if you go with a child to somewhere quiet and coach her about how to slow down and relax. This slows down both of you, and teaches her a coping strategy which she can use at another time. It works best if you can catch the behaviour early, before the child has become so worked up that she is really distressed.

The approach is quite simple: you go with the child to somewhere quiet, settle her into a comfortable chair and then ask her to take a few deep breaths so that her body can begin to feel better: no one enjoys being stressed. You wait until she is relaxed enough to sit quietly and without moving, after which you begin to count to ten. If she moves or talks while you are counting, then you start again. But you can be very encouraging: 'Oh no! You moved—and you were trying so hard too. I'll start again when you're ready. I know you can do it'.

When the child has managed to be calm for the full count, you can ask her how come she was able to calm down? Did she know she could do that? Does it feel nicer?

If the child does not usually get out of control of her feelings, then you won't have to be this formal about the procedure. You might find that all you have to do is remind her to breathe deeply and relax. On the other hand, if she often gets out of control of her feelings, then she might begin to thrash about, with the chance that she could hurt you. If this happens, then you will need to move to the next approach. Nevertheless, this is still a good sign, because it means that you were right to notice that her feelings were getting too much for her to handle by herself.

Of course, the method takes time. In the long run, it will take less time than having to address a child's disruptive behaviour over and over again; but in the short term, the whole staff team will need to plan how you can cover the staff member who is using the guided relaxation approach. At the same time, remember that you do not have to be slavishly consistent about using it. If no one is available to watch the other children while one of the staff stays with a disruptive child, then you can say so: 'Ruby, I know that you need my help to calm down but there would be no one left to look after the other children if I came and helped you. So I'm sorry, but I can't help you just now'. Your staff team might decide on a back-up plan for these occasions. You could use time away (although an hysterical child might not go there voluntarily) or you could remove the child from the play situation and have her stay beside you as you carry out your normal duties, on the understanding that she can resume playing when she has calmed down.

'Tantrums'

In chapter 11, I listed four types of tantrums—the word I use to describe a child's behaviour when he is out of control of his feelings. If a child is so out of control of his feelings that he might hurt you when you go with him for the guided relaxation procedure, or if he just wants a cuddle and some comfort from you, then it can help to hold him. If he is likely to hurt you, then you will have to hold him quite firmly because you have a right not to be hurt. If he just needs a cuddle, then give it.

The hold that I find works best for a preschool-aged child is to sit him on your lap but only on one of your thighs, and cross your other leg over his lap. If you have to, you can hold his wrists and cross his arms over his chest—but only if you think he might bite your forearms. Whether just cuddling or holding the child in this more confined way, the aim is to give him your physical comfort while he manages to get back in control of his feelings. While I am sitting with or holding a child, I tell him over and over again, 'I'll hold you until you feel better'.

You will see him go through four stages of emotional reaction:[1]

- anger
- sadness
- bargaining
- cuddling,

but not necessarily in a neat order. He might go back and forth between some of these stages again and again. When he protests during these stages, I often say, 'I understand that you're upset, and I'll hold you until you feel better'. At this stage, there's no point in reasoning with him, and so this is about all I do say. I might vary it a little, for example: 'I'm here for you while you find a way to help yourself feel better. Take your time. I'm here', but no doubt you will use your own words and style.

If you can last until the final stage, then the child has gained some experience of getting back in control of his feelings, while getting your help to do so. Once the child has learned how to calm down, all you will have to do in future is read his behaviour for signs that he is getting distressed and ask him if he needs your help to feel better again.

Guidelines for success

Do not punish. If you use the hold as just another or more effective form of punishment, then it will not work. It works because it is nurturing, not because it is restricting.

Make sure that you do not get hurt. If the child is too powerful for you to hold on your lap, or if you are pregnant, then you might have to hold him while he is lying on his back on the floor. To do this, you could straddle him at hip level, resting your weight on your knees, hold his wrists, and cross your ankles over his. This type of hold is obviously a last resort, and you'll want to turn it into a normal cuddle as soon as the child calms down enough. But if it's the only way of making sure that you don't get injured, then you don't have much choice.

Use the hold for all tantrum forms. Usually a passive tantrum (whinge-ing or uncooperativeness) comes before an active (protesting or social) tantrum. It will be quicker—and you might only need to cuddle rather than hold the child in a confining way—if you can use the hold to soothe a child having a passive tantrum before he builds up into the more active form. Sometimes, though, even when you do use the hold early, the tantrum still escalates into an active form, which just goes to show that the child really was disturbed by his feelings. At least getting them out in the open gets them over with.

Use the hold when practical. A related piece of advice regarding a tantrum-prone child, is to use the hold often, especially at first. On the

---

[1] I am grateful to Malcolm Robinson, Adelaide Family Therapist, for outlining these stages.

other hand, when you really *can't* use it, you don't have to. If you cannot hold a child even though you know he needs your help, you can say so: 'I can see you're feeling upset, and I wish I could help you to calm down, but I can't just now. I am sorry'. As long as you can use the hold sometimes, the child will be learning how to manage his feelings. True, the more often you can use it, the more practice he gets, but he can still learn even if he is not helped every time.

Be flexible. If another child needs you while you are holding a tantruming child, then stop the hold if you have to. Or if the tantruming child wants to be let go, make a deal that you will stop holding him, as long as he agrees not to hurt you. (Resume the hold if he does thrash about again and might hurt you.) If he can calm down without your holding him—maybe he calms down while you hold his hand or stroke his forehead—then do that. You will get to know what works for most children and for this particular child. Trust your instincts, and experiment with what works for you, and go with that. The less confining you can make the method—as long as it still works to teach the child how to get on top of his feelings without risking injury to you—then, the better you both will feel about it.

Accept his feelings, but not his actions. You must be clear that it is quite okay for a child to feel angry: don't tell him to calm down or be quiet. You are not holding him because he is angry but because he is acting on those feelings in inconsiderate ways—maybe by hurting someone.

Keep him comfortable. It will be hard for a child to calm down when he is uncomfortably hot. Offer to get him a cool facecloth for his temples—as long as he will stay put while you're getting it—and strip off his outer clothing if he wants you to, so that he can keep cool.

Encourage him. Tell him that you believe he can do it—he *can* calm down. When I've talked about growing up to the child beforehand, I've mentioned all the things he has already learned to do, and told him that I have faith that he can learn to manage his feelings as well. Then, while I'm holding him, I say things like, 'Take your time. I know you'll be able to calm down when you're ready. I *know* you can do it. I believe in you'.

Go the distance. Be certain to last out until the fourth and final stage so that the child has had enough time to get on top of his feelings, or he will get into more trouble straight away. When he is beginning to calm down, release your hold progressively in stages, until you are only cuddling him normally. If he begins to thrash around again, resume your hold for a bit longer.

Tell him about it in advance. It can help if you tell the child about the method before you start to use it. You might say something like, 'Sometimes, your feelings get you very upset and you can't help yourself to feel better. When you feel that badly, I'll help by sitting with you while you are settling down'.

Be sure that you obtain the parent's permission. If you anticipate that you will need to hold a child whose behaviour is often disruptive, then you will need to explain the method to his parent and get the parent's permission to use the approach. You might also want to check the idea with your centre director or a child psychologist so that you have a specialist's backing for your behavioural program. A consultant might be able to suggest a less intrusive method that you could try first, or find a way to vary one of the suggestions mentioned earlier in this chapter so that they will work for you and thus avoid the need for this more restrictive technique.

Sometimes though, you'll be caught on the hop: a child might require the hold unexpectedly, before you have gained his parents' permission. One way to avoid this would be to have a written behaviour management policy (see chapter 28) which parents receive when they enrol their child. On one of the enrolment forms which the parents sign, you could include a statement giving you permission to use any of the methods mentioned in the policy, on the understanding that you will follow up by talking with the parents as soon as possible after a behavioural incident.

Get medical advice. It is important to make sure that the child is not acting up for some medical reason: you cannot expect him to take emotional charge of a physical cause of his behaviour. To that end, you could ask his parents if they have ever considered whether a medical condition could be causing his behavioural difficulties, and perhaps give them advice about who they could consult to investigate possible causes.

Also, it might be dangerous to hold a child who has a medical condition—such as asthma or a heart condition— and so you will also need medical advice if these could be made worse by emotional stress, for example.

Advantages of the hold

The hold gives children your help to feel better. Helping them is kinder than making them sort themselves out—for instance, during time-out. It teaches them how to manage their feelings, and lets them know that you will support them, even when they are being difficult.

The method is active, at a time when the child cannot listen to reason and so talking would not work. It also works for children with delayed speech or comprehension who cannot understand a lot of talk, and for babies—say, when they bang their head over and over on their high chair tray. Because the method is active, it convinces the child that you are serious about expecting him to learn how to behave considerately.

The method works quickly and, because it is nurturing, you can use it before a child's feelings get completely out of control. It prevents tantrums both in the short and long term.

And it avoids all the disadvantages of punishments.

When numerous children are out of control

The hold seems unmanageable when a number of children are out of control at once. However, you still have a few options. You can begin by holding one child: perhaps the one you can catch, maybe the ringleader (as long as you identify a different ringleader each time; otherwise, one child will feel victimised); or, you could be random about whom you select. Once you are holding a child, the others will be watching and might decide to calm down independently. Or, when the first child is calm again, you could hold any children who are still out of control of themselves.

Another approach involves any adults who are free—although there are seldom many of them!—to hold one child each. Your choice of approach comes down to practicalities—and it doesn't really matter what you do because any of these methods will work.

If the same few children often get out of control of themselves as a group, then it might help if you can plan how to avoid future occasions. It might be that you will have to limit super-hero play or chasing games if these act as a trigger; you might have to move the children's rest time to earlier in the afternoon; you might find that one child is a ringleader and needs a concentrated effort to manage his behaviour. The rationale for examining triggers is that it will certainly be easier to avoid whatever you think sets the children off than it will be to calm them all down afterwards.

Reframing

Your response to a child's behaviour depends on what you think the behaviour *means*. You might believe that she can't help it and so you are not assertive about her behaviour. Or, you might think that the child is 'doing it deliberately', in which case you are likely to try to force her to stop it.

But if your approach is not working, maybe that is because your explanation of the behaviour is not helpful. To change the behaviour you will need to find a new way of looking at the behaviour. A new view of it is called a *reframe*.

For instance, if you have been ignoring the behaviour because you have thought that it was 'attention-seeking', you might find it useful to think of the behaviour as clarity-seeking. That is, the child is not clear that you are determined that she behave considerately, even when you are busy. So, you could abandon what you are doing and make it clear what you expect (see also chapter 11).

If you think that the behaviour started because of something which happened some time ago, then you cannot fix that, because you cannot undo the past. Instead, your new view of the problem will distinguish between what *started* the behaviour pattern versus what is *maintaining* it now.

A new way of looking at the behaviour is to avoid blaming the child, her parents, or yourself. It helps if you can find something positive in the child or her behaviour. For example, picking on another child makes that child look good—even though this is not what she intends—and so she is doing the other child a favour. She is getting into trouble, while the other child looks like an angel. Once you can notice that the effects of the behaviour are not entirely negative, then you can be more positive when you deal with it.

Yet another example of reframing is when the child has been intimidating or manipulating you. If a child has been scaring you, it can help to tell her firmly, 'You don't scare me'. A clear gaze and a calm voice while delivering this surprising message can be a very powerful way to let the child know that you are in control of yourself, and expect to be taken seriously in future.

Do the opposite

If all else has failed, try doing the opposite of what you have been doing about the child's behaviour. If you have been ignoring it, give it your attention. If you have been sending the child away to sort himself out, bring him close to you and give him your support to get back in control of himself. If you have been trying to talk him out of a behaviour, give him permission to continue with it—as long as it does not bother anyone. If you have been thinking that he cannot help himself, expect him to find a way to mend his ways.

The advice to try the opposite of what you have been doing, can be the basis of choosing between the range of suggestions which I give in Part five for dealing with specific behaviours.

Have fun

My final suggestion is to have some fun. By the time a child's behaviour has become a serious problem, life has got very earnest. The adults feel inadequate and, because you're human, you might dislike the child who causes you to feel that way. The child feels victimised by being told off all the time. So, if nothing else has worked, at least you could have some fun. When a child is throwing a tantrum, you could perform an ethnic dance, or have a tantrum yourself, or sing at the top of your lungs, or do a handstand . . . whatever. There isn't a child worth his salt who can carry on with a tantrum while you're being ridiculous. And if it doesn't fix his behaviour, at least you've enjoyed yourself and let off some steam.

16

• • • • • • • • • • • •

Why isn't it working?

If you have been dealing with a child's difficult behaviour in a way which you expect would have worked—and it isn't working—then the following list of questions might suggest a reason.

About you

- Are you letting yourself be intimidated by the child? You might not have come across a child with such extreme behaviour before, or you might be letting the child's diagnosis scare you from handling her as confidently as you otherwise could. If the child has been diagnosed, find out what you need to know about the condition by reading up on it or speaking with the child's parents or other professionals. Next, find some confidence—or pretend to feel confident (no one will tell the difference)—and take charge of the behaviour—through active means, not through talking.
- Are you being too patient? If you're having to nag, if you regularly give instructions more than twice, if you're feeling frustrated more than you think is reasonable, then probably you're being too patient. Act sooner, by being assertive about the child's behaviour, and by not reasoning with her while she is being unreasonable. Take some firm action, perhaps using one of the ideas in chapter 15.
- Are you worried that the child will not like you if you set limits on her behaviour? In fact, being unassertive *guarantees* losing her respect.

The child

- Could it be that the child's behaviour is communicating a need? He might be trying to tell you that he is stressed, is being abused, that he is unwell, that he has a food sensitivity or some other medical problem. His behaviour will not improve until you can deal with these issues—in consultation with the parents.

- Is the child stressed? worried about his family? If he is, and if he feels out of control of whatever is bothering him, then he will continue to behave poorly because he is too busy being worried about other concerns to take care of his own behaviour. He will be too stressed to cope with having so much responsibility and so little power.
- Have you been thinking that the child can't help himself? Maybe he has a disability, or you think he has an 'emotional disturbance'. You might have made allowances for him when his problems first appeared or when he started at your centre, and these lowered expectations still seem necessary because the problem has not gone away. Instead, he will need to know that you think that he is a whole person who can overcome obstacles. Clarify what you expect, make life more predictable to him, and accept no excuses. His particular problems can tell you that it will be more difficult for him to behave considerately than it is for another child, but if you allow that to excuse him from having to behave well, the other children will resent him, and the child will be disadvantaged by having the original disability plus a social disability.
- Have you identified the right child? Children often work as a team, with one provoking a child who has a short fuse. He blows up, gets into trouble, and the one who was teasing or provoking him gets entertained. Maybe you will have to address another child if working on the behaviour of one child is not working.
- If you have recently begun a new management approach, did you tell the child that you were changing how you were going to respond when he behaved disruptively? He might be trying to find out why the rules appear to have changed. Just tell him what you are doing.
- Are the child's parents recently divorced or separated? If they are, some children act up so that they can get their parents together—even if at a meeting to discuss their difficulties—in the hope that the two parents will sort out their differences. If this could be so, suggest that the parents explain to the child what is happening in their relationship, and let the child know that there is nothing he can do to change that.
- Is the child accustomed to throwing his weight around at home and is just transferring that into your centre? If so, don't despair, because children cope with a whole variety of expectations which are different for each parent, the neighbours, various relatives, home versus child care or preschool, and so on. You will just have to teach him what you expect at the centre, and explain that it might be different from at home but that you're sure he can remember both sets of rules.
- Is it possible that the child's home is violent? If it is, the child might take seriously only those discipline approaches which involve shouting or physical violence such as smacking. Your calm, reasoned manner might not impress him with your resolve. If this is possible, then explain to him in a firm voice (you can pretend to be stern—he

won't know the difference between mock sternness and the real thing) that even though you don't shout or smack, you still expect to be taken seriously and you expect him to follow the rules, because they keep everyone in the centre safe.

Your teamwork with your colleagues

- Could it be that a couple of members of staff are struggling to prove who is the more skilled person or who is right about how to manage the child? If a child with chronic behavioural difficulties senses that two people have different opinions and vastly different management methods, she will continue to behave poorly for both of you. It will be necessary for the team to decide to try one approach with which everyone can agree—even if some members of staff are sceptical about whether it will work.

Your approach

- Could it be that your explanation of the behaviour has suggested a management method that isn't working? You might have been thinking that the behaviour is a result of something which happened in the past—which you cannot undo; or you might be blaming the child's personality—which is difficult to change. These explanations will be telling you that the child's behaviour *cannot* change, not that it *can*. This might be paralysing you and making you indecisive when you respond to her behaviour.
- Is the behaviour which you are focusing on too difficult to fix? When you are trying to get the children to have an afternoon nap, you cannot allow one child to throw a tantrum and keep the others awake. But you can act when that child is uncooperative at some other time during the day. When she learns to take you seriously at other times, then she might lie down for a rest when you tell her that it's rest time. Likewise, it is difficult to deal with an active tantrum (see chapter 15) but easier to deal with a passive one such as whingeing or being uncooperative, so begin there, not with the most troublesome behaviour.
- Are you being too persistent with a method which, if it were going to work, would have worked by now? Even when what we actually do about the behaviour appears to have changed, usually we are only doing more of the same type of response. You might have been trying to force the child to stop her behaviour, you might have been ignoring it, you might have been feeling helpless about it. It could be worth trying something completely different—maybe doing the exact opposite of what you have been doing (see chapter 15).

Part five

• • • • • • • • • •

Specific behavioural challenges of young children

Part five applies the guidelines and general recommendations of the earlier chapters to some behavioural challenges that are common in the early childhood years. Many of the behaviours are understandable, given the children's developmental stage. But when the behaviours are happening too often, at the wrong time or place, or are still present at a later age than usual, you will need to take some action to help the children to progress beyond them.

Which suggestions you choose to use will depend on what you have already tried. If a behaviour has been difficult for some time, it might be useful to use an alternative strategy to the one you have been trying so far. On the other hand, sometimes a slight change in flavour—what I call 'fine-tuning' a method which you are already using—can be enough to make a difference, without having to instigate a completely new management plan.

If the ideas which I give here do not help, then don't keep going it alone. If a problem—even a small one—goes on for too long, it can become the whole focus of the centre, and the child who is experiencing the problem can quickly lose confidence in him or herself. To avoid this happening, it can help if you ask the child's parents whether you could consult a specialist in children's behaviour so that you can nip the problem in the bud before it becomes a habit.

The issues which are covered in the next three chapters won't all be relevant to you. So even if you have been reading the earlier chapters from beginning to end, the chapters in this section are intended for quick reference at the time when you are facing some challenging behaviour. Using the index, all you will need to do is look up the particular behaviour which is of concern, and read the section which addresses that issue.

17

• • • • • • • • • •

Self-management skills

At times, normally independent children will want help with tasks which they can usually do on their own. Physically they can do them, but sometimes they want extra nurturing.

Eating

Throughout the development of the human race, being suspicious of new foods has ensured our survival (Birch et al. 1995). For instance, children's preference for sweet food might be part of our species' make-up since, in the wild, sweet things are seldom poisonous (Birch et al. 1995). This means that it is natural that young children will be fussy eaters until they become familiar with a range of foods and realise that they are safe.

If your centre provides meals for the children, then these not only have to be nutritious, but also culturally and individually appropriate for the children. Even when you achieve this there will be times when individual children refuse to eat what has been prepared for them. In that case you might ask the children to taste the set meal in order to educate their taste buds. But forcing them to eat it can make them resistant to that food even if they otherwise might have liked it.

It pays to have something else as a stand-by for the children to eat instead. Some caregivers object to offering children alternative food on the grounds that it will only encourage them to be fussy eaters if they know they can have something else. However, children have a right to their food preferences and not to be hungry.

Meal times offer many opportunities for exercising choices and so are educational in themselves. They can also be a valuable time for talking with children about how to notice when they are hungry and when they have eaten enough. While some people eat as a result of external cues—they see food and eat it, or finish off the left-overs because they are there—others learn to eat in response to internal cues—to what their body is telling them about its needs. In the long run, internally cued people are less likely to develop eating disorders, and so education about internal cues at a young age can be important.

This underscores the importance of avoiding external controls around food. You should not reward children for eating, neither should you chastise them for not eating. You might ask them, 'Is your body not hungry right now, or just not hungry for pasta?'. If the child is not hungry, then perhaps you can set aside a bowl of food which he can eat later; if he is not hungry for this particular meal, then you will need to offer a substitute.

If refusals are common a change in the menu is indicated, not least to satisfy the children, but also because wasted food is expensive. If just one or two children are refusing to eat the meals you could consult with their parents for their suggestions. A child who is an especially fussy eater can still be encouraged to eat the centre's meals, but perhaps the parents themselves could provide a snack as back-up in case the child refuses to eat.

Another reason not to force children to eat the prepared food is that sometimes they refuse food which upsets their body. They cannot tell you this, but somehow they know to avoid particular foods. This can result in refusing a certain class of foods. However, it is more likely that the child will simply notice that food upsets him and so he will become suspicious of all foods (although keep in mind that being suspicious of foods is natural in young children). This child is likely to be small for his age.

The opposite pattern comes about when food to which we are intolerant gives us a quick 'fix' or pick-up, followed by a let-down. To avoid the withdrawal effect, the child needs another dose of the same food. The pattern follows that the child will choose the same food or a restricted range of foods over and over, will ask for particular foods when he is tired as they will pick him up, and might be constantly eating, with possible over-weight resulting.

The most suspect foods fall into three categories: children with a family history of allergies (such as asthma, eczema or migraines) can be sensitive to whole foods—that is, dairy products, eggs, wheat, corn, cereals and caffeine (in chocolate, coke, tea and coffee). The second class of triggers for food sensitivities are additives such as colourings and preservatives; and the third class are naturally occurring chemicals and foods such as sugars, salicylates, MSG (chemical number 621) and amines.

If you notice either of these patterns of fussy eating in a child, it might help to talk with his parents to see if they want to investigate possible food sensitivities.

Another possibility is that the children are copying their parents' attitude to food. If a parent is constantly on a diet or has anorexia, for instance, then the child might learn that food is dangerous and so will avoid eating. Again, this is a subject which you could raise tactfully with parents if you think this might apply to a child in your care.

An underweight or sickly child adds extra pressure on adults to help the child to eat. While you are establishing better eating patterns the parents might be willing to see a doctor for an overall health check for the child, and also for a recommendation about vitamin supplementation, so that if a child continues with a limited diet at least you will not feel obliged to pressure him to eat out of your own concerns for his nutritional well-being.

Toilet learning

It is very difficult to toilet train children before the age of two years and three months and, even at this age, they are really toilet timed, responding to frequent reminders from adults to go to the toilet, rather than deciding for themselves that they need to go. If a child has older brothers or sisters, she might make up her own mind to be trained before this, but you cannot force the pace.

If the parents become anxious about toilet training or want the child to be trained by a certain date, then she might pick up on their anxiety and in turn might refuse to be trained at all. As with eating, you can only encourage and ask for appropriate behaviour such as taking off her knickers or sitting on the potty or toilet, but you cannot force a child to be toilet trained unless she decides to be.

It is important to avoid toilet learning becoming a major focus of your program (Greenman & Stonehouse 1997). If you feel that a child is under a little too much pressure to learn toileting, then perhaps you can tactfully suggest to the parents to back off for a few weeks and start again later. In the meantime, you could explain to the child that now that she is growing up on the outside, you know she will soon be ready to grow up on the inside as well, by learning to do a wee like a big three-year-old (or whatever age she will be at her next birthday).

Some children acquire toileting skills quite successfully until they turn three and then they have a series of accidents again. This comes about because, now that they are three, they can concentrate for a longer time on what they are doing and so there aren't as many natural interruptions during which they could notice that they need to go to the toilet. You might deal with this by reminding the child that needing to do a wee can sneak up on her and so she will need to think extra hard to remember to be boss of her sneaky wees. You can also revert to the earlier toilet-timing method of suggesting that she go to the toilet at natural breaks, until she gets back in control of her toileting again for herself.

It is important not to punish a child for toileting accidents. On the other hand, don't praise her either or tell her that she's 'a good girl' when she uses the potty or toilet because this implies that she is a 'bad girl' when she has an accident. And avoid reward systems such as star charts because they make you more responsible for a child's behaviour than she is. (See chapter 11 for more disadvantages of star charts.)

Separating from parents

Children differ in how they deal with being separated from their parents, depending on their age and how often they have been apart from their parents in the past. They will also differ in the strategies which they have developed to cope and in the circumstances in which they were placed (Waters 1996). This means that each child will react differently to separating from his or her parents when beginning child care or preschool.

Some youngsters will enjoy the early days in the centre but when they realise that the arrangement is permanent they will develop problems; other children have separation problems from the beginning. Sometimes a new stage of cognitive development signals a new understanding of being left in care, and separation difficulties begin unexpectedly after some months (Greenman & Stonehouse 1997).

A staggered start, with frequent visits before their actual start date can help, but many parents do not find or do not use child care until the last minute before they return to paid employment, with the result that some children are introduced into the centre 'cold turkey'.

To help settle a new child, you can allocate one person to be the primary caregiver, and then move the child on to other adults gradually once she has formed a steady attachment. You can ask parents to bring in the child's favourite comforter from home, and try to give her some favourite activities and foods, especially in the early days. Beginning with a small group of other children of her age can help, if that can be arranged.

A goodbye routine can be useful. It might be that the child puts her bag in her locker, is helped by her parent to begin an activity, they have a hug, and then the parent leaves. Babies might need a longer handover ritual than older children. It might help to make the child active in saying good-bye to a parent, perhaps by opening the door for the parent (Greenman & Stonehouse 1997).

Preparation. At enrolment, talk with parents about how they might respond to any separation difficulties (Greenman & Stonehouse 1997). Ask how their child has responded to previous separations and what they think will work for their child if separation problems occur, and also pass on your suggestions.

Accept a child's feelings, even complaints about feeling ill. Agree with his concerns, rather than telling him that it's his imagination. Comfort him when he is distressed, rather than trying to distract him from his feelings.

Explain exactly when the parent will return. Don't tell a child that 'Daddy will be back soon', when 'soon' can mean anything from a few minutes to a few hours (Greenman & Stonehouse 1997). Instead, explain that Dad will be back after a particular activity.

Communicate your faith that he can cope. You can tell him that you know that he can cope, and that he will enjoy playing with the other children once he has decided to find ways of getting over his feelings. You might talk with the parents about other times the child has overcome his feelings and remind the child of these occasions, expressing your faith that he can do it again.

Ask the parent to join with the child before going. It can help if the parent and child find a quiet corner in which to have a close hug. It can be easier for the parent to leave once she and the child have made emotional contact. In the busy-ness of getting out of the house, the parent might not have been able to give the child the emotional closeness which he needs to get through the day.

Ensure that the parent never sneaks out on a child when she is leaving him, even if telling him that she is going leads to the child becoming upset. If a child has no warning signals to distinguish when he has to be self-reliant versus when someone is available to comfort him, he will be anxious all the time. Also, suggest that the parent *tells* the child she is leaving. If she *asks* him if that's okay, the child is likely to say 'no', leaving everyone frustrated and miserable and the child feeling betrayed since the parent will go anyway.

Try keeping goodbyes brief. Suggest that the parent states briefly and calmly that she is leaving now, and hands the child over to a familiar staff member. Encourage parents to leave once they say they are going, and not to return, rather than prolonging the farewells (Greenman & Stonehouse 1997). If the parent has to leave a distressed child with you, then invite her to call you later to check how the child responded after she left.

Make the child responsible for a solution. Having listened to the child's concerns or ills, you could ask him how he can help himself to feel better. He might play with an imaginary toy or friend, begin a favourite activity when he first arrives, or make special friends with one of the other children. If he is determined to be miserable though, then you cannot change that.

Help him to deal with his feelings. When a child has a long history of separation problems, he can become upset, not so much that his parent is going, but that he feels so badly. When a child becomes hysterical he needs his parent—not a caregiver or teacher—to help him. This means asking the parent to stay until the child is back in control of his feelings. If she has inflexible working hours, she might not be able to stay the first time this happens, but you could plan for the parent to arrive 15 minutes earlier for a week, so that she has time in the mornings to sit with the child if he becomes hysterical. While the parent is with the child, he or she will be holding him (as I described in chapter 15 for tantrums) until he is back in control of his feelings. Once he knows that he can get himself calm again, his feelings will no longer frighten him into hysteria, even though he might continue to be sad.

Check that the child is not feeling responsible for his parent/s. Some children have taken on the job of looking after their parents, but they cannot take care of their parents unless they are with them, and so they refuse to separate. You can find out if a child thinks this by asking who looks after whom in his family. The child should be able to say that Mum looks after herself and Dad (if there is one in the family); Dad looks after himself and Mum; and both parents look after the children. The child might be able to tell you that the children look after the pets or dolls. If, however, he tells you that he looks after either parent, then there's your clue about a possible cause of some of his separation anxiety. You can report this back to his parents and ask if they are willing to explain to the child that he is making a mistake to think that it is his job to look after them. His job as a child is to have fun, learn to paint, run, jump etc., and to be boss of himself. It is the adults' job to look after themselves and other people. Remind the parents to thank the child for working so hard up till now to take care of them, and to let him know that now it is his turn to be looked after. The parents will need to back this up by taking better care of themselves, to convince the child that they do not need him to look out for them.

Recommend another placement. Centre-based child care does not suit every child. If a child cannot settle at all in your centre, even after patient and sensitive handling, then it might be that a home environment (such as family day care) could suit the child's personality better than centre-based care. You might have to recommend this to the child's parent, explaining your reasons.

Reunions

Even those children who separated reluctantly from parents might be off-hand when their parents return to collect them or might resist going home. Alternatively, they might see the parent and experience renewed sadness that they have been parted all day and so become distressed. Greenman and Stonehouse (1997) explain that these reactions have nothing to do with the child's preferring to be in child care than at home. Instead, children's reluctance to leave can be an attempt to involve their parents in this important part of their lives; their distress can be a reaction to being exhausted and reacting when their defences are worn down; and ignoring the parents might simply reflect the fact that they were certain that their parents were going to return.

When parents collect the child, suggest that they avoid telling her that they miss her, in case she thinks that they need her company and so will refuse to separate. Instead, they can tell her that it's lovely to see her, which is what they mean anyway.

Children who are picked up later might experience growing distress as they see other children going home. It can be useful to reserve some special activities for this time of the day and to make use of the improved adult–child ratio to give these children some special attention (Greenman & Stonehouse 1997).

Clinging to staff

There are a few reasons why children might cling to an adult rather than becoming involved in the centre's activities:

- a child who is new to the centre might need some initial security before being confident enough to join in;
- a slow-to-warm-up child might need the same extra security, but for longer;
- the child's development might be out of step with the other children's. For example, a child who is not steady on her feet could feel at risk of being knocked over by boisterous bigger children; a child whose development is advanced—that is, who is gifted—might have grown out of the activities which the other children are doing but cannot find an intellectual peer with whom she could play more sophisticated games;
- the child's parents might have recently separated and now that she is being separated from her remaining parent, she is grieving or is frightened that she might lose that parent too;
- the child might not know how to make friends.

Whatever the reason, you can begin by giving the child the extra time she appears to need. If, however, that only makes her more rather than less dependent, you can begin to help her to separate by drawing in another child to be with the pair of you. Introduce the children to each other and tell them about an interest which they have in common, even if it's simply that they are the same age. You can also give the child small tasks to do—perhaps first with you, then in parallel with you, and then on her own or in a pair with another child. Make sure that she doesn't just transfer her dependence from you to one other child, by bringing in different children every now and then (Mitchell 1993). Now that she can move away from you for a short time, extend the time she can manage without you by going off to another area to do something, while promising to return soon.

If these efforts do not work and the child cannot join in with the group because she doesn't have the social skills to do so, then the suggestions in chapters 8, 9 and 18 might help.

Group time disruptions

Young children cannot sit still for long and they do not pretend to be interested in something which is boring them: they will just get up and leave. You can use the children's signs of restlessness in group time as a signal that it is time to end an activity, and when some children leave altogether, then that is valuable feedback about how interesting—or developmentally appropriate—the activity was to them. All of us have experienced planning an activity which we were sure would excite the children, only to find that it fell flat. You will have to accept the children's verdict, not yours, and use that information to help plan your program in the future.

Some teachers and caregivers want children to comply with sitting in the group for activities by way of training for group sessions at school. But a task is much easier to learn when a child is developmentally ready for it, and so if a child is not ready yet it doesn't mean he won't be by school age. I prefer to keep group time voluntary. When you make the activities relevant and attractive to the children, they will choose to take part.

It is also important to keep the number of children in a group manageable—not only manageable for you, but for them. Fields and Boesser (1997) suggest that a child needs the number of children in a group to be no more than the number of birthdays he has had. While this may not be practicable in most centres, this guideline might serve as a reminder of the difficult task you are setting when you ask children to be part of larger groups, and so might help you to tolerate their inattention.

It is also important to keep group time short—no longer than 15 minutes in the preschool years. And finally, it will help children to participate in group activities if they can be actively involved.

With group time structured along these lines you can then invite a restless child to leave the group and do something else so that she doesn't disrupt the activity for the other children. When children know that they can leave, those who stay will voluntarily manage their own behaviour.

Fears

Some children say that they are frightened of a variety of inoffensive objects—such as balloons, the sound of a toilet flushing, the sound of the hand drier, or going outside. Since these fears restrict their activities, you will need to help them to overcome their fears. The following are some possible methods for doing this.

Listen. First, listen to a child about his fears. If there is a good reason for his fear, try to remove its source. Understand that he is fearful even if you don't understand why. But even if the fear seems ridiculous, don't tell him to 'stop being silly'. If you tell a child that he is not allowed to be frightened, he will become frightened that no one will help him, and worried that he won't be able to hide his fear from you. These two feelings make the original problem worse than it was.

Take the panic out of being afraid. Normalise what he is feeling. You might explain that everyone gets frightened at times, or you can teach him the difference between being frightened of something, versus disliking it, versus being surprised by it. Sometimes we appear to be afraid of a cockroach, say, when we really have been surprised to find it somewhere unexpectedly. Being surprised or disliking something is not as scary as being frightened of it.

Have faith that he can overcome this. Armed with information from his parents, tell him stories about other times he has overcome problems, and express to him that you are confident that he can do so again. Let him know that you think he is very brave to be trying to be boss of his fears.

Make him responsible for a solution. Ask him how he plans to overcome his fears. Since they are a product of his imagination, only he can change his thinking. You might explain that his fears are sneaking up on him and a child who is growing up on the inside as well as the outside will find a way to out-sneak them. Once he has decided to become boss of his fears, you could offer to be his 'fears adviser'. You know about magic spells that can get rid of fears, and he knows about his own brain and so, because young children believe in magic, together you could invent a magic spell that will make the fears go away.

Repeated refusals or uncooperativeness

At around the age of two, children learn that they are separate individuals and they learn that they can make decisions. Sometimes, they say 'no' when they mean 'yes', and sometimes they change their mind and decide that they want something which they previously refused. All this is normal and healthy. You can avoid some hassles, however, by:

* avoiding over-use of your power to make rules which you then have to police. Let the children participate in deciding on rules which affect them (but not that there will be rules) so that they become committed to keeping them.
* offering children a choice about how they will do something which is compulsory, but not whether they will do it, so that they can still exercise some autonomy without rebelling against you.
* not asking if they want to do something when they have no choice about it. For instance, don't ask foolish questions such as, 'Do you want to wash your hands before lunch?'.
* asking a child what her objection is when it seems that your wishes conflict with hers. It is easy to assume what the problem is, when it is something entirely different. Once you know her objection you might find a simple solution.

Copying inappropriate behaviour

Sometimes children will copy the silly behaviour of a friend. This is normal and it can take the heat out of the situation by simply clicking your tongue in mock annoyance and saying something like, 'Four-year-olds! Still, at your age, you need times when you can have fun and be silly. Looks like this is one of those times'. Another thing you can do is point out quietly to the child who is following the other that something is funny the first time, but humour (which has to do with the unexpected) soon wears out when it goes on and on. You might say that it's fun to be silly, as long as it doesn't go on for too long. Also, you could teach children to discriminate—that is, think about—what is appropriate and what isn't by asking them whether what they are doing is a good idea.

Stealing

During the preschool years children have a vague understanding of ownership, and so can't really be said to be stealing. If a child in your centre is taking home items which are not his, you could explain that the centre needs all of its toys so that there is something for the children to play with, or that another child will miss a personal item if he takes it home.

A child who is insecure emotionally—maybe because one of his parents has died—might hoard things he does not even want, and might steal them so that he can store them up. He knows that he can lose things without warning and so needs to stock up, just in case. Rather than focusing on the hoarding, it will help if you can find ways for him to feel emotionally secure at your centre and if you can talk with him about grief (see chapter 21).

18

•   •   •   •   •   •   •   •   •   •   •

Social and play difficulties

Even when you can meet most children's needs most of the time, there will still be some occasions when children have social difficulties. Some of these come about because a child lacks a more mature skill; sometimes it's because the behaviour—antisocial as it is—works for the child: it is quicker to snatch a toy than to ask for it. At other times you might not know the cause.

The purpose of this chapter is to offer a range of suggestions for particular social difficulties which are common with young children. If you have already tried one of the ideas and have found that it has not worked in your particular situation, then any of the other ideas might be useful.

Isolated children

In chapter 9 I made a distinction between solitary play—which can be active or passive—versus reticence, when a child hovers on the outside of a group, appearing to be interested in joining the other children but not knowing how. Solitary play is likely to be positively beneficial for every child at some time during each day, but reticence is associated with shyness and loneliness and so it can be worthwhile for you to help the reticent child.

Solitary play

Every individual of any age needs some time to be alone: to rest, prepare for new situations, or observe those around her (Readdick 1993). Solitary play does not mean that the child is failing to advance to the next stage of development: it is a normal part of any day.

Over the course of a day, children fluctuate in their ability to be sociable and their personalities differ too, so that some children need a lot of solitude while others are comfortable with being surrounded by people for much of the day. However, all children are more likely to tolerate having others around when there is enough space, when the group is a comfortable size rather than being too big, when there is a lot of opportunity to play in small groups, and when noise and temperature levels are reasonable.

1 Because so much time in child care or preschool is shared with other children, it is doubly important for you to provide a safe, inviting area in which individual children can be alone. This might be a window seat or a big chair with soft toys and quiet play activities—maybe some books—to which the children can withdraw when they need to be by themselves.

2 Accept when children need to be by themselves. Forcing them to play with others when they do not want to could make them less rather than more willing to be sociable. Therefore, do not force children to take part in activities such as listening to stories. If the story is attractive enough they will choose to give up their solitude to take part.

3 You can directly teach children how to signal when they need to be alone. You also need to read the signals which children may be giving verbally or—mostly—nonverbally. Children might signal that they need solitude by saying they want to be alone, by creating territorial boundaries with their toys, by turning away from the other children and engaging in solitary play, or by withdrawing from the company of others (Readdick 1993). Children sometimes use aggression as a communication that they are not coping, and this can be handled as suggested in a later section.

Lonely children

Loneliness can come about because of a recent loss in the child's life, such as the loss of a friend or a family member through death or separation, or a change of child care centre or preschool (Bullock 1993). Children who are suffering recent loss often feel lonely, just as adults do, and they need the same understanding which lonely adults require.

1 Listen to the lonely child and accept her feelings, even though you might feel distressed for her. Avoid reassuring her that things will get better, since this tells the child that she is not allowed to feel as she does. Instead, listening lets her know that you care about her and accept how she feels now.

2 Arrange soothing activities—such as water play—which are best done alongside, or with, other children. Once the child is comfortable with this parallel play, you could then introduce some cooperative games— see Appendix B for suggestions.

3 Children's books about the type of loss which the lonely child is experiencing can be useful—see Appendix E for suggestions.

4 Talk with the child's parents about anything which might have happened at home to cause the child's loneliness, about what they suggest you could do to help the child, about what you are doing at the centre which they might want to support—say, by inviting one of the centre's children over to play—or suggesting books or outside professionals for

the parents to read or consult if the child is having difficulties at home as well.

5 If the problem does not get better in the centre, together with the parents you might need to refer the child for help from other professionals.

Reticence (not joining in)

Sometimes a particular child does not manage to enter a group or develop friendships because she lacks the necessary social skills. In turn, a lack of friendships means that the child does not have enough opportunity to practise and develop her social skills, and so the initial problem can grow. In the preschool years, shyness and withdrawal are not good indicators that a child has or will develop social problems later, although young children will feel lonely when they are isolated, and so reticence in young children is worth doing something about.

On the other hand, children will wander around aimlessly when their caregivers are not responding to their needs (Doherty-Derkowski 1995). Therefore, check that your program is suitable for a reticent child and that you respond to that child appropriately and promptly.

If you believe that the child needs coaching in particular social skills, then as well as providing cooperative activities and coaching her about how to join in other children's play (see chapters 8 and 9), you could also:

* structure an activity with only a small group of children, beginning with one other child, then adding two, and then more.
* ensure that the children know each other's names, by introducing them, asking one child to name who is next to her, and singing songs which include their names.
* keep larger group activities short at first. Allow any of the children to go off by themselves when they need to.
* accept that all children will feel shy at times. However, when shyness is causing a child acute pain, she needs some help to overcome it.

Shyness

Whereas disruptive behaviour comes about because a child is not monitoring his actions and thinking about them in advance, the shy child is monitoring too much, worrying about the impression he is creating. Not everyone has to be outgoing, but shyness can be very painful and limiting to a child, so it will be beneficial if you can help him to overcome it.

Improve his self-esteem. Use acknowledgment rather than praise to teach the child not to rely on other people's opinions of him.

Normalise shyness. Acknowledge that we all feel unsure of ourselves in groups of strangers and that maybe what he is feeling is normal. This removes his worry about being shy and so halves the problem.

Give him time to recover himself. When a young child becomes self-conscious, as they all do, don't encourage this by calling it shyness ('Ooh, have you gone all shy?'). Instead, don't comment but give him a moment or two to recover himself.

Expect appropriate social behaviour. Expect him to greet people, but not necessarily when everyone is watching him. He might need a few minutes, after which he can approach you and say 'hello' less publicly. Insist, however, that he does so, otherwise the shyness will become an excuse for poor social skills.

Make him responsible for a solution. Talk with the child about being boss of the shy feelings which sometimes overwhelm him. Just as other fears are a product of his imagination, fears about what others think of him are too, and so he will need to take charge of them.

Have fun. If nothing else has worked, you could prescribe the shyness—perhaps by telling the child not to say 'hello' when he arrives at the centre, because you would get such a fright, or because he couldn't cope. This exaggerates how silly his shyness is, making it obvious that nothing dreadful would happen if he overcame it.

Prejudice and discrimination

Some children reject others who look or behave unusually.

Prevention. Establish an anti-bias curriculum and policy which is written down and given to new parents when they enrol their child in your centre. You cannot demand that parents share your centre's values, but parents need to know what behaviours you will and will not condone in the centre.

Use books and natural events to talk with children about the differences between people (Crary 1992). The children's awareness of differences can be increased through inclusive wall displays or planned activities and discussions about how other people feel and live. However, this multi-cultural perspective should not degenerate into a 'tourist curriculum' which focuses on a culture's exotic customs rather than daily life (Derman-Sparks & the ABC Task Force 1989). A tourist curriculum is likely to perpetuate stereotypes—for instance, not all Aborigines are rural, and so the daily life of urban Aborigines needs to be a focus also. A true anti-bias curriculum can be supported by inviting parents, community members and staff to share with the children some of their cultural experiences.

While bigotry assumes that differences mean that people are unequal, 'colour-blindness' assumes that differences do not matter (Stonehouse 1991b). Neither perspective is accurate. Instead, an anti-bias curriculum acknowledges and celebrates differences openly and honestly (Saifer et al. 1993) by giving children straightforward information about gender, race and ethnicity. From a very young age, children are aware of differences between people and so need their questions to be answered in a way which conveys the sense that differences are interesting, rather than deficiencies.

Establish a general rule of using words which do not hurt other people (Derman-Sparks 1992). Ensure that the children know that they cannot exclude another child from their play for reasons of race, gender, or disability (Derman-Sparks & the ABC Task Force 1989).

Intervention. When an incident of teasing or verbal abuse has occurred, withdraw the recipient and the offender together. Talk to the recipient of the teasing. Listen to her. Tell her that you understand that what the other child said hurt her feelings. Meanwhile, allow the offender to hear this conversation, without being lectured to or shamed. When a child has not been humiliated, the teasing or abuse is more likely to stop.

As long as you can do so without preaching, give the perpetrator some simple information which clarifies a stereotype or misconception (Crary 1992).

Teach the victim to be assertive in reply to teasing, using general statements such as, 'Don't say those things to me. I don't like it' or more specific rebuttals, such as, 'That is not friendly. I won't play with you if you're not friendly' or, 'That's not true. I'm not (whatever the other child has accused her of)'.

Teasing can be a child's way of gaining power in situations where she otherwise feels powerless (Mitchell 1993). You therefore need to ensure that perpetrators of discrimination in the centre feel accepted and powerful. Ensure that you offer many opportunities for choices and for making real contributions to the centre and that you acknowledge—but do not praise—children's achievements so that they learn how to value themselves and each other.

Refusals to allow another child to participate in play

At times, a child or small group of children might refuse to let another child join their play, not because of the child's devalued status (although they might claim that this is the reason), but simply because they cannot absorb another player or they want to be alone. You can ask them about their play and whether there is room for one more child. Complaints such as, 'Matthew wants to be the baby and we already have a baby', could be met with suggestions that this family could have twins, or that Matthew could adopt some other role. If the children reject these suggestions, you could explain, 'Well, it looks like there isn't room for you in this game just now, Matthew. Children, how long do you think you'll be playing this game before you can let Matthew join in? How long will Matthew have to wait?'. This gives a certain end to their exclusion of Matthew and lets Matthew know that his exclusion has to do with the demands of the game, rather than himself.

Aggression

Aggressive children's verbal and nonverbal behaviours often disrupt the play of other children, with the result that they will have problems developing friendships. Aggression is inconsiderate of the feelings of other children. Therefore you will need to respond to aggressive behaviour, both for the aggressor's own sake, and to protect her peers.

When crowded and competing for too few toys, it is more likely that the children will use available toys as missiles or will snatch toys from each other. Therefore, sufficient space and enough equipment is crucial in preventing aggressive play.

Your aim when responding to aggression is to comfort the recipient; to teach the aggressor another way to meet her needs and solve problems; and to reassure onlooking children about their ongoing safety—both from attacks on them by the perpetrator and from being dealt with harshly if they were to make a mistake by becoming aggressive. The basic premise is that non-violence is better than violence at solving problems (Slaby et al. 1995).

Babies

Babies are sometimes accused of playing aggressively when they hit another child. However, they usually hit in an attempt to touch, but because they cannot control their own strength they can hurt the other child. (The same can be true of older children with particular physical disabilities such as cerebral palsy.) However, the behaviour is not 'naughty' because the child cannot help it.

The baby's physical skills will develop in time. In the meantime, you can separate the children involved, distract the perpetrator, or just show her how to touch 'gently'. Even though this will not work immediately, in the long run the child will learn that you appreciate gentle treatment of other children.

Stressed children

Children who are distressed at home might find it difficult to deal calmly with being sad or angry. Their aggression can be a reaction to stress in their lives. Nevertheless, they cannot be permitted to harm other children. Ways to help them cope with their feelings are given in chapter 20. One of these is to arrange a solitary area where they can withdraw until they feel better.

Children with additional difficult behaviours

Children who have too much power at home often extend this over-control into their play with other children at the centre. These children's feelings frequently overwhelm them, resulting in a range of disorganised behaviours (see chapter 11), only one of which is direct aggression. I gave a series of suggestions for responding to tantrums in part four of this book, among which were:

Act on earlier forms of lost control. Where possible, help the child to calm down before she becomes aggressive. The passive forms of tantrums—uncooperativeness and whingeing—often show up before aggression. If you can help before a child's feelings become actively out of control, they might not escalate into aggression.

Address the victim, not the perpetrator. Take the perpetrator and victim aside and reflect the victim's feelings. 'That hurt you, didn't it? . . . Yes, Shelley forgot to use her words . . . She might be feeling frustrated or angry, do you think?'. Next, nurse the recipient's injuries and invite the child who inflicted them to help, so that she is encouraged to be responsible for her actions.

Teach assertiveness. When the immediate crisis is over, coach the victim to tell the aggressor that he will not play with her if she hurts him.

Explain—later, briefly, and without anger. Remember that 'you can't reason while a child is being unreasonable' and that you can only talk with the perpetrator once she is back in control. If you can do so without humiliating her, explain why aggression is hurtful. However, keep these explanations brief because the child is likely to have heard it all before and already knows what you are saying—she just couldn't act on the information (much like adults when we know we shouldn't eat an attractive food, but do it anyway).

Do not give an angry child a substitute target to which to direct her aggression (Slaby et al. 1995). Instead, teach the child how to use words when she is cross, instead of hitting out at someone or something else.

Separate the children if necessary—but not as a punishment, simply as recognition that their behaviour tells you that they cannot play together at the moment. You might have to help them to begin a new activity if they are too worked up to generate alternative ideas themselves (Slaby et al. 1995).

Acknowledge prosocial acts. When you see a child who is frequently aggressive using more prosocial behaviour, acknowledge that you (and her playmate) appreciate that. Remember not to praise, though, for the reasons discussed in chapter 6.

Referral. If a child does not respond to the above methods, then you will need to suggest to her parents that they consult a specialist in children's behaviour. If they are unwilling to do this and your efforts ultimately prove unsuccessful, you might have to consider asking the parents to withdraw the child from the centre, in the interests of keeping the other children safe. This sounds harsh but might be therapeutic in that it could shock the parents into helping their child; it also protects the other children, who have a right to feel safe in your care.

Rough-and-tumble play

Some children use rough-and-tumble play as a way of inviting another child to play with them. They do not mean to be aggressive, but they might not notice the other child's protests.

- Remind children to use words when they want to invite another child to play.
- In group activities, separate children who find it difficult to keep their hands off each other.
- Make the group activities as attractive and active as possible to maintain the interest of the more busy children.
- Teach the children to discriminate quiet times from active times. If they are in a large group which calls for passive participation but they cannot control their activity level, you can direct them to play somewhere else so that the group is not disrupted.
- At other times, provide a mat for tumbling and offer cooperative games which allow children to touch each other safely.
- Explain how the other child is feeling about unwanted touch. If, after these reminders, the child cannot control his behaviour, then he is out of control of his feelings: it is no longer a social problem, but a behavioural one. This can be dealt with as described in chapter 15.

Biting

Biting is a common problem, particularly with younger children. Dealing with it is complicated by the fact that it is so emotive. Your responses will depend on the age of the biter and how often the child bites.

General guidelines

- Your job is to protect children—all of them—and this means taking decisive—although not frantic—action when one child is hurt by another.
- Biting is like any other behaviour which hurts or injures a child's playmates. Try to get it into perspective, and not over-react emotionally. Your reaction itself might keep the behaviour going, because it is so entertaining.
- If you discipline by using power, you cannot do anything until after one child has bitten another. If instead you use guidance, you might be able to detect when a child is showing early signs of stress or feeling out of control and help him to deal with these feelings before another child has to get hurt.
- Ensure that the program offers enough equipment, a balance of active and calming activities, sufficient challenges—but ones which are not so difficult that the children become frustrated—and enough space so that frustration or the sheer proximity of other children does not invite biting.
- Do not make the perpetrator apologise. A child hates losing face just as adults do, and so feeling shamed might provoke another incident.

Also, there is no value at all in forcing children to say they're sorry if they're not.

- Keep explanations brief. Mostly, children know that biting is hurtful, but at the time they could not overcome their emotions and act on this knowledge.
- Sooth the injury in the usual way, and if the skin is broken consult a medical practitioner in the rare chance of infection.
- Without telling parents of the victim who has bitten their child, notify the parents of both children about the incident. However, make it clear that you have sorted it out and that you do not expect the parents to solve it for you. You don't want the perpetrator punished at home for something which has happened at the centre. On the other hand, parents have a right to know about their child's behaviour or injuries. It can take courage to tell the parents of the perpetrator, and so suggestions for these types of meetings are offered in chapter 26.

Babies

The first type of biter is the under-one-year-old who, without malice, bites another child who happens to be there. Babies put things in their mouths, and that 'thing' can occasionally be another child. In addition to all the general guidelines already mentioned, you could:

- Check that the baby is not uncomfortable in the mouth because of teething. Administer medication such as paracetomol for acute pain, and offer teething rings to soothe low-grade pain.
- You might choose to say 'no' firmly to the baby who has bitten. (I reserve the word 'no' for dangerous behaviour, and avoid it for simple mistakes.)
- Offer the child something else to bite or eat, explaining, 'Teeth are for eating. Here is something you can eat' (Mitchell 1993).
- Meanwhile, you could separate the babies, and calmly nurse the injured child.

Toddlers

A second type of biter is the two-year-old who appears not to be malicious and yet repeatedly bites other children. Perhaps this child has learned that biting works: it gets her the item that she wants, and it is quicker than using words, which do not yet come automatically to her.

Just as for younger children, make sure that the toddler is not experiencing too much frustration, is comfortable, uncrowded and is receiving sufficient—but not too much—stimulation in the centre.

1 Teach and support verbal children to use words rather than biting to express what they want.
2 Explain *briefly* that since she cannot be friendly, she cannot play with other children, and redirect her to a solitary activity or an activity with an adult. She needs time away from other people to calm down. *This is not a punishment*, because punishment will not work: it's just a chance for a breather.

3 Shadow a child who has been habitually biting, so that you can observe her behaviour and possibly identify any early signs that she is getting worked up or is likely to bite. She might be complaining, tearful, aggressive or uncooperative in safe ways before she gets worked up enough to bite someone. Or she could be competing for too few toys, and bites in order to get a turn. If the biting is chronic, it will be useful to record your observations. Writing them down makes it easier to identify patterns in the child's behaviour (Mitchell 1993).

4 Avoid large group activities and break the children into smaller groups, while also avoiding placing a repeated biter with her favourite victim (Greenman & Stonehouse 1997).

Children with additional difficult behaviours

A third type of biter is the child whose behaviour is out of control in lots of ways, only one of which is biting other children. This pattern of biting is just another form of aggression. Despite knowing what is right, the child cannot behave appropriately because her feelings overwhelm her. Suggestions for responding to this pattern of biting were given in chapter 15 and in the earlier section on aggression in this chapter. An additional suggestion is to intervene with an easier behaviour instead of tackling the biting directly, which is hard to fix. Once children know that they have to take you seriously about a lesser behaviour, they might take you seriously when you instruct them about biting.

Bullying

Bullying is the ongoing intimidation of one child by another. In early childhood, rather than using aggression which is directed systematically at a particular child, bullying usually involves excluding a child from the group.

• Bullying tends to occur most when there are big differences in power or status between children and when they are not supervised enough by adults. To avoid this, ensure that the program highlights equality among the children and between adults and children.

• Recognise that repeated exclusion from a group is bullying and intervene to protect vulnerable children.

• Tell the perpetrator that the behaviour hurts the victim's feelings, and that it is not okay.

• Ensure that the perpetrator does not draw other children into excluding a particular child. Have her speak for herself, saying something like: 'I don't want to play with you just now' instead of, 'We don't want to play with her, do we?'.

• Teach a vulnerable child to be assertive about her rights to play where and with whatever equipment she likes. She has a right to a turn.

• Assume that the perpetrator has low self-esteem: the only way she can feel good is if she has power over other people. Work on her self-esteem in ways suggested in Part two.

• If the bullying does not stop, then it is a simple tantrum: the perpetrator is too out of control to behave considerately. Respond to this in some of the ways described in chapter 15.

Super-hero play

When TV programs with themes of power and subordination become popular, some children will carry over the violent themes into their play at the centre. Super-hero play can help children work out issues of good and evil and power and powerlessness (Saifer et al. 1993). Or, the play can simply be an imitation of what they have seen, in which case it is merely ritualistic and does not help children make sense of their world (Gronlund 1992).

Dawkins (1991) suggests that we cannot ban violent play in early childhood centres because it helps children to understand their world. She believes also that children need an exciting environment which is full of adventure, challenge and exploration, rather than a boring and bland middle-class, sterile, safe and stultifying setting.

On the other hand, violent play has some significant disadvantages. First, it can mean that children whose play is often violent are not experimenting enough with their play themes as they concentrate almost exclusively on their super-hero play. Second, super-hero play can deteriorate quickly into outright aggression (Gronlund 1992). Third, children who weren't originally involved in the violent play can imitate the other children's aggression both at the time and later—although this effect mostly occurs for children who were already aggressive (Dawkins 1991). Fourth, the violence of the play can intimidate the children who are observing it. Fifth, victims of the make-believe violence usually do not enjoy it (Bergen 1994). These disadvantages give rise to some suggestions for limiting the potential negative effects of play which has violent themes:

- Give children opportunities to make choices and take responsibility so that they are powerful in their own lives. This avoids the need to use dramatic play to resolve issues of powerlessness.
- Become familiar with the programs so that you understand their attraction for the children (Cupit 1989) and so that you can incorporate them into your educational program and, in so doing, moderate any negative effects the programs can have on the children (Dawkins 1991).
- Let the children teach you about their heroes so that you can share rather than disparage their interests (Gronlund 1992). This communicates that you accept their experiences and feelings, allows you to ask questions which help them to be critical of what they see on TV, gives you credibility when you discuss aggression with them, and ensures that their play does not become surreptitious. More important, however, it allows you to provide support for the children as they work out scary feelings and reach their own conclusions about hurting other people (Gronlund 1992). You can also balance the gender bias of violent games, involving girls who usually are onlookers only,

and thus giving girls opportunities to resolve issues of power and submission too.

- Explore issues of power and safety by using alternative topics such as dinosaurs, space adventures, or nightmares. Protectiveness training can also address safety issues for young children.
- Help the children to extend their super-hero play scenarios into more positive themes. You can begin with their script but add new parts and new conclusions which are more positive (Gronlund 1992).
- Provide alternative game scenarios which do not involve violence but which still give children power (Saifer et al. 1993). Move the danger source from a person to an event, and have the children conquer the danger—for example, by tracking down a wild animal or putting out a fire. Using miniature figures such as toy animals can help the children to distance their play from real people (Bergen 1994).
- Have available a range of attractive dramatic play materials which can encourage the children to play other games as well as their favourite super-hero games.
- Ensure that there is enough time and equipment for gross physical activity, so that the more active children are able to use their energies without needing to play the super-hero games exclusively.
- Facilitate cooperative activities, as mentioned in Part three.
- You could cordon off a section of the outside play area in which the super-hero play is permitted, so that the remaining area feels safe to the other children.
- At the same time insist that the play has to be pretend play, and that no one is to get hurt. Gronlund (1992) recommends teaching children that on TV, the real actors use stunt men and women who practise the moves carefully to ensure that no one gets hurt, and so the children also need to practise making the moves safely.
- Ensure that girls as well as boys can participate in the games and discussions about power and safety. Boys may be the main instigators of games with powerful themes, but girls need to participate as well so that they become aware of their own power.
- If necessary, set a time limit on the super-hero play. It might be easier to use natural changes of routine—such as fruit time—as a signal to stop the play and settle into a new activity.
- Continually check with participating children that they still want to play the game. It is important to suspend the play if any of the children are not feeling safe (Bergen 1994).
- If you watch TV or videotapes during your session, you can teach the children to be active viewers rather than passive recipients of what they see. Once they have learned to be active viewers and evaluate what they see on TV, they can begin to make judgments about the violent programs which they are copying in their play (Dawkins 1991).
- Finally, it can be useful to talk with parents whose children do not seem to be growing out of the super-hero phase. The parents might not know that their child is obsessed with the violence and, once aware

of the problem, might decide to limit the child's TV viewing. It can also be useful to encourage parents to buy toys which allow for creative play rather than TV-related toys which have only one purpose (Gronlund 1992).

Being unwilling to share

Adults commonly report that young children will not share. However, it strikes me that we often expect children to be better at sharing than we adults are. Just like us, children need some territory which is theirs alone, and they have the right to choose with whom to share. With this said, some ways of promoting sharing include:

1 Have enough toys of each type in the centre to avoid repeated struggles over equipment. Ensure that there are enough attractive alternatives so that a child is just as happy with one item as with another.
2 Give children permission to finish playing with a toy before being expected to hand it over to another child. This allows them some control over sharing, which increases the likelihood that they will be happy to share appropriately.
3 Explain non-judgmentally that it is friendly to share toys with your friends, and also acknowledge or thank (but do not praise) a child for being friendly when he has shared with another child.
4 It might be useful to ask children to bring to the centre only those personal toys which they are happy for other children to touch. If they do not want other children to touch them, then it is better to keep them at home. (The exception will be the child's soft toy which he cuddles at sleep time and which he does not have to share.)
5 It might help to allocate special spaces for each child for sleeping and for eating. This helps them to perform the task which is allotted to that space, and also gives them something at the centre which they do not have to share.
6 When a baby has snatched a toy from another child and the other is not protesting, then ignore this (Greenman & Stonehouse 1997). If the other baby is protesting, then see if you can help them both to find a toy which interests them. When an older child has snatched a toy from another child, you could give him a restricted choice, for example: 'You can give that back to Tran, or you can put it down over there'. This allows him to save face while still returning the contested item.

Children who have suffered a profound emotional deprivation such as the loss of a parent through a death or separation, tend to be less able to share. It is as if they have learned early to grasp anything that is going, because they never know when it won't be there any more. It could help if you can let a grieving child bring some precious items to the centre without having to share them, support him in his grieving (see chapter 21), and choose disciplining techniques that are firm but gentle, to give the child confidence emotionally in the adults who remain caring for him.

Taking turns and waiting

Fields and Boesser (1997) say that making children wait is disrespectful: it wastes their time (as well as being an invitation to behavioural problems). This makes it important for you to manage transitions between activities so that the children who are ready early do not become restless while they wait for the late-comers. It can help to:

- give advance warning of a change in activity so that the children can disengage in time;
- allow children to finish an activity in which they are engrossed even if that means that they will have to start the new one late;
- break the group into smaller groups for activities such as hand-washing.

When children are having to wait for turns on equipment, an egg timer can help them to be aware of the passage of time. Or, you can have the children write their name on a 'waiting list' so that they don't have to hover idly near the desired equipment, which wastes their time and puts pressure on the children who are using the equipment to defend their place. If a child is too young to write her name, you could have each child's name written on a small card with a velcro dot attached to its back. The child can find her name card and then stick it to a waiting list board that has velcro patches on it.

On the other hand, you do not want to be overseeing these arrangements completely. Help the children to be responsible for negotiating turn-taking, or else you will have to be judge and jury in a constant stream of disputes and will be asked to respond to repeated cries of, 'It's not fair!'.

Telling tales

Children will often approach you with a description of what another child is doing wrong. Telling tales usually comes about because of normal development. Young children go through a natural stage of having too much respect for rules and they cannot yet distinguish important rules (which ensure safety) from other less crucial ones. So the child reports everything, is told off for doing so, and then gets told off when she hasn't let you know that another child is in danger.

Telling tales can also come about when adults rely heavily on rewards and punishments in their discipline. With only so many 'goodies' (so much approval) to go around, the children will compete with each other for the most. From a child's perspective, this means making another child look bad so that she can look good in comparison.

Some strategies for dealing with telling tales include:

- Involve verbal children in making the rules so that, in this process, they learn the reasons for rules and can eventually learn to distinguish important rules from the less crucial ones.
- Explain that it is vital to tell if there is danger, but not otherwise.

- A child who tells tales might simply be noticing behaviour which is not allowed at home and is assuming that it is not allowed at the centre either (Mitchell 1993). In this case, you could explain that it is not a problem because it is not hurting anyone and is safe. Children are able to adjust to different rules in different settings and so they will cope with this.
- Ensure that you do not punish a child who has broken a rule. Punishments create competition between children, lowering their self-esteem and encouraging them to tell on each other so that the tale-bearer looks good by pointing out what another child is doing wrong.
- If a child tells you something which you have already noticed, or identifies a culprit when you're more interested in a solution, then you can thank her briefly and let her know you will deal with it (Mitchell 1993).
- Encourage children to tell a rule-breaker that they do not like her behaviour.
- Teach them that if they have done this and it hasn't worked, they can come to you and ask for your *help* to get the child to stop. In this way, they are not coming to tell tales, but are letting you know they need some help.
- If a child continues to tell you whenever another child does not live up to her expectations, then you could encourage her to notice positive things which the other children do and report those to you instead (Mitchell 1993).
- Never make a young child responsible for supervising another child. This can teach her to tell tales out of fear of under-reporting something serious. She is not yet mature enough to judge what is serious and what is not.

Destructiveness

Children can destroy toys as part of a general behaviour problem, although more usually they break things in an attempt to find out how they work. Being a natural and useful stage of development, exploring how toys work should not be discouraged, rather:

- Buy toys which are made for pulling apart or are indestructible, or have a stock of toys that are already broken so that children can experiment with them.
- If a child is touching something you don't wish her to, then substitute it with something similar which she *can* touch. For example, if she handles the knife while helping you cut up fruit, give her a plastic knife or a spoon instead.
- To avoid damage to books, some centres keep the most interesting books out of reach of children. However, this leaves only the dull books within easy reach. Despite their high cost, good quality books need to be within easy reach of the children. Better to have to replace some books than to have children learn that books are dull.

Tidying up equipment

Planning how to tidy up a whole area of toys in logical steps can be too difficult for a youngster to do without help. (It's like having to tidy up the kitchen the morning after a party.) Also, it's one thing to do a task when asked, but quite another to be responsible for deciding whether, how, and when it needs to be done. Some suggestions which could help children to participate in tidying up after an activity include:

- Help the children to plan how to go about tidying up, or ask if they would like some suggestions.
- Turn tidying up into a game which helps organise the task, for example, 'Simon says, put away everything that's red . . . and now, everything that has wheels' and so on.
- Help them to tidy up. Like most activities which children do, they want some social contact and so your company can encourage them to take part in tidying equipment away.

If a child's refusal to put away toys is part of a general pattern of non-cooperation, then you could act on the other behaviours first. Once he takes you seriously on the big issues, he will follow minor instructions such as to tidy up the equipment which he has used.

Suggestions for further reading

For an examination of issues to do with prejudice and an anti-bias curriculum:

Creaser, B. & Dau, E. (1995), *The anti-bias approach in early childhood*, Harper Educational, Pymble, NSW.
Stonehouse, A. (1991), *Opening the doors: Child care in a multi-cultural society*, Australian Early Childhood Association, Watson, ACT.

The following titles examine many issues pertaining to an anti-bias curriculum and contain an extensive list of children's and adults' books which have an anti-bias theme:

Derman-Sparks, L. & the ABC Task Force (1989), *Antibias curriculum: Tools for empowering young children*, National Association for the Education of Young Children, Washington, DC.
Thompson, B. J. (1993), *Words can hurt you: Beginning a program of anti-bias education*, Addison-Wesley, Menlo Park, California.

For promotion of pro-social behaviour, you might like to refer to:

Slaby, R. G., Roedell, W. C., Arezzo, D., & Hendrix, K. (1995), *Early violence prevention: Tools for teachers of young children*, National Association for the Education of Young Children, Washington, DC.

19

• • • • • • • • • • •

Developmental concerns

Most of young children's difficult behaviour comes about because of their level of development. Some of this behaviour can be irritating or can limit the child's ability to behave considerately, and can sometimes be avoided with sensitive handling.

Changing activities

If you suddenly spring a change of activity on young children—such as telling them to come inside now—you can cause a tantrum. Because young children cannot easily change what they are paying attention to, they might not be able to stop what they are doing unless you give them some advance warning.

Comprehension

Children can usually understand sentences which are two or three words longer than the sentences they speak. If you exceed this, however, then they might not understand you. Some children whom I have seen for behaviour problems ('non-compliance' in particular) are in fact not understanding adults' instructions, especially when they contain many parts. To help, you can simplify what you say. If you tell a child that if he eats his lunch, he will be able to have some ice-cream for dessert, the only word he might understand is 'ice-cream', and want it straight away.

In the same vein, keep your instructions to one or two parts. If you add extra words into your instruction, children might remember only the first thing you said, and so might begin to do as you asked but then forget the rest of what they were supposed to do.

If the children are old enough, you could ask them to tell you what you have just said, so that you can be sure that they have understood.

Not responding to instructions

We probably over-estimate young children's ability to carry out something which they are told to do. It is hard for them to interrupt their train of thought or to translate a verbal instruction into action. Some children appear not to do as they are told, when instead they just cannot manage to put words into action. Repeating a verbal instruction is not likely to work if it hasn't already worked after two attempts. Instead, you could move across to a child when he is not acting on your instruction and help him to get started. If he had understood what you wanted but was refusing to do it, and he still won't follow your instruction once you are helping him, then you can respond in the ways suggested in chapter 15 for dealing with uncooperative tantrums.

Refusal to talk (elective mutism)

Some children refuse for months to speak in a particular setting such as the preschool, whereas in other places they talk freely. Unlike most childhood behavioural difficulties, their refusal to talk in safe environments represents over- as opposed to under-control of their behaviour. Do not ignore elective mutism, because it can delay the child's development since it restricts his participation, isolates him from other people, and channels his energies away from learning into exercising such restrictive self-control. The following strategies could encourage a silent child to talk.

Take him out of the spotlight. When a child first enters a room, we often put him under a social spotlight—everyone watches him. Under this public glare, it can be more difficult for him to talk, so let him know that it's okay not to greet others right away, but encourage him to say hello later instead.

Gentle teasing. If taking the pressure off does not help, then you can try teasing him out of silence. You could instruct him not to talk to you because you would be so shocked that you'd probably fall over in a faint, and then what would he do?

Indirect communication. A next step if this fails is to have him talk through a toy—perhaps a doll, teddy, or hand puppet—to your equivalent toy.

Let him save face. To ensure that the child does not lose face by finally beginning to talk, you might sit back to back with him and let him talk to you less directly, or you could ask him to whisper or sing what he wants to say, so that he can talk (which is your aim) but on his own terms.

Allow him to retain his cultural language. A bi-cultural child might be refusing to use English even when he knows it, out of loyalty to his family and the language they speak at home. You might ask his parents to reassure him that they are happy for him to use both languages.

Articulation errors

By school age, many children are still not yet accurate at saying the single sounds: th, r, l, sh, ch and s; and have difficulty with blends containing r, l, and s (such as 'tree', 'play' and 'spoon'). Difficulty with these sounds will also depend on whether the sounds occur in the beginning, middle or end of a word. Multi-syllabic words (such as animal, hospital and ambulance) are often still difficult for children who are nearing school age. Most substitutions for these sounds are developmentally normal; others indicate a speech difficulty. If in doubt, consult a speech pathologist.

When a young child is learning to talk, don't point out her articulation errors, but simply model the correct sound. For instance, when a child has called a cat a 'tat', you can respond positively with, 'Yes, that's a cat'. The child will hear the difference and learn how to say the word correctly. In the meantime, don't try to force her to say it properly. That will come.

But if it does not, and her articulation errors make it difficult for other people to understand a child at an age when you would expect her speech to be getting quite clear, then a review by a speech pathologist is a good idea. It can prevent the child from becoming frustrated, it will avoid social difficulties which can arise when other people do not understand her, and it can avoid reading difficulties at school. Sometimes, children's speech is unclear because they do not discriminate the sounds which make up the language (this is called 'phonological awareness'), and if they cannot distinguish the sounds they could have trouble learning to read later. It is far more successful to treat this and other speech problems before school age than after.

Overuse of speech rules

Once a child has learned a grammatical rule—for example, how to turn verbs into the past tense—he might overuse the rule, resulting in some errors: the past tense of 'wash' is 'washed' whereas the past tense of 'run' is not 'runned'. In the same way, infants can think that the term 'horse' means any large four-legged animal, and so they call all farm animals 'horses'. Only later will they learn the different words for each animal. As with articulation errors, don't overcorrect these kinds of mistakes. It could discourage their attempts at communicating.

Baby talk

Four-year-olds often like to use baby talk. If there's a new baby in the family, parents sometimes think that the older child is trying to get their attention; if the child has just moved up to the kindy room from the toddler room, you might think she is not coping with the change. But most four-year-olds use baby talk, so it does not mean anything significant. Young children just enjoy playing with their voices and finding out what sounds they can make. Nevertheless, it can be irritating, especially when it means that you cannot understand what a child is saying and so, after letting her enjoy her voice for a while, you can ask her to speak in her big, four-year-old voice again.

Asking repeated questions

Children learn how to make statements before they learn how to ask questions. But once they've got the hang of questions, they know that asking one gets you to speak to them, even if they already know the answer. This can be fine for a while, but the twentieth 'Why?' can be irritating. So, you could answer the same question just once or twice, or ask the child what he thinks the answer is. Then, when you have to move on to another task, you could tell him this, so that he learns to discriminate between when it's time for asking questions and when it's time to be quiet.

If all else fails, turn the child upside-down and shake the questions out of him in a joking way. (Hold his neck and only very gently jiggle: *never* shake a child.) Ask him if he thinks his questions are all out while you 'watch' them fall on the floor.

A rare difficulty is a language disorder, in which a child will ask repeated questions which seem appropriate to the activity, such as asking, 'What you doing?', but he does not absorb the answer or appear to notice that you have answered him. There would be other signs of a disorder, such as a delay in speaking, poor attention to words, and a difficulty with comprehension. If you're in doubt about a child's speech, consult a speech pathologist, because the sooner a speech or language difficulty can be addressed, the more promising are the results.

Telling lies

Children under four years of age might say things which you think are a lie, but which are really just fantasies or wishes. You can handle these 'tall stories' by going along with and extending the fantasy, or by asking gently or playfully whether what the child is saying is a wish or hope. It takes a few years for children to distinguish fact from fantasy, and in the meantime you can guide them about the difference.

Later on, nearer five years of age, children might tell lies to get themselves out of trouble. Sometimes a child will say that she didn't do something, when all she really means is that although she did it, she did not mean it to turn out so badly. At other times, a lie is an outright denial of having done it at all. You can avoid lies by not looking for a *culprit* but instead involving all the children in finding a *solution*.

When a child has committed some misdeed, you must react predictably and reasonably or else next time she will fear your reprisals and will not own up. You will have taught her to tell lies. Also, don't preach to her about a mistake when the outcome has already shocked her. Let her save face.

Ensure that the child has a healthy self-esteem so that if she has been a 'little bit wicked' and enjoyed every moment of it, she will be able to face other people's disapproval since her opinion of herself can remain intact.

Lack of manners

Children are more likely to say 'please' or 'thank you' if you don't praise or punish them when they do and don't. If you just respond to a 'thank you' with, 'You're welcome' or something similar, children will want to please you by saying it again.

If you want to insist, however, you would wait until the child says 'please' before giving him what he wants, and keep holding on to it until he says 'thank you'.

I don't insist every time because I remind myself how often children have to ask for things, and that if adults had to ask that often, we'd get fairly abrupt too. Nevertheless, I accept that everyone is different in how strict they are about manners. Children's manners will get more automatic over the years, and if you are willing to wait, your example will work its magic in time.

Expressing anger at you

Children will often say that they hate you when they actually mean that they are angry. They do this because they don't have many words to describe their feelings. To respond to a child's expressions of hate, you can say, 'You're angry with me at the moment', or you might even reflect the first feeling that caused her to be angry—namely, being hurt or frightened (see chapter 5). Often, listening is enough to tell her that what she feels is okay. If she seems to need help to calm down again, you could ask her what she can do to make herself feel better.

When a child is angry with you, resist the temptation to tell her that you love her. Telling her that you love her when she is angry with you might make her feel guilty for being angry. Likewise, this is not the time to say that you love her but don't like her behaviour, because that is a difficult concept for a young child, and in times of stress it is even less likely that she will understand it.

'Answering back'

If you find that a child 'answers back' when you tell him off, or uses a tone of voice which you think is 'cheeky', this could mean that you are using controlling discipline approaches, and he is rebelling against them. When your own tone of voice is courteous and you try to lead rather than boss children, you will probably find that they treat you with the same respect in return.

But even so, if a child continues with a disrespectful tone of voice you could ignore him while he speaks to you in that way—although this will work best if you say that this is what you're doing. Or you can be assertive when his tone of voice is offensive. If he persists after you have told him how you feel about what he is saying, you can treat his behaviour as a sign that he is out of control of his feelings—that is, he is in the midst of a social (verbal) tantrum and needs your help to get back in control of himself—see chapter 15.

Swearing

There are two types of swearing: expressing frustration, and verbal abuse of someone else. My belief is that it pays to ignore frustrated swearing which is directed at objects, unless the other children are likely to copy the swearing or unless a child is using it often—in which case it is a sign that she is feeling overwhelmed.

Ignore first occasions of frustrated swearing. The first time you hear an offensive word, it can pay to ignore it—and it may pay to tell the child what you are doing. If you light up like a Christmas tree, she might only say it again for the effect. Telling her that you are ignoring it also lets the onlooking children know that you have noticed and are doing something about a behaviour which they realise is not acceptable.

Permit chanting. Almost all children go through a stage of chanting—and they will choose swear words so that they can experience what it feels like to be a bit wicked. Because this is so normal, you might decide to tolerate it for a while, but to say when it stops being funny. Or you might tell a child that it's okay to chant like that to yourself, but that other people will think that she is calling them names, and so she cannot do it out loud to someone else. When you do not let it trouble you, the chanting will stop naturally once that developmental phase ends.

Be assertive. If the swearing is really offensive, you could try telling the child that someone has taught her the wrong words to use, and that you will teach her the right ones. Or you could assert your rights: 'I feel yukky when I hear words like that'. If she argues that other people use these words, you can simply state that other people might not mind them, whereas you do, and you have a right to ask her to respect your needs.

Expand the child's vocabulary. You might ask the child if she knows what the word means and say that it's better not to use words we don't understand. You could replace the swear word with another, more interesting word: when she tells you about a 'bloody big dog' you can agree that, yes, it's *enor*mous.

Avoid punishment. Washing a child's mouth out with soap or putting mustard or Tabasco sauce on her tongue, won't stop her from swearing: instead, she will repeat the words under her breath to prove that she can get away with it. This isn't surprising, given that punishments seldom work.

Verbal abuse. Swearing at another person—child or adult—in the centre is verbal abuse. It is a sign that the child is out of control of her feelings. You will need to state firmly that it is never acceptable to talk to anyone in words which could hurt, and then help the child to regain control of herself, in any of the ways suggested in chapter 15.

Insistent demands

Sometimes a child will be so insistent about his demands that they wear you down until you indulge him by giving him what he wants even when you don't really want to. On the other hand, it is fine to change your mind when, after thinking about a child's protests, you realise that giving him what he wants would not inconvenience you. If you decide that what the child was asking for is reasonable, and that you were too hasty when you said 'no' in the first place, then you can consider changing your mind. You might explain to him that you have changed your mind because you realise that he is right, rather than leaving him with the impression that you are giving in because he has worn you down.

One way to avoid making hasty decisions when a child asks for something, is to pause and give yourself time to decide whether it is reasonable, saying something like: 'I'll think about it'.

If what the child wants is unreasonable, clarify that you will not be changing your mind. If he cannot live with that, then it is clear that he is out of control of his feelings. See chapter 15 for ways to deal with tantrums.

Part six

• • • • • • • • • • •

Helping children with particular needs

Part six addresses some family and personal issues with which young children sometimes have to cope. Each chapter will address how you can talk with young children about the issue and what you can do to help them overcome obstacles.

Distressing as some of these issues are—such as child abuse—it is important to keep them in context. Despite what we sometimes think, modern family life is not very different from the way it was in the past. The difference is that we are now talking about some of the problems more than we did in the past. There are fewer secrets. And since secrets are a burden—especially for children—accepting reality relieves children of much of the stress of not being able to disclose what is happening in their families. It also means that by talking about it we are able to help children and their parents grow through family crises.

The chapters in this section just gives a taste of the issue being discussed. Each chapter will serve as an introduction only: the recommended readings at the end of each chapter and the books listed in Appendix E will offer some more information and guidance.

20

• • • • • • • • • • •

Stress and resilience in children

> We want more for our children than healthy bodies. We want
> our children to have lives filled with friendship and love and
> high deeds. We want them to be eager to learn and be willing
> to confront challenges ... We want them to grow up with
> confidence in the future, a love of adventure, a sense of
> justice, and courage enough to act on that sense of justice.
> We want them to be resilient in the face of the setbacks and
> failures that growing up always brings.
>
> Seligman (1995, p. 6)

When people are reacting negatively to external events, we say that they
are *stressed*. This chapter focuses on the stress reaction and how you can
promote its opposite—resilience—in young children. My assumption
is that while there may be little that you can do to change the home
circumstances or personality of individual children, you can nurture
stressed children while they are in your care and help them to rise above
their circumstances.

When children are stressed they can experience both social and emotional difficulties (Slee 1993), probably because stress teaches them that
they are not in control of what happens to them (Rutter 1985).

Definitions

The stress literature is replete with definitions of terms which have
both lay and particular meanings and which, therefore, call for some
clarification.

Stressors

Stressors are specific external or internal demands which we believe tax or exceed our ability to cope (Compas 1987). They are an everyday part of childhood experience and reflect children's need to cope with the demands of reality and with differences between adult and child perceptions (Dickey & Henderson 1989).

There are two types of stressor. The first sort is when too many changes happen at once—even if those changes are positive. The affected child has the skills to cope with each one of them, but not all at once. The passage of time will help while, in the meantime, you can let the stressed child know that you understand that it can be scary to have so many changes happen at once.

The second type of stressor comprises negative events in children's lives which are largely beyond their control (Slee 1991). These can be everyday hassles or traumatic life events (Luthar & Zigler 1991) such as: losing a parent through death or marital separation, their parent's remarriage, death of a relative, birth of a sibling, hospitalisation of a family member, a parent's physical or emotional illness, parental unemployment, their parent's job being stressful, or financial worries.

Traumatic life events will have different effects depending on when they occur in a child's life; how recently they have occurred; whether they are one-off events or chronic life conditions such as poverty; and whether they are internal to the child—such as an illness—or whether they arise from external sources such as parental separation (Goodman et al. 1993; Honig 1986; Slee 1991 1993; Rutter 1985).

The stress reaction

The stress reaction is a *physical* response in the body involving four stages: an adrenalin-based alarm reaction; cognitive appraisal of the situation; searching for a coping strategy; and implementing a selected strategy (Honig 1986). These physical responses occur when we think that we will not be able to cope with the demands which are being placed on us.

Anxiety and worry

In contrast to stress which is a physical reaction, *anxiety* has emotional, behavioural, physical and cognitive components. A second difference is that stress is a reaction to events which have actually occurred, whereas anxiety is a response to anticipated events, or events which might never even happen (Silverman, La Greca & Wasserstein 1995).

Worry is the cognitive component of anxiety. Worry can be adaptive: by anticipating events, children can rehearse an adaptive response but, on the other hand, if their worry is not resolved and the danger is being rehearsed without a solution ever being found, then worry is maladaptive (Silverman et al. 1995).

Coping

Coping is the process of changing our thinking or behaviour to manage stressors—that is, to minimise our distress and maximise our performance (Compas 1987). This occurs in a number of stages, as individuals first assess the stressor and their own resources for coping with it, and then take action (N. Ryan 1989).

The coping strategy which we use can be directed at solving the problem itself—that is, the strategy is *problem-focused*; or it can be directed at our own emotional reactions—that is, *emotion-focused* coping (Compas 1987). Emotion-focused coping includes methods such as accepting, tolerating, avoiding, distracting, reframing, and relaxation, and emotionally distancing ourselves from a negative situation which we cannot change (Rutter 1985).

Children will use different coping strategies at different stages of development and in different phases of problem-solving—such as before, during or after the event (N. Ryan 1989). For example, problem-focused strategies are used more frequently when children perceive that they have some control over a situation, whereas emotion-focused strategies might be used to deal with issues which they cannot change (Spirito et al. 1991). The most effective coping style is likely to be one which is flexible and adaptive to circumstances (Compas 1987).

Resilience

The fifth and final concept which we need to define in order to discuss stress in children, is the notion of *resilience*. Of the most high-risk children who experience multiple stressors, fewer than half go on to experience adult adjustment problems (Rutter 1985; Zimmerman & Arunkumar 1994). The fact that so many people cope with adverse circumstances is often attributed to 'resiliency'. Resiliency refers to the ability to overcome adverse experiences (Bland, Sowa & Callahan 1994).

Resilience does not come about by avoiding stressors, but by encountering them *at a time* and in a way which enhances children's self-confidence because of their experience of mastery and taking appropriate responsibility (Rutter 1985). In short, successful coping can strengthen children.

Although resilience seems to be a positive attribute, it can in fact be masking children's distress and so you will need to be alert for a range of signs of stress in children.

Signs of stress in children

Children who have too much responsibility for events or other people show their stress in some typical ways.

Lack of independence

Stressed children might not be as independent as you would expect for their age—such as sleeping alone, separating from their parent, and controlling their feelings (for example, fears, shyness, frustration). Some suggestions for overcoming these difficulties were given in Part five.

Uncontrolled emotions

Stressed children might show their stress by acting in impulsive, silly, reckless or inconsiderate ways. They might be taking so much responsibility for events which they cannot control, that they do not have enough resources left over to take charge of their own behaviour. Because they are already feeling overwhelmed by external events, they find it hard to cope more constructively with any new challenge or provocation.

Under-achievement

With more responsibility than they can handle already, out-of-control children cannot pay attention to learning the skills which are usual for their age. They are also not steady enough in their approach to tasks to guide themselves through them step-by-step. So, they achieve below the level you would expect for their age and abilities.

Low self-esteem

The behaviours which stressed children display attract negative responses from others—but, more importantly, the children themselves know that they are out of control and they dislike being that way. Therefore, it is little wonder that children who are stressed can have low self-esteem. In reverse, their low self-esteem will cause them to think that they do not have the skills to cope with demands. Therefore, you might see any of the signs of low self-esteem which I listed in chapter 4.

Conclusion

In summary, children who are out of control might fluctuate between acting too old for their years, and behaving very immaturely—such as by throwing tantrums. Very little of their behaviour is typical of their actual age: it is either too mature, or too silly. It can be said then, that they need to grow *down* before they can grow *up*.

Methods to prevent stress

Given the importance of children's self-esteem to their coping capacity, the measures which promote a healthy self-esteem which I described in Part two will also help children to cope with stress. In addition, the following suggestions target stress in particular.

Be emotionally available

Children need to feel connected to the adults in their lives. Emotionally meaningful relationships between adults and children will protect the children from becoming stressed and will promote their healthy self-esteem.

Structure a cooperative setting

Children need to know that it is safe to make mistakes (Jenkins-Friedman & Murphy 1988). Mistakes need to be seen as part of the learning experience, rather than a measure of their worth as people. By fostering acceptance and cooperation within your centre, you will be increasing the children's confidence that they will receive emotional support when they need it.

Allow children some control of their environment

Children are less able to predict events and to control their surroundings than adults (Carter & Cheesman 1988). This is normal. But if children repeatedly find that they cannot control their physical and social surroundings, they can learn that they are helpless to affect what happens to them. The result is that even when they could exert control they do not try to do so, because they have never learned that they can. These children think that external forces control them, rather than believing that they can make a difference in their own lives.

In his research into helplessness, Martin Seligman (1975) concluded that caregivers can 'inoculate' children against learning to be helpless, by giving them repeated experiences of control over even small aspects of their environment. The following are some suggestions arising from his and others' research.

- Ensure that suitable activities and objects are within the children's reach. If a child can pick up a small toy, she has learned that she can. While exploring the item teaches her important things, realising that she can exert control is even more important.
- Prepare children in advance for changes, as long as you do not give them the impression that you are worried that they cannot cope with the change.
- When something is about to happen which might distress the children, be honest and say so. This allows them to distinguish threatening situations from safe ones, with the result that they will become anxious only when they are under threat, instead of being nervous of any new situation.
- Allow children to solve their own problems. This gives them experience of not being helpless. Seligman suggested that when a baby drops a toy, for example, rather than returning it to her hand, you could move the child near the toy, or put the toy near her, so that she can retrieve it for herself.
- Show children that you believe that you can make a difference to what you think, feel and do. They will copy this.

Promote children's autonomy

In chapter 15 I suggested that we can give children choices at three levels: whether to do something which is optional; or how to do something, or how to feel about something which is compulsory. Allowing children to contribute to decision-making about issues which affect them, will both enhance their self-esteem and raise their confidence in their coping skills.

Realistic expectations of children

If we expect too much of children, we can stress them. David Elkind (1988) discusses a modern epidemic which he called *The hurried child syndrome*. He said that, these days, we are trying to teach children skills earlier and earlier, disregarding whether they are ready to learn them. The result is that, although they might learn skills earlier, they lose interest and confidence in learning because it always seems so difficult (Katz 1988). Elkind quotes research that children who were pushed to read too early did not enjoy reading later, nor chose to read recreationally.

Teach children to generate realistic explanations for their own successes and failures

To promote their resilience, it is important to teach children to evaluate their performances accurately so that they can learn to accept responsibility for their actions (Seligman 1995). When children are unsuccessful, they need to define the event as *temporary* rather than permanent; *specific* to the event rather than a sign of a general or all-pervasive failing on their part; and they need to accept personal responsibility without taking blame—that is, they need to explain the event in terms of their *behaviours*, not personalities (Seligman 1995).

When you hear children blame their personalities for failings—such as when they say, 'I'm hopeless at this'—and when they assume that the problem is permanent ('I'll *never* be able to do it'), you can gently correct their statements with something like, 'You're right. It hasn't worked out, has it? What could you do to make it better?'.

You could explain to the child the link between her actions and their outcome: 'You look like you thought about how to make that before getting started', or 'Perhaps you need to stop and plan what will work, since having it fall over is getting you cross'.

In the same vein, don't teach children that objects or bad luck caused them to fail. Sometimes, in order to be playful or to distract a young child from a hurt, we might give the step from which she has fallen a smack, saying, 'Naughty step. You tripped Mandy over'. Instead, it can be helpful to soothe the child and also to say something such as, 'Didn't you see the step?' or, 'Did you forget to get your balance before you jumped off?', so that she learns about the link between her own actions and their outcome. You don't have to confront the child with failure, but to deny it is not helpful either. Small as this point may seem, blaming objects is just one more way that children learn that outside forces are in control, not themselves.

Evaluation

When we can teach children to evaluate their own successes, they will be more willing to accept responsibility for their failures as well.

Teaching them how to form realistic self-expectations and to evaluate for themselves whether their performances meet these, will avoid much of the stress of high expectations.

Authoritative behaviour management

When children can control their own behaviour and when they can trust that they will be protected from the behavioural excesses of other children, they will be less vulnerable to stress. On the other hand, the methods which you use must nurture even disruptive children so that they feel safe from adults as well as from other children.

Encourage children's friendships

Helping children to make friends will provide them with the emotional support which will help them to overcome stress.

Methods to promote resilience in stressed children

All of the above methods will be useful to prevent stress reactions. In addition, the following suggestions will help children who are actively stressed.

Allocate responsibility to its rightful place

Children become stressed not so much because problems exist, but because they feel in some way responsible for doing something about them. When parents or a child let you know that the family is experiencing more than its usual share of problems, the most helpful thing you can do (or advise the parents to do) is to tell the child that he is right: yes, something is worrying his parents. However (you go on to say), it is an adult's—not a child's—problem. And the adults are working on sorting it out. In other words, he does not have to worry because the adults are still in control of themselves.

Be a mentor

You may be aware of some stressors in certain children's lives, but are equally aware that you can do very little about the traumatic events themselves (Weinreb 1997). In these instances the temptation is to feel powerless to help the children, but Weinreb proposes instead that you can act as a resiliency mentor to them. For instance, although you cannot change a child's violent home circumstances, you will strengthen a child when you believe in him, provide warm hugs, and offer 'incidental' (but deliberate) comments which guide him in how to cope (Weinreb 1997). As Weinreb states, 'Resilient children are children who have hope and a positive outlook that they can deal with problems' (1997, p. 16). You can give them this hope.

Teach coping skills

It does not so much matter *how* children cope with stressors but simply *that* they take action about a stressful event (Rutter 1985). Doing so teaches them that they are in command of their lives. Therefore, rather than teaching children some specific coping strategies, it will be more useful if you can identify which skills they are already using, and then help them to use these more successfully (N. Ryan 1989).

Teach relaxation skills

As well as traumatic events, children can become stressed from internal stressors—such as being ill, suffering medication side-effects, being sensitive to foods, having a poor diet, not getting enough exercise or sleep, or being over- or under-weight. Whether a stressor is internal or external, it can be useful to teach children how to relax. Relaxation is one of the few coping strategies which are available to children—they aren't usually allowed a glass of wine with dinner!

Children can learn relaxation indirectly through play, when you include a range of busy and quiet activities throughout the day. Or, specific games can teach them how to relax their bodies. For instance, they can relax various muscle groups to a version of the 'Simon says' game. This and other relaxation activities are described in Appendix B.

Relaxation increases the resources which children have available for coping with stressors. When they are relaxed they will feel well, in control of themselves, and know they can use their new skill of relaxing in order to feel less stressed.

Fun

Fun is the intangible joy which we experience when our intellectual and emotional needs are met (Glasser 1986), and so is a natural by-product of the other measures covered in this book which are designed to meet children's needs. In addition, you can ensure that your interactions with children are playful and fun, in order to balance out the many demands which they can experience.

Counselling

I regard most early childhood 'counselling' as incidental comments which are aimed at boosting children's faith that they can surmount obstacles. These comments can arise as a result of the children's play or from books about stressful events. If you feel that a child needs some formal counselling, however, you might suggest that his parents consult a child psychologist or similar professional.

Conclusion

While there are many aspects of children's lives over which you have little influence, you can communicate to stressed children your faith that they can cope. Fostering their healthy self-esteem will raise their opinion of their own ability to overcome obstacles; nurturing them emotionally will give them confidence in your support.

Suggestions for further reading

The following book suggests a range of activities and lists children's books which can support stressed children:

Oehlberg, B. (1996), *Making it better: Activities for children living in a stressful world*, Redleaf Press, St Paul, MN.

You might also find the following title useful:

Young, B.B. (1995), *Stress and your child*, Harper Collins, Sydney.

21

• • • • • • • • • • •

Helping children cope with grief

When children suffer a loss because of the death of or a separation from a family member or close friend, their reactions are as profound and as varied as adults'. As well, children might not have been prepared in advance for a death or for their parents' separation, and so afterwards they can suffer more than adults. Parents' confusion about how to help their child understand and cope with his feelings can add to his pain. Early childhood workers, then, are in an ideal position to help a child when his family is too overwhelmed to give him the support he needs.

Children's reactions to loss

In general, children's response to a loss is determined by their age at the time it occurred. The following section gives a thumb-nail sketch of typical reactions of children through to adolescence. The reason to discuss later ages is that some children whose development is advanced might experience a reaction which is more typical of older children.

0–2 years. While babies or toddlers will understand very little about death or other losses, they can sense when other people are feeling bereaved and can miss the person from whom they have become separated through a death or marriage break-up. Sometimes, children of this age wander off because they feel lost and confused. Also, if their mother is feeling bereaved, they might miss out on the extra nurturing which they need to receive from her.

3–4 years. Children of this age think that death is temporary and so they can appear to ignore the death callously. They will become more and more bewildered, though, as they come to realise that the death is permanent. You might need to explain to the toddler that the person or pet whom he loved is 'dead dead' or 'real dead' rather than 'pretending dead like on TV'.

5–8 years. This is the age of magical thinking. A child who has said in anger 'I wish you were dead', is likely to think that she caused the other person's death, since every child knows that wishing makes things come true. This guilt and terror can be paralysing. For many months afterwards, the child might try to be especially good to reverse the hex—that is, to return the person to life.

Older children can express sorrow in the same way that adults do: they can become apathetic, withdrawn, hostile, angry, and might cry a lot. This is healthy and normal. It is important that adults allow children to express these feelings—including anger—because bottling them up can make them unwell. Older children and adolescents might want to relate to their peers after a death of someone they love, but they still rely heavily on their parents as well. They can begin to worry if their parents' marriage is unhappy at the time, in case their parents might separate, bringing on another loss for them.

Helping children to deal with death

It helps children if they can stay with their family and be involved in the activities surrounding a death and the funeral. They can become frightened if they are separated from their parents and, if they are kept away, children sometimes assume that they being blamed or punished for the death.

If a death has already occurred in the family of one of the children in your care and she did not attend any memorial or funeral service, then you might suggest to her parents that together they plant a tree to commemorate the person or pet they have loved. The child can help to water, feed and tend the tree as a way of remembering the lost one. If the child attends your centre often, you could even set aside a special part of your outdoor area for the child to tend in memory of the person or pet she has lost.

Explaining death to children

When talking about death to children, tell them the truth. They need facts and they need honest answers to their questions about death. It can help if you get information from the child's parents about the circumstances and cause of the death so that you can be honest about the specific events, otherwise children might fill in missing details with their imagination, which can be even more frightening than reality.

You will need to explain to a young child that the person she loved died because his body grew very old or he became very *very* sick from an illness or an accident—so sick that nothing could be done to make him better. In the case of the death due to illness of a baby or child, you might say that the baby's body hadn't been made properly and so he could not live in that body any more. Remember to tell the child that the dead person did not want to leave her, but that he could not stay in his body any more.

Children often ask where the dead person goes. That sort of question might best be answered by the child's parents, or you can ask them what they would like you to tell the child. However, in general, the grieving period is not the best time to complicate young children's feelings with religious explanations: these are best saved for before or well after a loss. Whatever explanation you settle on, you can say that the spirit of the person—or the love that the child felt for that person—lives on in the child's heart and memories, which will always be there.

Some children's books can help you to find appropriate words to use when you are talking with children about death and marital separations. Some titles are listed in Appendix E.

Separation and divorce

A divorce presents children with many challenges to add to the normal demands of growing up. Over the course of some months or years, they must acknowledge the reality of their parents' separation; disengage from their parents' conflict so that they can get on with their own lives; resolve their grief, anger and self-blame about the divorce; accept that their parents' separation is permanent; and form realistic expectations for their own future adult relationships (King 1992). Young children will not achieve all this during their early childhood years, but they can make a start.

Children's reaction to divorce

Children's adjustment to divorce depends on the circumstances which led up to their parents' decision to separate, plus the children's age at the time, their sex, and their temperament, including their ability to adjust to change. They are also affected if there is a sudden loss of household income following their parents' separation. Children's healthy adjustment is helped when: they have other people to support them; their relationships with both parents are warm before and after the separation; their custodial parent can get on with his or her own life and does not remain angry with the former spouse; the two parents can still cooperate in the children's interests following their separation; and when their separation ends any conflict which might have been present during their marriage.

In the short term, preschool children might be more upset and confused by their parents' separation than adolescents would be. For the first two years they can react to their parents' separation with profound distress, sadness and anger, exhibiting a number of new or more intense emotional and behavioural problems.

However, in the long term, young children tend to forget the unhappiness surrounding their parents' separation, whereas memories of the separation can still upset older children some years later. There can also be a 'sleeper effect': children can adjust very well for many years, but sometimes problems surface again during school age for boys—whose behaviour can become under-controlled—and during adolescence or early adulthood for girls—whose difficulties can show in heterosexual relationship problems. Nevertheless, almost all children are better adjusted after a divorce than are children from intact homes where the parents are fighting (Burns & Goodnow 1985).

Effects of divorce on children's development

A divorce can affect three aspects of children's development (King, 1992). The first is their ability to manage aggression. Their extreme grief about their parents' separation can make it difficult for children to manage their anger, and if their parents separated as a result of violence, then the children might not have learned non-violent ways of managing conflict. As a result, children might act out aggressively, or over-control their feelings, resulting in depression or drug use at later ages.

The second aspect of children's development which is affected by divorce is their ability to separate from their parents, especially when they are worried that their custodial parent would be lonely without them.

The third effect is establishing a gender identity. Boys whose father is absent can worry that they are effeminate because of not having had a male parent as a role model; girls might feel that their female role model—their mother—was rejected and so they do not value their femininity. The absence of a father tends to affect girls' later attitude toward men, their decision to marry, their choice of a marital partner and their satisfaction with their marital relationships.

Your awareness of these long-term effects can allow you to make special efforts to ensure that a male caregiver or teacher has a supportive relationship with any child whose father has left the family home; or you could model constructive attitudes to men and women, and to relationships between boys and girls in the centre.

What to say about marital separation

It can be difficult for a child's parents to know what to tell him about their marital separation and they might ask you to help their child to understand. Once again, you can help because you are less involved and are not sharing the pain which the family is experiencing, making you an ideal person to listen to the child and to pass on the information which his parents might ask you to convey.

A young child needs to know that:

- his parents have left each other but that they have not left him;
- parents leave each other because they stop being friends;
- it is not the child's fault that his parents have separated;
- both his parents still love him, even though they don't love each other enough to live together any more.

If the remaining parent tells you that a child has been abandoned by the absent parent, then you will need to explain this in a way which fits the facts as the child sees them. When he is feeling sad, you could state that you understand. You might explain that some people are lazy about showing how much they love other people. The child needs to be told over and over again that being abandoned is not because he is unlovable.

Minimising compound losses

After a death in the family or a marital separation, women are often forced to go back to work, and so the child's care arrangements can change suddenly. The sudden loss of her mother and the need to cope with new care arrangements can add to a child's original grief.

If a child is beginning in your centre or increases her hours after a recent loss, you will need to give her extra understanding. Increase the amount of support you give her so that she is able to meet your expectations, but do not lower your expectations. In this way, she has something stable in her world on which she can rely.

Avoiding parent protection

Even young children will watch their parents closely when there has been a loss in the family. They might take on the job of looking after their parents—instead of the other way around. This can be encouraged when people tell a child to 'look after Mum now that Dad is gone', or they try to comfort a boy with the notion that he, 'is the man of the house' now. These instructions force the child to grow up suddenly, at a time when he is least able to cope, and they rob him of his childhood.

Some children try to behave extra well to protect their parents from further upset. Some don't tell their parents about their own grief, in case it makes their parents feel worse—and because their child says nothing, the parents think that he is coping okay. The result is that the child does not get the support he needs. Other children develop severe behavioural difficulties, which can be understood in one of two ways. The first is that the behaviour is a sign that the child is grieving and so it will go away as he begins to resolve his feelings. The second explanation is that, by having to respond to him, his behaviour distracts his parents from their own grief. If this is what the child is about, then the behaviour will go away only when the parents have resolved their feelings.

To avoid burdening a child with looking after her parents, you could suggest to her parents that they explain to her that they are very sad at times but are still there to look after her. Although everyone in the family will feel sad—sometimes very sad—they will cope and, eventually, they will find new ways of being happy. To back up this message the parents will have to show the child that they are looking after themselves, so that she does not take on that job for them.

Coping with intermittent parent absence

If one of the parents in a child's family works away from home for extended periods, you might find that his behaviour is unsettled at home and in your centre as the family go through repeated cycles of grieving and reuniting. To help the child cope, accept his feelings and explain that the remaining parent can still look after him while the other parent is away.

Suggestions for further reading

Ahrons, C. (1995), *The good divorce: Keeping your family together when your marriage falls apart*. Bloomsbury, London.

McKissock, M. & McKissock, D. (1995), *Coping with grief*, 3rd edn, ABC, Sydney.

Teyber, E. (1992), *Helping children cope with divorce*, Jossey-Bass, San Francisco.

Westberg, G.E. (1992), *Good grief*, rev. edn, Fortress, Melbourne.

22

•   •   •   •   •   •   •   •   •   •   •   •

Children who have been abused

When children are abused, it is most often by a close family member. (More than any other fact, this should tell us how hard it is to bring up children without supports.) Distressing as it is, some children are abused by adults who have no qualms about exercising their power over a child. To be able to watch out for children in your care, you will need to know the signs to look for and some facts about child abuse and its perpetrators.

Types of child abuse

The term *abuse* refers both to neglect—that is, not doing something to care for children—and active abuse—which involves doing something harmful. Both are defined as causing injury, either physically or emotionally.

Neglect involves not meeting the child's physical needs for food, clothing, shelter, protection, medical care and safety from injury. *Physical abuse*, as the title suggests, refers to non-accidental physical injury inflicted on a child, even before she is born. For example, women are at greater risk of assault during pregnancy than at other times. *Emotional abuse* can involve not being responsive to the child, verbally abusing her, threatening physical abuse, or being overly controlling. *Sexual abuse* includes any sexual behaviour imposed by an older person on an individual under eighteen. It includes verbal or visual contact (such as seeing sexually explicit videos, or exposure), unwanted kissing or touching, lack of privacy, intercourse, and using the child for prostitution or pornography.

Facts and myths about child abuse

While child abuse seems totally foreign to those of us in the early childhood professions, it is a fact that a person's chances of being murdered are highest in her first year of life, that in as many as one in five homes (20 per cent) physical abuse is used to control children, with perhaps another one in five households using verbal (emotional) abuse. Neglect is even more common, and harder to detect. It accounts for more child deaths than active abuse. As well as physical abuse and neglect, one in six children (both boys and girls) is sexually abused, usually by a family member. If these children are not helped, then they are likely to be abused again, and the perpetrator is likely to go on to abuse other children as well.

Abuse occurs in all sectors of society, although the special pressures which poverty brings can make impoverished families more prone to abusing children. Some people excuse adults who abuse children, saying that they are mentally ill or were abused as children themselves and so they can't help themselves. But I have met many parents who overcame dreadful childhoods to be wonderfully caring parents—and if they can do it, then other people can too.

Child abuse is a straightforward abuse of power. We abuse children—and women—in our society, because we can get away with it. Some people even condone it.

Effects of abuse on children

We cannot always predict the harm which abuse and neglect will do. The effects will differ for each type of abuse or neglect, and will depend on the age of the child when the abuse happened, and on how long it continued. By far the most significant single effect is that the child learns that the adults in his life—those whom he should be able to trust most—are unjust and untrustworthy. In the short term, it makes the child constantly vigilant for danger and so will distract him from learning the skills he needs to acquire (Caughey 1991). In the long term, this lack of trust is a poor basis for forming close relationships in the future.

Abuse makes children responsible for adults, causing them to sacrifice their personal development and happiness (O'Donnell & Craney 1982). They try to take control of the abuse, even though they cannot—perhaps by trying to behave in a way which will not attract abuse, or even provoking it to 'get it over with' and to make it predictable (Caughey 1991). In later life, the individual who was abused as a child is likely to experience severe confusion, feeling a range of conflicting emotions including anger (at the abuser and often at a non-abusing parent for not protecting him), sadness, fear, guilt and self-doubt. The anger can often be directed at himself too: an adult often expects that as a child he should have been able to stop the abuse. However, children do not have the same power as adults, and so by themselves they can never stop abuse from happening. Finally, the most predictable outcome of child sexual abuse is sexual dysfunction in adulthood.

Signs of abuse

To be able to detect abuse early, you need to be aware that it can happen in any family. Hence the saying: 'I wouldn't have seen it, if I hadn't believed it'.

No single sign can indicate with certainty that a child is being abused; however, unexplained behaviours or sudden changes in a child's behaviour pattern should alert you to look into the possibility of abuse.

Physical signs

Physical signs of neglect include: bruises, welts, burns, broken bones, head and internal injuries, complaints of hunger or rummaging for food, malnutrition, lack of hygiene, chronic or untreated illnesses including nappy rash in babies, delays in speech or other skills unexplained by other causes, and a failure to thrive. The abused child might show no response to pain.

Physical indicators of sexual abuse include: pain in the genital or anal areas when going to the toilet or when picked up; bruises, redness, rash, swelling or tears in the genital or anal areas; or any unusual discharge from the vagina or anus. The child who has been subjected to oral intercourse can develop throat infections or have difficulty swallowing.

Emotional signals

Emotional signals of abuse include a fear of physical contact, being watchful of adults or cringing away from them, a reluctance to approach adults for help (since the child does not trust them to protect her), extreme aggression or withdrawal, fears and nightmares, and low self-esteem. The child might become clingy and refuse to separate from her parent, show fear of certain people or places, or show unusual fear, anxiety, or embarrassment when receiving routine medical treatment or being treated for injuries (especially those inflicted by sexual abuse). A child who is being sexually abused might stop wanting to hug adults, even when they are not the perpetrators of the abuse (Briggs 1993).

Behavioural indicators

If the abuse has been going on for some time, the behavioural signs are hard to detect, since they too will have been going on for some time. But if the abuse has just begun, you might see a sudden change in a child's behaviour which corresponds with the onset of the abuse. Behavioural signs include poor sleeping and eating habits, renewed bed wetting or soiling, poor social play skills, and self-destructive behaviour. Overall, the child might regress, behaving in immature ways which she had previously grown out of.

The child who is being sexually abused might start being secretive, or might talk about a friend or toy who has a secret or to whom something bad is happening. She might ask questions about secrets, and whether she should tell a secret even when she has promised not to. You can reply that it is wrong for anyone to tell her she has to keep a secret forever, and that nothing is too awful to talk about. She can speak with you about anything.

A child who is being sexually abused might display sexualised behaviour such as blatant flirting, provocation, excessive masturbation, using new terms for genitals, or displaying inappropriate knowledge of adult sexual behaviour in advance of her years. Or, she might re-enact what is happening to her, with her dolls, drawings, or toys. She might also play in a sexualised way with other children. A child who is abusing someone else has been abused: she would not know about these things otherwise.

If you suspect abuse . . .

In only a few cases will children tell you directly that they are being abused (Briggs 1993). Mostly, they will reveal the abuse by accident or their unusual behaviour will raise your suspicions (Briggs 1993). If you have reason to believe that a child in your centre might be being abused, then as a mandated reporter, you *are legally obliged* to notify the local child welfare agency. To do this, you ring the agency and ask for the duty officer in the child abuse team.

Remember that, by making a notification, you are *not accusing* anyone of abusing the child, but you are simply asking for experts in the field of child abuse to *investigate* whether the child is safe. The officer who takes your call will tell you what action the investigating team will take as a result of your information. In all circumstances, the name of the reporting person is absolutely confidential. Even freedom of information legislation does not allow the agency to tell anyone who notified them.

How to help an abused child

In the short term, the single most important thing you can do to help a child when he tells you about being abused, is to believe him (Briggs 1993). Almost all reports, of sexual abuse in particular, turn out to be true. This is logical, since while children might tell lies to get out of trouble, they don't usually tell lies which get themselves into trouble. After you have listened to the child, then the next thing to do is to support the family as they strive to limit the effect that disclosure will have on the child and the rest of the family.

Physical abuse

Ask the child how he received an injury which you have detected. If he tells you that some form of abuse caused the injury, reassure him that help is available. Do not make negative comments about the abuser, but be clear with the child that he is not to blame for the ill-treatment he has received.

Emotional abuse

An emotionally abused child might behave in ways that seem to invite ridicule or sarcasm. Refrain from this at all costs. Encourage him to talk, although do not force him to confide in you. Listen, without trying to change his feelings. Comment on his strengths, and encourage his efforts to cope. Enhancing an emotionally abused child's self-esteem is especially important.

Sexual abuse

First and foremost, believe what the child tells you, but do not ask for detailed descriptions of what happened (Briggs 1993), and do not ask leading questions: child abuse specialists are best suited to finding out this information in a way which will not add to the child's distress. Maintain your usual level of caring for the child so that you do not inadvertently appear to be rejecting her but, on the other hand, do not smother her either, or communicate to her that you think she cannot cope.

As an early childhood caregiver or teacher, by law you *must* report the abuse, so do not promise that you will keep it a secret, since you cannot. Even when an investigation is begun, do not suggest that the child should forget about what has happened. She will still need to talk about it and might choose you as her confidante. If threats were used by the abuser against the child, explain that these were tricks to try to get her to keep it a secret, and that they were not true.

No matter how hard it is, stay calm. Act in a matter-of-fact way so that your reactions do not increase the child's guilt and embarrassment or make her worry about hurting you by telling. Be clear with her that the abuse is not her fault, and that you are pleased she has told you. You might tell her that, unfortunately, what was done to her happens to lots of children, and that she was not to blame for anything that happened.

Helping the family and the child

Except for suspected child sexual abuse, you will need to tell the parents about the child's claims and that you are obliged to report them. (Unlike the other forms of abuse, sexual abuse is a crime and investigation of it will involve the police, who prefer possible perpetrators not to be warned about an impending investigation, in case it gives them time to think up a plausible explanation for the allegations.)

At no time should you express any suspicions to the parents about who could be the perpetrator. After making the report, your role is to support the child. This includes supporting her family, even if she has named a family member as the perpetrator. The non-offending adults will need immediate emotional support (Briggs 1993). As well, it might be useful to give the family some reading material on coping while the investigation is happening. They might also appreciate the names of psychologists or family therapists who could support them during the investigation. Or, they could benefit from getting in touch with a parents' support group (Briggs 1993). Your local child welfare agency might know if such a group operates in their area.

After a child has revealed that she has been abused, she can be subjected to further institutional and societal abuse, including scorn, blame and disbelief from friends and acquaintances, upheaval and possible dissolution of the family, being removed herself from the family home (being punished for being a victim), and repeated assessments from treatment agencies. Although a medical assessment might seem only to add to these intrusions, it is an important step in letting the child know that she has not been permanently injured by the abuse (Briggs 1993).

Meanwhile, for as long as the child remains in your centre, you can be a significant—sometimes the only—source of stability while these and other upheavals occur. As Briggs (1993: 66) advises, 'Be loyal to child victims'. Even when their behaviour appears to invite contempt or frustration, accept them and find ways to show them that they can be safe again.

Conclusion

In the longer term, you will need to understand that abused children will view their world as dangerous but also you must suggest an alternative point of view (Caughey 1991). You might sit beside a child and participate quietly or comment on what she is doing or saying, to help her notice that she is having a positive experience (Caughey 1991). Caughey also suggests that we allow children to express negative feelings in a safe way, perhaps with creative activities or dramatic play with toys, so that they can come to terms with their reactions to their circumstances and learn that their feelings are not frightening or likely to get out of their control.

Child protection training

To keep children safe from abuse, your centre can have a formal program for teaching children to recognise their feelings and to notice when their feelings are telling them that something is wrong. The guiding concept here is: *If you don't feel safe, you aren't safe.* You might ask children where in their bodies they feel unsafe feelings—say, when they are at the top of a high slippery-dip; and later teach them the difference between being excited-scared and bad-scared. Children still need to be able to take risks and have fun, and so being good-scared is okay.

The next aspect of child protectiveness training is to tell children that *nothing is too awful to talk about.* You can teach children that good secrets always finish: when they keep a secret about someone's birthday present, the secret ends on the birthday. But if someone tells them to keep a secret forever, then that means it is a bad secret. Children must feel free to tell adults any secrets like these that worry them.

Next comes the networking stage. This involves helping children to identify to whom they could talk, if they had a problem. One activity is to get children to draw around their hands, and on each finger or thumb write the name (or draw a picture, or glue a photo) of one person that they could ask to help them if they ever needed it. They are likely to nominate their parents, and after that they might need some prompts to think of other adults. If they nominate a child, pet or favourite toy, you can ask, 'And who would he tell?' and then put that adult's name on the outline.

The final stage is teaching children to be persistent. If the first person on their network is not there, cannot help them, or does not understand, then they can ask the next person, and the next . . . and so on. Mem Fox's *Hattie and the Fox* and other children's picture books can reinforce the theme of persistence.

Finally, you might arrange for the children to visit an ambulance, fire or police station, or show them an emergency vehicle in a story or on TV. You can explain that in an emergency, these vehicles are allowed to be noisy and to rush. In the same way, if the children ever feel frightened, they don't have to be polite to someone who is scaring them: they can scream as loudly as they want to and can run away for help.

The beauty of the child protectiveness training approach is that you do not have to scare children with stories of bad people enticing them into cars or of people who hurt children. The children can apply the ideas to any frightening situation—such as finding a live snake. They can be empowered to ask for help, without first depowering them by scaring them. An alternative could be to warn them about strangers but we know that most child abuse is perpetrated by someone whom the child knows, and so it will be more effective to give them the skills to notice early warning signs of danger and to feel confident enough to act on them and get help.

Conclusion

When you teach children to be considerate instead of compliant, when you are assertive about your needs and teach them to be likewise, and when you listen to and accept their feelings—even the inexplicable ones—then you will have inoculated them against being abused. Abuse can only occur within power-based relationships, and if the children do not experience these, then they will be able to detect and avoid abusive relationships.

Suggestions for further reading

Briggs, F. (1993). *Why my child? Supporting the families of victims of child sexual abuse.* Allen & Unwin, Sydney.

Appendix E also lists some children's books which can help you to talk with children who have been abused, or which can be used to supplement your protectiveness training program.

23

• • • • • • • • • • •

Children who have a disability

There are two ways of looking at early childhood programs for young children with disabilities. The first is the remedial approach which tries to bring these children's development nearer to normal development by making adjustments to regular curricula. This approach sees education as the process of making everyone similar, and so children who are different are regarded as deficient (Mallory & New 1994).

The second approach is true inclusion, in which programs are designed with diverse needs in mind, so that the resulting programs, by definition, include all children. The inclusive approach regards high-quality child care and early childhood education as a fundamental right of all children and their parents, rather than an opportunity to correct the 'deficiencies' of some children.

Attitudes versus supports

Some writers say that successful inclusion of children with disabilities is a matter of caregivers' and teachers' 'attitude' (e.g. Chandler 1994) but, in fact, it has more to do with the level of resources which are available to the centre (MacMullin & Napper 1993). Sufficient supports make it possible to meet the needs of children with disabilities at the same time as not disadvantaging the children without disabilities (Shimoni, Baxter & Kugelmass 1992). Caregivers and teachers are rightly concerned about the needs of the other children in the group when they are aware that they do not have the resources to meet everyone's individual needs.

Some key terms

Children whose needs fall outside the normal range for their age consti-tute around 5 per cent of any group. Many of these children have an *impairment*—let's say some damage to their brain—which, in turn, leads to a *disability*—perhaps a physical disability such as cerebral palsy—which, in its turn, can lead to a social *handicap*. A handicap occurs when individuals with disabilities are unable to participate maximally in activities because the environment or social attitudes present obstacles for them.

Known disabilities

There are two situations when you will need to care for and teach children with disabilities. The first is when the children's disability is known at the time of enrolment. The second is when your observations lead you to seek further assessment of a child whose development seems atypical. Let's deal with each in turn.

Goals of early childhood programs for children with disabilities

Bailey and Wolery (1992, p. 35) list the following goals for your work with children who have disabilities:

- to support the children's families in achieving their own goals for their child;
- to promote the children's participation, independence and mastery of the early childhood curriculum;
- to promote children's development in all skill domains;
- to build and support the children's social competence;
- to promote the children's use of skills in other settings as well as in your centre;
- to prepare children with disabilities for the normal experiences which are provided for all children;
- to prevent children's disabilities from affecting other developmental domains.

It is important to keep in mind that it is unlikely that you can 'cure' their difficulties (Chandler 1994). You can prevent a child's difficulties in one area of development from 'spreading' to other areas—such as when a child's language disorder causes social problems—but it will be rare for you to cure the original disability. The aim of inclusive curricula is not to make these children 'less deficient', but to meet their present needs, however these are manifested.

Programming for children with disabilities

Not all children with a particular disability are the same. The label 'children with disabilities' is used consciously—to signal that they are children first—individuals who differ as much from each other as all children do. The term is also used to signal that everything you know about programming for typical children can also be used for programming for children with atypical needs.

However, while your programming *process* is the same for all children, whatever their ability levels, the special needs of children with disabilities can necessitate adjusting some parts of the regular program *content* and instruction *methods*.

In terms of content, on the whole you will choose to teach all children the next skill in the sequence in each developmental domain, because these skills are usually functional for them. However, when a child with a disability is not acquiring that next skill, you need to ask yourself whether it is worth persisting with teaching it. That decision will depend on the child's environment. For example, if a child is having difficulty learning to balance on one foot, in many circumstances this skill might not matter. But if the child's peers enjoy football at play times, then the child's social inclusion will depend on being able to kick a ball, and so teaching him to balance on one foot will be important.

Placement of children with disabilities

Children's significant developmental delays will affect your placement decisions. On the one hand, it might seem best to place them within a group of younger children who have similar developmental levels to their own. But this ignores the fact that there are still likely to be differences not only in *what* the various children can achieve but also in *how* they achieve it (McCollum & Bair 1994). Also, the older child's physical size—plus the notion of age-appropriate practices—might mean that placement in a younger group is not suitable.

On the other hand, placement in an older group can put the child in danger if, for instance, he is still mouthing or eating materials such as glue or nails which are part of the older children's activities, or if the climbing equipment which suits older children is dangerous to him.

Placement decisions are crucial, since it is essential for all children to experience success (Chandler 1994). Success is even more crucial for children with disabilities, because they are likely to face repeated failure, particularly in their impaired skill areas. (The importance of genuine success was emphasised in chapters 6 and 7.)

Process modifications

Since children learn by interacting with the adults in their world, you will need to facilitate the learning of children with disabilities somewhat differently than you do for non-disabled children (McCollum & Bair 1994). For instance, whereas non-disabled children are likely to initiate activities which advance their skills, children with intellectual disabilities might need more encouragement to explore and play and, once engaged, might need extra cues, prompts and encouragement to continue to be involved (McCollum & Bair 1994).

Autonomy

When you think about it, the very first thing which a baby learns is that she can look at something which interests her and somehow manage to roll, creep or crawl towards it to investigate it. By approaching the object of her interest, the baby is able explore it and, in so doing, learn about the object. But, even more than this, the baby realises that she can meet her own needs and can act on her own ideas.

Therefore, when a young child has a physical disability, she is at risk not only of having less opportunity to explore and learn, but also of not finding out that she can make things happen. This means that it will be crucial that your program gives the child opportunities to exercise choices and to develop autonomy.

Children with speech or language disabilities

Speech refers to what ideas a child can express. *Articulation* refers to how clearly she can say speech sounds. Various articulation errors can be normal in the early childhood years, or they could represent lack of control of the muscles of the lips and tongue. *Comprehension* or *language* skills refer to how much a child can understand.

Children can experience delays in any of these three areas. Or, their development might occur out of the usual sequence or order—in which case it is said to be 'disordered'. Children with delayed speech or language are relatively easy to identify when you have same-aged children with whom to compare them and when you are aware of the normal developmental milestones. (Most of us need to refer to our favourite chart for these.)

However, disordered speech or language can be difficult for a non-specialist to identify. The child can appear to be using language in the right time and place—such as asking 'Where we going?' while sitting in a car—but does not appear to understand the reply. The child might understand some complex language and yet confuse easier concepts. Or, the child might not be able to translate instructions into action at an age when other children can.

Language skills are absolutely crucial for children's ongoing cognitive development and for forming friendships. The longer speech or language difficulties go unchecked, the more areas of their development that become affected. Therefore, it is crucial to talk early with parents if their child appears to have difficulties with speech or language. With their permission it can be useful to seek professional advice and to ensure that the child's hearing has been checked thoroughly.

Children with sensory impairments

The level of background noise in the centre will make a huge difference to how well a child with a hearing impairment will function. You will need to be familiar with the child's means of communication—sign language, lip reading, or a combination of these. When speaking with the child you will need to ensure that you are at eye level, have good overhead lighting but not to the point that your nose throws a shadow over your lips, that your mouth is not obscured—say by a beard or moustache (in the case of males, obviously), and that you speak slowly and clearly but not exaggeratedly so.

Children with visual impairments will range from those who have complete blindness to children whose partial vision allows them to see light and dark only, to those whose vision is impaired only at a distance or with close work. The child's specialist advisers will need to visit your centre and explain the child's particular needs and give you guidance about how to adjust your program to suit the child's vision.

Strategies for social inclusion

Research tells us that while the number of interactions between children with and without disabilities increases when they are in care or educational settings together, the children do not necessarily become friends (Guralnick, et al. 1995). This is because children choose friends whose development and interests are similar to their own. Therefore, it is not enough simply to place children with a range of abilities together and hope that they will develop friendships.

If a child with disabilities is ignored (neglected) or rejected by the rest of the children, then she or he can be lonelier in a regular setting than if there were other children present who had similar needs and abilities. It is for this reason that most writers and researchers acknowledge that inclusion of children with disabilities in regular settings is not *always* the best alternative for them (Cook, Tessier & Klein 1996).

Talking with the non-disabled children

When parents first enrol their child who has special needs, it will be important for you to gain their permission to explain to the other children about the child's disability, in order that the other children will understand him. The other children will need clear, straightforward information about the child's disability, and they will need permission to ask questions about it. At times it will also be important to comment on how the child with a disability is similar to the other children.

Young children might be scared of 'catching' a disability and they might assume that it imposes limitations on all aspects of the child's development—for instance, when they see that a child cannot walk, they might think that he is intellectually delayed as well (Doherty-Derkowski 1995). As a result, they might not think of him as a suitable playmate, or they might help the child too much.

Once the child with a disability is attending your centre, it can help if you give the child himself words to explain to the other children about the disability (assuming that the child is verbal).

If the child who has a disability is harming the other children in any way—even if it is not deliberate—then the other children should not have to tolerate that. They have rights too. You must allow them to express their anger or frustration and protect them from harm. For instance, I recall a two-year-old who had a severe language disorder and whose only way to make social contact at child care was to chase the other toddlers, often resulting in their falling or being pushed over. They were told to say to the child, 'Stop it. I don't like it'. But, because he did not understand language, he thought that this was simply what you said when you fell over. He did not realise that it actually *meant* that he should stop chasing the other children. Despite the fact that he had no malice whatsoever, the effect of his behaviour on the other children was to intimidate them. To protect the other children, he needed firm guidance to find other ways to play, and physical prompting to stop chasing.

Finally, it is crucial that you do not burden young children with caring for a child who has a disability. Not only would it patronise the child himself, but it would be too much responsibility for the other children. One way to avoid this is by showing the children how to talk naturally to a child who has a disability. The children will copy your behaviour towards the child, and will be over-solicitous and protective only if you are.

Communicating with the other parents

The other parents have a right to know that a child with a disability will not be taking up one-to-one attention of a staff member, resulting in reduced care of their own child. However, you will need to decide on a case-by-case basis how much information you should tell the other parents about the attendance of a child with a disability. If you tell parents in advance, it could create unnecessary anxiety or be a tacit invitation for protests (Chandler 1994). If you do not, then some parents might feel that you are not listening to their legitimate concerns.

Supporting parents of children with disabilities

In the long term, most parents adjust to their child's disability and can love their child, even at the same time as occasionally feeling sad on her behalf because of her limitations. This is still different from acceptance, which would mean that they did not mind about their child's disability. But in the early childhood years, the diagnosis is likely to be recent and so they will still be dealing with their initial emotions and with the demands of negotiating an unfamiliar service system.

Understand the parents' emotions

Mothers can be reacting not so much to the disability, but to the restrictions which their child's high care needs impose on their own lives (Koegel et al. 1992). Meanwhile, fathers might feel left out of the service system, with the results that they lack support for their own responses and feel superfluous to the child and family. This makes it important that you support fathers as well as the mothers. Another important family member is the grandparent. Because people with disabilities used to be hidden away in institutions, grandparents might lack information about their grandchild's needs (Meyer 1993). Therefore, when you have contact with grandparents, giving them information about their grandchild can increase their confidence in their ability to support their adult son or daughter.

At the same time, children with disabilities make a positive contribution to their parents' lives (Mullins 1987; Turnbull, Guess & Turnbull 1988). Many parents report that their marriage becomes stronger as they work together to advocate for their child's needs (Abbott & Meredith 1986), and that they learn about their own personal strengths, develop deep respect for their child's triumphs over adversity, and develop closer family ties (Meyer 1993).

Therefore, when you are talking with parents whose child has a disability, do so with a listening ear, rather than with preconceived notions that they will be stressed, grieving or in need of sympathy. Each person's reactions will differ, and will change from day to day and depend on how recently they have discovered their child's disability. Whatever they are feeling, they need to know that you regard them as whole people who have the personal resources to run their own lives—just as they had before their child's birth.

Introduction to the centre

Some parents will feel insecure about leaving their child with special needs with strangers. Other parents will be at the end of their tether and will want to hand over their child to you. Either because of their own separation anxiety or their imperative for some respite, in their haste to leave they might not give you enough information to cater adequately for the child's special requirements. You might be able to avoid this by having a longer than usual period of introduction to the centre, not only for the child's sake, but also to reassure the child's parents and the staff about your ability to care for the child.

Giving parents information

Parents can teach you about their child's disability, the disability service system and their child's particular needs. At the same time, there is a lot that you can teach them about what to expect of their child, since it can be difficult for parents to have realistic expectations when their child's development is not typical.

When passing on information to parents, my own experience of working with children with disabilities leads me to give two suggestions. The first is to explain to parents the terms you use when you are discussing their child's needs. For instance, I recall explaining to a parent that her child had an intellectual disability, to which she responded, 'I'm so relieved! I was really worried that she was retarded'. I then had to explain that the two terms meant the same thing.

My second recommendation is that, while it is important to be positive and to highlight what a child is achieving, you need to be clear about the child's special needs too. When you are describing the child's progress, you will need to add what that means. For instance, it is not enough to report that a four-year-old child is now putting two words together—you might have to add, 'And so that means that he is speaking more like a two-year-old, which is an exciting development compared with when he first started here and wasn't using words at all'.

Expectations of parents

Just as your expectations of children with disabilities need to be realistic, so too is the need for you to maintain realistic expectations of their parents. Parents of children who have disabilities are in a marathon: their period of intense parenting lasts longer than for most parents (Turnbull & Turnbull 1997). Professionals, on the other hand, go home at night, and so it is easy for us to invest great energy in one child and forget that the parents have themselves, their marriage and perhaps other children to look after, not just their child with special needs.

Communicating with other professionals

On occasions, you might have the role of coordinating a child's various specialist services, especially when they are being delivered at your centre. This coordination and planning role can take extra time and will need to be planned for. It cannot be an add-on duty which you are expected to carry out in your lunch time, but neither can it remove you from your direct care or teaching responsibilities. Centre management will need to find ways of making you available for this aspect of your care and education of the child with special needs, while also not compromising the centre financially and not reducing the care which the other children receive.

When attending case conferences, it could be easy to be intimidated by the sheer number of other professionals in attendance and their seemingly lofty qualifications. Except for the parents and yourself, everyone else who is involved in the child's care or education will be a specialist. But you might be the only person among them who specialises in early childhood. Also, you might be the only person (other than the child's parents) who can see the child as a whole person. Your holistic view can humanise the whole planning process and so your contribution is invaluable.

Learn from other professionals by listening and by asking questions when you do not understand what they are telling you; and teach them about your own area of knowledge. Part of learning will mean asking the child's parents and consulting a medical dictionary or some similar reference text about the child's condition, so that you have some background knowledge of the diagnosis.

Another part will be reading assessment reports which have been written by other professionals. However, these can be written in a language which is difficult for people outside that profession to understand. The main thing that you need to know in interpreting other professionals' reports is a statistic called a *standard deviation*. This figure is used when describing a child's skill levels and will be expressed as a number which falls somewhere between −3 and +3. The standard deviation tells you whether a particular child's skills fall near to or a long way from the mean (average). If a child's skills are near the average, then he or she is likely to be well provided for by a regular program. We assume that scores between −1 and +1 represent a normal amount of variation from the average. Scores between −1 and −2 tell us that the child is significantly delayed; while standard deviation scores of below −2 indicate a disability.

My purpose in listing these statistics is so that when you read another professional's assessment report which includes standard deviations, you will be able to interpret how significant is a child's developmental delay. This knowledge allows you to prioritise his or her most serious needs. For instance, if the speech pathologist reports that a child's language skills are at −3 standard deviations, and the physiotherapist says that the child's motor skills are at −1 standard deviations, then it becomes clear that the child's language skills are furthest away from the average and so are the highest priority for intervention. Your ability to understand the assessment reports of other professionals will also allow you to translate them for the child's parents when necessary.

Another area in which your expertise will be especially valuable is translating assessment information into practice. A diagnosis—such as Down syndrome—does not indicate what curriculum a child needs. Your knowledge of child development and curriculum planning will allow you to plan activities which are targeted at the child's specific developmental needs.

Identifying disabilities

Sometimes a child will be participating in your centre and, over time, you may observe signs of atypical development. You cannot diagnose the cause of these as that is outside your realm of expertise (Chandler 1994). However, your keen eye and knowledge of child development is the child's greatest asset, especially when combined with knowledge about which professional to whom you could refer the child for an assessment.

Your first action will be to talk with the child's parents about your concerns. I suggest ways to approach parents with such sensitive information in chapter 26. However, keep in mind that not all parents will react with alarm or hostility. Sometimes, they will be relieved because your concerns confirm their own. Often the mother has been worrying quietly or mentioning her concerns to family members or her local doctor, but has been told that she is over-reacting or being 'silly', or that the child will 'grow out of it'. And so your sensitive queries can confirm that she is not imagining things and can initiate a search for more information. The diagnosis, when it finally comes, can be a relief.

Conclusion

It is important to understand the difficulties under which children with disabilities are functioning but, wherever possible, not to make unreasonable allowances for them. It is important to treat the children as normally as possible, maintaining realistically high expectations for them, since if you expect less *of* children you will gain less *for* them. And to permit antisocial behaviour would make them doubly handicapped.

Suggestions for further reading

For a simple guide to stages of development:

Allen, K.E. & Marotz, L. (1994), *Developmental profiles: Pre-birth through eight*, 2nd edn, Delmar, Albany, NY.

Chandler, P. A. (1994), *A place for me: Including children with special needs in early care and education settings*, National Association for the Education of Young Children, Washington, DC. This is a practical and basic book, without jargon. It will be a good introduction but on its own won't be in enough depth to guide day-to-day practice.

For useful overviews of young children with disabilities:

Cook, R.E., Tessier, A., & Klein, M.D. (1996), *Adapting early childhood curricula for children in inclusive settings*, 4th edn, Merrill, Englewood Cliffs, NJ.

Umansky, W. & Hooper, S.R. (eds.) (1998), *Young children with special needs*, 3rd edn, Merrill, Upper Saddle River, NJ.

For detailed discussion of working with parents whose child has a disability:

Seligman, M. & Darling, R B. (1997), *Ordinary families; Special children*, 2nd edn, Guilford, New York.

Turnbull, A.P. & Turnbull, H.R. (1997), *Families, professionals and exceptionality: A special partnership*, 3rd edn, Merrill, Upper Saddle River, NJ.

24

• • • • • • • • • •

Hyperactive children

Attention-deficit hyperactivity disorder (ADHD) is a relatively new term for a condition which was first identified almost a hundred years ago (Anastopoulos & Barkley 1992). Earlier labels were: hyperactivity, minimal brain dysfunction and hyperkinesis.

The condition is 'an extreme and sustained condition of restless, inattentive and impulsive behaviour' (Lambert 1990, p. 43). Today's label recognises that there are two types of attention-deficit disorders: ADHD, which comprises inattentiveness *and* hyperactivity; and ADD, which involves inattentiveness only. This chapter will mainly focus on ADHD, partly because ADD is less likely to show up in the early childhood years, and partly because ADHD is the more disabling condition.

Prevalence

Most estimates say that around 3–5 per cent of children and adolescents have ADHD (Wodrich 1994), with little variation across socio-economic groups. Most children show their first signs of the condition between three and four years of age (Anastopoulos & Barkley 1992). As many as three to six times more boys than girls are diagnosed with the condition (Anastopoulos & Barkley 1992; Barkley 1988; Goldstein 1995), possibly because there actually are more boys than girls with the condition, or maybe because boys' behaviour is more obviously disruptive because of their social conditioning (Lambert 1990).

Signs of ADD and ADHD

Most practitioners use the DSM-IV criteria (American Psychiatric Association 1994) as a starting point for diagnosis (Blum & Mercugliano 1997). These criteria are reproduced in Appendix C. To be diagnosed with ADD or ADHD, these symptoms must:

- begin prior to seven years of age;
- continue for at least six months—and longer in the early childhood years;
- be present in at least two situations; and
- not be the result of other conditions.

Attention deficits

Children can lack attention in any one of three ways (Zentall 1989):

- having difficulty coming to attention;
- not being able to sustain their attention (concentration span); and
- not being able to filter out irrelevant information and pay attention to the important features of a task—that is, selective attention.

Children with ADD or ADHD have a short attention span, especially when there are attractive alternatives to which they would rather attend. This is due to their *impulsivity*: they flit from one activity to another, not in any planned way, but as the mood takes them.

Hyperactivity

Children with ADHD may be physically or verbally overactive. Verbal overactivity is described by Christopher Green and Kit Chee (1997) as insatiability—once the child gets an idea in his mind, he goes on and on about it. Physically, the child is constantly on the go but, unlike normally boisterous activity, ADHD activity levels are excessive, task irrelevant, developmentally inappropriate, and pervasive across settings (Anastopoulos & Barkley 1992). In short, children with ADHD fail to regulate their activity levels to suit the context.

Impulsivity

Impulsive children respond too quickly and make mistakes as a result (Zentall 1989). Impulsive behaviours include (Anastopoulos & Barkley 1992; Hinshaw & Erhardt 1991):

- finding it hard to wait for a turn;
- beginning tasks before instructions are completed;
- taking unnecessary risks;
- having difficulties adhering to rules and requests;
- difficulties with problem-solving;
- problems with moderating their behaviour to suit the context—that is, self-regulation.

Once they are old enough, impulsive children know how to act appropriately, but do not pause long enough to allow this knowledge to influence their behaviour (Goldstein 1995). This leads to repeated offences which appear to be deliberate but which usually just reflect a lack of planning (Goldstein 1995).

Variability of symptoms

The core behaviours occur in a variety of situations but are most notice-able when the children are: tired, expected to concentrate for long periods, and are in a group rather than in a one-to-one situation; when the activity is boring or repetitive and is highly structured; when move-ment is restricted; and when there is no supervision (Anastopoulos & Barkley 1992).

Secondary features

As well as the primary symptoms which I have just summarised and which are outlined in Appendix C, children with ADHD often show other secondary symptoms associated with the condition. These sec-ondary problems are not included in the criteria for diagnosis but they can complicate management considerably and so it is helpful for care-givers and teachers to be aware of any associated difficulties which a child might be experiencing.

The secondary features include:

- behavioural problems such as uncooperativeness, aggression, and temper outbursts (past the normal age);
- emotional difficulties which include having sudden changes of mood, being emotionally immature and having a low tolerance for frustration;
- relationship difficulties with peers and at home;
- learning disabilities despite having average abilities overall;
- a higher than normal rate of health problems, such as incoordination, sleep disturbances, middle ear and upper respiratory infections, asthma, and allergies (Anastopoulos & Barkley 1992).

These children's social difficulties can be the most significant. Their peers tend to reject them because of their physical aggression—which is up to ten times higher than normal—and their verbal aggression, which can be three times higher (Goldstein 1995). Not surprisingly, this behav-iour leads both to difficulties with establishing friendships and, even more importantly, to sustaining friendships, except perhaps with other children who are experiencing similar difficulties to themselves (Barkley 1988).

Causes of ADHD

The cause of ADHD is not known. Those who take a biological (as opposed to an environmental) view of the condition contend that the behaviours are due to immaturity in the child's development—perhaps in how the frontal parts of the brain function. This area of the brain is responsible for planning.

However, the cause of this apparent neurological immaturity is not clear. It is likely that it arises from an impairment in *how* the brain func-tions, rather than to the brain's actual *structure*, but this is difficult to test. The disorder appears to run in families, although families also share the same environments and so genetic and environmental causes—such as poor nutrition, food sensitivities, environmental lead levels, anaemia (iron deficiency)—are both possible (Goldstein 1995). The conditions of pregnancy or birth appear to be unrelated to ADHD (Goldstein 1995; Lambert 1990), although the mother's overall quality of life could in turn affect her legal and illicit drug use during pregnancy, and so may be related to a higher incidence of ADHD in children (Anastopoulos & Barkley 1992; Barkley 1988).

In the past it was thought that ADHD behaviours were the result of poor discipline practices of the parents, but most practitioners now believe that negative parenting styles are instead the *result* of having a child with ADHD in the family (Anastopoulos & Barkley 1992). This conclusion is supported by the observation that once the children's behaviour improves—say, as a response to medication—the parents' discipline style becomes more positive (Wodrich 1994). It also stands to reason that the parents are not the cause in families where one child has the condition and other children don't have it.

Whatever the cause, these children's behaviour can be very uneven and unpredictable, and so it can look as if they are being deliberately disruptive, with the result that parents and caregivers can become very frustrated with them.

Prognosis

The long-term outcome for children who have been diagnosed with ADHD is still not clear (Hart et al. 1995). A significant number of them—perhaps as many as two-thirds—do not display the symptoms a year later (Hart et al. 1995). For those who still have ADHD a year after diagnosis, the inattentive symptoms then remain relatively stable throughout the child's school years into adolescence (Barkley 1988), but then improve substantially during early adulthood (Hart et al. 1995). Throughout childhood the hyperactive-impulsive behaviour progressively improves (Hart et al. 1995).

Attempts to identify those children with ADHD who are most at risk for a poor adult outcome have generally been unsuccessful, although some factors which are associated with problems in adulthood include: low intelligence, poor peer relationships during childhood, emotional instability, aggressiveness, parental disturbances, and low socio-economic status (Barkley 1988; Goldstein 1995; Hart et al. 1995). The severity of childhood symptoms appears *not* to determine the prognosis in adulthood (Hart et al. 1995).

Assessment

ADD and ADHD are difficult conditions to diagnose accurately, for a number of reasons:

- Children will differ in which core symptoms are most prominent for them and in the severity of their symptoms.

- More so than for other children, the performances of children who are diagnosed with ADHD can fluctuate widely across settings and time, both in terms of accuracy and productivity, (Anastopoulos & Barkley 1992; Barkley 1988).
- ADHD is difficult to distinguish accurately from other conditions such as a language disorder, intellectual disability, learning disability or emotional problems.
- There is a particular problem in the early childhood years since many of the behaviours of children with ADHD are typical in less extreme forms of very young children. This makes it difficult to distinguish ADHD from young children's normal lack of planning and exuberance.

These difficulties create a danger of diagnosing too many children with the condition, or of under-identifying young children and so denying them timely treatment (Goldstein 1995).

Because affected children's behaviour will fluctuate across settings, an accurate diagnosis is possible only when information is gained from many sources, including parents, caregivers or teachers, and developmental and medical assessments. The aims of the latter are to rule out other possible conditions and to gain an understanding of the secondary problems which are associated with ADHD.

Treatment

The most common forms of treatment are medication, behaviour management programs, educational and dietary measures.

Medication

Quite by accident, stimulants were discovered in 1937 to help ADHD but did not come into more common use until the late 1950s (Green & Chee 1997). Medication still appears to make more difference to the symptoms of ADHD than any other form of treatment (Goldstein 1995; Fox & Rieder 1993), especially after the age of five years and for children with moderate to severe symptoms (Anastopoulos & Barkley 1992; Barkley 1988). Nevertheless, the debate about which children benefit most from medication, and at which doses, continues (Levy 1993). Also, the medication works only if the child has been diagnosed accurately: the medication has less effect for children who appear to have ADHD but actually have some other condition (Fox & Rieder 1993).

The most common medication which is used to control hyperactive symptoms is methylphenidate (ritalin), an amphetamine. Paradoxically, it is a stimulant. It is assumed to work by stimulating those parts of the brain (the frontal lobes) which are thought to be under-functioning in ADHD. It begins working within 30–45 minutes after taking the tablet and remains effective for up to four hours (Anastopoulos & Barkley 1992; Barkley 1988; Goldstein & Goldstein 1995; Irwin 1994; Levy 1993). About four to eight hours after taking the medication, some children's symptoms get worse than they were without any medication at all, although the severity of this 'rebound effect' varies considerably among children (Goldstein & Goldstein 1995; Irwin 1994).

While the child with ADHD is on the medication, most of her symptoms reduce to the point where she is indistinguishable from other children who do not have ADHD. The exception is aggression, which drops from ten times higher than normal to three times higher. Nevertheless, this improvement leads to better relationships with peers and at home and, in turn, is likely to improve the child's self-esteem (Green & Chee 1997).

These gains come at the cost of some medication side effects, which are relatively common, especially at higher doses. Most of these unwanted effects improve after the child has been on the medication for a while, but some remain troubling for around 4 per cent of children (Levy 1993). These temporary side effects include nausea, reduced appetite and headaches from increased blood pressure (Fox & Rieder 1993; Goldstein & Goldstein 1995; Levy 1993). For children with a family history of Tourette's syndrome (which involves involuntary motor and vocal tics), ritalin is not recommended as it can bring on the condition permanently.

Some side-effects were originally suspected to exist but have not been found. Those which have been ruled out include over-sedation, tolerance for the medication, depression or other emotional disorders and increased seizures resulting from taking ritalin. Although children lose their appetite and, as a result, their growth slows when they are on amphetamines, it would appear that they ultimately achieve their expected adult height or weight (Fox & Rieder 1993; Goldstein & Goldstein 1995). But even temporary growth suppression can mean that already under-weight children should not take ritalin.

Alternative medications

Methylphenidate (ritalin) is not usually recommended for children aged under six, since there might be more negative side effects and fewer benefits in young children, although more studies are needed to confirm this (Goldstein & Goldstein 1995). After this age, ritalin produces equal benefits for both school-aged children and adolescents (Goldstein & Goldstein 1995).

Although 25 per cent of children with ADHD make no gains on ritalin, some studies have shown that most of this group of children will usually respond to a different dose or to another stimulant (Fox & Rieder 1993).

A third, smaller, group of children—perhaps only 1 per cent (Goldstein & Goldstein 1995)—who fail to respond to any of the amphetamines or who develop unwanted side effects from them, sometimes respond instead to a central nervous system depressant, usually one of the tricyclics. The tricyclics' treatment effects can diminish over time, and overdose is possible (Fox & Rieder 1993); therefore antidepressants are not considered suitable in the long term (Anastopoulos & Barkley 1992). Also, even if a child is both depressed and hyperactive, it is not wise to combine anti-depressants and stimulants, since they can be toxic when used together (Fox & Rieder 1993).

Conclusion: Medication

Given the possible side-effects, it would seem that, for children with mild symptoms, drugs should not be the first treatment option. On the other hand, the impact of severe symptoms on affected children and their families might justify administration of drugs. The decision to use medication, then, will depend on:

- the severity of the condition;
- whether other methods have been tried and have failed;
- the child's age;
- the child's and family's attitude to medication; and
- the ability of parents and caregivers or teachers to supervise a medication regime adequately (Goldstein & Goldstein 1995).

Medication does not have to continue indefinitely if the parents do not want it. It can be useful for an older child to receive medication for a short time to give herself and her family a rest from the demands of coping with the condition before they get ready to change their behaviour management plan; at younger ages, with medical advice, it could be useful for a child to be placed on medication—even for a few weeks—when first settling in to a new centre or to increase her cooperation with a restricted diet.

Educational measures

To *motivate* children to attend to activities, you will need to: ensure that the tasks which you give them to do are developmentally appropriate; capitalise on the children's interests; explain how tasks are relevant; and provide a wide variety of activities. At the same time, to make it *easier* for the children to pay attention, you will need to provide a high degree of organisation and structure, have clear expectations, and reduce distractions (Goldstein 1995).

Behaviour management

Because children with ADHD lack self-control, the temptation is to try to control their behaviour by using star charts, time-out, loss of privileges, and other controlling discipline methods. But you need to remember that these approaches will only teach children to do as they are told—if they worked—whereas these children's problem is that they are not taking charge of their own behaviour. If you manage their behaviour for them, they will never learn how to do it for themselves.

Therefore, I recommend that you use the methods which were described in chapter 15—especially the latter ones—to teach affected children how to take charge of their own behaviour. It might take longer than for a child who does not have ADHD, and it could be more difficult for these children to learn to think before they act, but in my view the alternative of controlling them externally will never teach them how to take charge of their own feelings and behaviour.

Also, many children who are diagnosed with ADD or ADHD feel unable to meet the expected standards for their behaviour. So, while improving their skills is important, it is also crucial to ensure that your expectations of the children are appropriate (Zentall 1989).

Dietary management

There are three classes of foods to which children can be sensitive: for those with a family history of allergies the first class—whole foods—are suspect. These include dairy products, eggs, wheat, corn, cereals and caffeine (in chocolate, coke, tea and coffee). The second class of triggers for food sensitivities are artificial additives such as colourings and preservatives; and the third class are naturally-occurring chemicals such as sugars, salicylates, MSG and amines.

Food intolerances are more likely with children who have severe symptoms of the condition and who have family members with allergic conditions such as eczema, asthma or migraines, and so these children might benefit from dietary restrictions (Goldstein 1995). As to the rest of the ADHD population, it is possible that the lack of findings about food sensitivities is due to the trigger food being particular to each individual, rather than all sufferers of ADHD being sensitive to the same food or food group. Unless the particular food to which a child is sensitive is removed from his or her diet, then the symptoms would remain; removing an irrelevant food would obviously produce no improvement.

Elimination diets or orthodox medical or homeopathic tests can diagnose food intolerances. (The local Allergy Association or Attention-Deficit Disorders Association will have lists of practitioners who are interested in this field.) The research evidence for dietary restrictions is still scant, although many practitioners consider that, in the meantime, at least *some* children who have been diagnosed with ADHD can benefit from dietary modifications, and that these children may suffer unnecessarily if we withhold dietary management while awaiting unequivocal evidence. Naturally, a nutritionist would need to ensure that any restrictions do not compromise the child's required nutrient intake.

Some practitioners are reporting promising results with a controlled carbohydrate diet, on the understanding that children who are diagnosed with ADHD have high insulin levels which drop their sugar levels too low for organised brain functioning (Blum & Mercugliano 1997). Therefore, a controlled carbohydrate diet could be worth pursuing, especially for individual children with a family history of diabetes.

Food sensitivities are likely to affect the child's mood—especially irritability—rather than her actual ability to concentrate (Dengate 1997). Nevertheless, parents report that this improvement in the child's mood is a huge gain for family life.

Working with parents

ADHD excites a large share of scepticism and victim blaming. As a result of their child's increased needs and their own reduced confidence about meeting these needs, parents of children with ADHD 'very often become *overly directive and negative* in their parenting style' (Cuningham & Barkley 1979, in Anastopoulos & Barkley 1992, emphasis mine). But because of this pattern of parenting, many people blame the condition on the parents when, as I said earlier, their 'poor' parenting can be a result—not a cause—of the management difficulties of children with ADHD.

It is important that you believe parents who tell you that their child has the symptoms of ADHD, even if the child does not display them in your centre. Part of this syndrome is that affected children's behaviours will vary across settings. As well, it is easier for children to behave better in a centre than at home because of the structure of the centre and because children who are having difficulties can observe and learn from other children who are behaving appropriately. Also, many children behave less well for their parents in the confidence that their parents will love them anyway. And you can expect that parents will be more stressed by a child's unrelenting difficulties, and so are more likely than you are to find them overwhelming.

It will be necessary to exchange information with a child's parents about what you both find works and doesn't work when guiding the child's behaviour. If the parents like to read, you could suggest some books on discipline which might offer some additional management suggestions.

You might find that you can manage the child without any medication on the days he attends, and so his body and nervous system can get a rest from medication side-effects. Nevertheless, don't use your apparent better success with the child as a weapon against the parents or as evidence that their child does not have ADHD.

In a few, very rare cases, a diagnosed child actually has fewer emotional problems than his parents. This puts prescribing doctors in a dilemma: I have known some doctors to prescribe medication for a child—not so much because he needed it, but because his parents were feeling frustrated with his behaviour for reasons of their own. The doctor's reasoning was that if the medication made the child more placid, then he was less likely to be abused. Although this is not ideal, some doctors decide that it is better than the alternative. Therefore, don't be too hasty to assume that a prescribing doctor misunderstands these types of situations. If you are ever in doubt about a child's diagnosis or method of treatment, you can ask the parents' permission to talk with their specialist and hear first-hand their practitioner's thinking.

Conclusion

ADD and ADHD are complex conditions, whose accurate diagnosis and treatment are especially complicated in the early childhood years. It is important to keep in mind that, unlike some diagnoses, the ADD/ADHD label is not prognostic: a child born with Down syndrome will always have Down syndrome, but the same cannot be said for children with attention deficits. Neither is the label explanatory. This is evident in the circular nature of the diagnosis: 'Why does your child behave that way?', 'Because she has ADHD.' 'How do you know she has ADHD?', 'Because she behaves that way'. At this stage of our knowledge, the label is simply descriptive: it is a shorthand way of describing the characteristic behaviours of this group of children. It neither explains nor predicts their behaviour, however.

In short, there are huge gaps in our knowledge of the attention-deficit disorders. Nevertheless, our relative ignorance is not a reason to blame children, their parents, nor their caregiver-teachers for the condition. It is true that labelling children can allow adults to avoid responsibility for making children's environments more responsive to their needs (Mendaglio 1995). On the other hand, criticism or a lack of treatment will condemn children and their families to an array of primary and secondary difficulties which can severely lower their achievements and self-esteem.

Whatever combination of treatment programs is used, it is clear that treatment needs to be designed specifically for individuals, include a combination of approaches, and be continued for extended periods of time.

Suggestion for further reading

For a clear overview of ADHD written for lay or professional audiences:

Green, C. & Chee, K. (1997), *Understanding ADHD: A parent's guide to attention-deficit hyperactivity disorder in children*, Random House, Sydney.

25

• • • • • • • • • • •

Children who are gifted

Young gifted children are doubly disadvantaged when it comes to acknowledging their special needs. As a society we do not want to give advantages to children who already seem to 'have it easy', and we tend to value intellectual giftedness less than, say, top sporting achievements (Gross 1993; Fraser 1996). Overlaying this general distrust of intellectual giftedness, some fear that identifying gifted children at a young age will make them conceited or pompous (Gross 1993; Mares 1991). However, as Mares (1991, p. 12) observes, 'This is sheer nonsense. The child is gifted, whether she is identified or not'.

We are also reluctant to expose gifted children to 'hot housing' in which they are pressured to achieve and, ultimately, lose interest in their special talent, become withdrawn from social and playful contact with other children, or come to define themselves as valuable only because of their talent (Mares 1991). This, however, is not a fault with identification but with misusing assessment information.

Others feel that, while they are young, gifted children are not aware of feeling different from others and do not suffer any of the emotional or social difficulties of older, gifted children. Instead, precisely because they *are* intellectually aware from a young age, gifted young children do notice that they are different from their agemates and so early childhood can be the most lonely time of all for gifted children (Whitmore 1980), possibly setting the foundation for under-achievement and a low self-esteem for many years to come.

Identification of gifted young children

During their preschool years, it can be difficult to identify children with special gifts, for a number of reasons:

• assessing young children's skills is even more challenging than assessing their older counterparts;

215

- young children might not yet have been exposed to the area in which they will later develop a special talent;
- children can be gifted in a variety of ways and, while we might easily notice verbally gifted children, we can be less accurate at noticing children who are gifted in less obvious ways;
- some young children's advanced skills are hidden by their, as yet immature, social or emotional behaviours (Kitano 1990), or their inability to direct their own learning: they might not concentrate for long enough to display their talents, for example (White 1985);
- children's personality or culture contributes to the ease of identification: if a child is slow to become involved in activities, he might not be identified as being gifted, whereas a boisterous child is more likely to come to your attention.

Some of the characteristics of giftedness which you could look for are listed in Appendix D. You can gain useful information from parents about these characteristics and their child's milestones. Despite a popular myth that all parents think their child is gifted, it is more common for parents to under-estimate their children's abilities than to over-estimate them (Chitwood 1986), especially when the parents are well educated (Roedell, Jackson & Robinson 1980).

The IQ score and its meaning

It is increasingly recognised that children can be gifted in any developmental domain, including creative activities and personal relationships (Gardner 1983). However, teachers are mainly concerned with academic—or intellectual—giftedness. This is usually identified through what is termed an 'intelligence' test. This yields an IQ score or 'intelligence quotient'. It is well accepted that the label 'intelligence' test is a misnomer because this type of test measures just one specific form of giftedness (Borland 1986; Sternberg 1997). Nevertheless there are no reliable tests of the other forms of giftedness, particularly in the early childhood years. Therefore, for convenience, I will focus on intellectual giftedness.

Children are usually regarded as being intellectually gifted if they have an IQ score above 130, although because the test results cannot be completely accurate, children whose IQ scores fall between 125 and 130 are said to be mildly gifted. Table 25.1 lists the categories of giftedness, quoting the IQ score range on the most common IQ test, which in the early childhood age range is called the Wechsler Preschool and Primary Scale of Intelligence—revised edition—or the WPPSI-R (pronounced whipsy-are) for short.

However, when a child is given an IQ score, that number can seem fairly meaningless. The easiest way to interpret an IQ score is to know that the average IQ is 100, and so when a child has been assessed to have an IQ of 150, then she is developing 50 per cent faster than normal for her age. So, at four, her mental age is six; at the age of six, her mental age will be nine years. By way of a second example, an IQ of 130 means that the child is developing 30 per cent (or almost one-third) faster than other

Table 25.1: Levels of intellectual giftedness with their associated Wechsler IQ scores

Wechsler IQ range	Degree of giftedness	Proportion of population
125–129	Mild	1 in 20
130–144	Moderate	~1 in 50 (2.14%)
145–159	High	~1 in 1000 (0.13%)
160–179	Exceptional	1 in 10 000 (0.01%)
180+	Profound	<1 in 1 million

Source: Gross 1993.

children. For technical reasons, this calculation is not exact, but it helps you to calculate the child's mental age and so to know what level of intellectual stimulation she or he might need.

Emotional vulnerabilities

The gifted education field has debated for most of this century about whether gifted children are more vulnerable to emotional difficulties because of being gifted. One side of the debate says that because the brain does two tasks—thinking and feeling—the increased brain functioning which leads to advanced learning can also lead to emotional sensitivity and intensity (Silverman 1994). This view is like the folklore that geniuses are often insane. However, this notion receives very little support by research. In fact, it seems that, in the long term, gifted children adjust emotionally at least as well as—and frequently better than—non-gifted people (Grossberg & Cornell 1988; Moon, Kelly & Feldhusen 1997). This is thought to come about because they have the intellectual skills to solve problems (Clark 1997).

Nevertheless, in their early years gifted children might be more aware of issues which provoke an emotional response in them, while still being too young to resolve these issues intellectually. Therefore, they can appear to be emotionally sensitive or intense. These traits often have the appearance of social or emotional immaturity and so can be misinterpreted as evidence that the children are *not* gifted, when in fact these characteristics are part and parcel of giftedness at this age.

Frustration

Children with particular gifts or talents usually do not develop equally in all areas. They will learn some things virtually automatically, but will struggle with others. Fine motor skills are the most likely to lag behind the other skill domains (Chamrad & Robinson 1986; Tannenbaum 1992). This lag shows when children understand how to do up buttons, but their little fingers can't make the button go in the hole, or when they have an idea in their mind about what they want to draw but cannot execute it on paper. Their resulting frustration can lead to emotional outbursts which seem immature, especially compared with their advanced skills in other areas.

Self-esteem

Gifted children's self-concept develops early (Delisle 1992). This, in turn, hastens their awareness of being different from other children of their age (Clark 1997; Harrison 1995). This awareness can lead them to assume that there is something 'wrong' with them, unless adults explain the real reason for the difference.

Overall, gifted children tend to be confident about the domain in which they are gifted, even if they are less confident in their physical or social skills (Sekowski 1995; van Boxtel & Mönks 1992).

Perfectionism

While gifted children are often said to be perfectionists in the sense that they strive to do things excellently because they can, they are not normally dysfunctional in their perfectionism (Parker & Adkins 1995; Parker & Mills 1996). Perfectionism becomes dysfunctional when the children are not happy with their performances, no matter how well they do.

Even striving for excellence can have its drawbacks, however. Some children concentrate only on their area of special talent, with the result that the gap between their upper and lower skills widens, and they progressively lose more and more confidence in their less developed skills. Or, they might put off starting something in case they cannot do it perfectly. In that case, it is wise for adults not to take over and do a task for them, or else the children will think that you do not believe that they *can* do it themselves.

Involvement

Because verbally gifted children understand adult issues and conversations, they might involve themselves in adult business. They might debate with you about your instructions, and might even think that you have no 'right' to tell them what to do. This gives them too much power, and can result in stress levels which will lead to inappropriate behaviour.

From a very young age, gifted children worry about the big social issues too—such as the environment, poverty and wars. At the same time they have no power to do anything about these problems, and so they can become stressed or lose confidence in themselves (Galbraith 1985).

To minimise these problems it can help if you discuss with the children only those issues about which they can do something. You can also keep reinforcing the message that adults are taking care of adult business, and that it is the children's job to be children and to grow up at a manageable speed. At the same time, however, you might need to let gifted children do age-appropriate things—maybe dictate a letter to a politician—which allows them to feel satisfied that they have done what they can about social issues which are concerning them.

Fears

Gifted children's advanced cognitive and social awareness causes them to develop fears earlier than other children (Derevensky & Coleman 1989), when they might be too young emotionally to cope with their precocious imagination. It can help to explain to them that they need to take charge of their imagination so that their ideas and feelings do not overwhelm them.

Behavioural nonconformity

Because of their independence, gifted children tend to resist attempts to control their behaviour (Delisle 1992; Kitano 1990). Although their intellectual risk-taking is often reflected in advanced learning, it can also result in breaking 'rules' in unusual and unanticipated ways and so can appear to be 'mischief-making' (Mares 1991).

Social challenges

The emotional problems which gifted children can experience are mainly due to feeling different from other people (Whitmore 1980). Naturally, the more gifted the children are, the more they are likely to notice that they are different from other children, particularly since there will be few other children in any group who are like them.

Play

Young gifted children often learn to play games with rules earlier than other children (Mares 1991). They have advanced play interests and behaviours, and so they might attempt to structure the play of a group of agemates in too complex a way. The result can be that the less able children wander off and lose interest (Morelock & Morrison 1996). Gifted children can easily interpret the other children's lack of interest as a rejection of them, rather than realising that the other children cannot yet play at more sophisticated levels.

Loneliness

Friendship problems are most acute in early childhood because same-aged peers do not share gifted children's interests and level of organisational and conceptual play (Whitmore 1980), and yet older children are seldom available in child care or preschool centres. As a result, gifted children's play can become solitary or they might gravitate to adults.

Lost friends

Another social problem which young gifted children experience is that they often make friends with the oldest children in a group, but these children graduate to the next group in the child care centre or go to school, before they do. They have to make new friends but, at the end of the next term, the same thing happens again, which can be discouraging. As gifted children near the age to move on, of course, there will be fewer and fewer children who are older than them and who can provide the intellectual stimulation they need. The result is that gifted children's last six months before starting school can be a particularly lonely time.

Part of the solution can be acceleration—see that section later in this chapter. As well as this, it can help if parents can link moderately or profoundly gifted children up with other children with similar ability levels, so that they can gain some experience of true peer relationships.

High demands of others

Gifted children can develop perfectionist standards for other people as well as for themselves. As a result, they can become very bossy or competitive with other children. They might think that other children are being 'deliberately stupid' or silly. These attitudes are not likely to endear a gifted child to the other children, and are another reason why it is important to counsel gifted children about their giftedness.

Moral development

Gifted children typically have an advanced sense of justice (Baska 1989; Clark 1997) as a result of being more empathic than is usual for their age. However, when other children do something which is developmentally normal but which the gifted child knows to be 'wrong', gifted children can be offended and confused. Their moral values can also drive their personal interests, leading to a disdain for popular activities—such as sport—which have no 'meaning'.

In the long run, these differences can mean that gifted children need to learn the benefits of being tactful, while never forcing them to go against their strongly held views just to be popular.

Educational challenges

These emotional and social characteristics are supplemented by some educational challenges which can create difficulties for gifted young children.

Lack of independence

Because young gifted children need a lot of stimulation, they sometimes learn to rely on adults to supply this. They can also become dependent about self-care tasks such as dressing, especially after they know they have mastered the activity and it holds no new intellectual challenge for them. Their resulting dependence can mean that they cling to you rather than associate with other children and can limit their risk-taking, with the result that they do not gain a sense of achievement about everyday tasks.

Low self-confidence in their learning ability

Because many things come easily to gifted children, they might not realise that they know how to learn. You can help gifted children by pointing out the processes which they use to solve problems, and congratulate them on their logical approach to a task, on using their memory well, or on planning how to go about an activity. Also, when they fail at something, explain how their failure was caused by the approach they used. They can turn failure into success by changing their approach.

Boredom

Young gifted children can display some seemingly inappropriate behaviour if they have little else to do to entertain themselves. The last two terms of preschool can be particularly trying, especially if they are not allowed to begin school early or if they cannot be linked up with other gifted children of their own age.

Short attention span

Sometimes gifted children appear not to persist at activities. It looks as if they have a short attention span when, in fact, having done the activity well the first time, it offers them no new challenge to repeat it, and so they refuse to do it again. They might then wander aimlessly around, unless you can offer them something stimulating to do.

Implications for practice

These characteristics—and others which are detailed in Appendix D—necessitate some adjustments to early childhood practices. Gifted young children are advantaged relative to older children because early childhood professionals are inherently child-focused, have a flexible enough structure to allow them to cope with the demands of a mixed-ability group, and are aware of the imperative to focus on children's social, emotional and physical needs as well as their intellectual skills. This will serve all children well, but especially children with atypical development.

Realistic expectations

It can be hard to know what to expect of gifted children, not least because their precocious development in some domains inadvertently tricks you into developing high expectations of them in all areas. The stress of living up to high expectations has an effect rather like stretching out a piece of elastic and then letting it go. The gifted child stretches to cope at an advanced level and then, when the stress gets too much, he drops his bundle and behaves even younger than his years.

Unlike the child's parents, however, you have worked with hundreds of children of this age before and, if you momentarily forget about normal development, you have a dozen or so other children of the gifted child's age to remind you.

On the other hand, the stress of coping with low expectations can be debilitating also. Knowledge of normal developmental milestones or a fear of pushing children can set a ceiling on adults' expectations of children. As a result, you might offer gifted children age-appropriate activities because you do not expect them to be able to do more, and so they do not get the extension which they crave.

Explain giftedness to children

You will need to come clean with a bright child, and explain to him that his brain is learning more quickly than other children's. It is wise, however, to avoid the label 'gifted' because it is so easily misinterpreted and creates pressure on the child to be perfect (Cornell 1989).

After this, you can deal with other issues which are particular to that child. For instance, with social difficulties, you might explain that it is not the other children's fault that they do not understand the things which a gifted child does. When the child is frustrated with his less advanced skills—let's say his fine hand abilities—it might help to explain that, while his brain is learning things very quickly indeed, his hands are growing at the same speed as other children's, and so his hands cannot do everything which his brain tells them to.

For emotional outbursts or behavioural difficulties arising from giftedness, you could explain to the child that, while his brain is a good learning machine, it's like a good car. But even good cars still need someone to steer them, to be in charge of them. Therefore, he needs to find ways to take charge of his brain so that it doesn't trick him into thinking or feeling things which aren't real.

Authoritative discipline

Gifted children's advanced intellectual skills mean that they are particularly prone to rebelling against arbitrary or authoritarian discipline because it robs them of their autonomy. Also, their perfectionism can make them very sensitive to criticism (Mendaglio 1994, 1995). This means that it is especially important not to punish them for inappropriate behaviour and to give them a chance to save face if they do make a mistake (see chapter 13). At the same time, it is important not to praise them for being 'clever', as they might believe that they are worthy *only* when they do well. Rather, you will need to teach them how to notice their own achievements, using acknowledgment (see chapter 6). And make sure that you acknowledge *how* they use their talents, not *that* they have them. For example, instead of telling a child that she is clever—which she inherited and so cannot claim any credit for—comment on how hard she tried, how well she planned what to do . . . and so on. Those are achievements for which she *can* take some credit.

Curriculum differentiation

Curriculum *differentiation* refers to the provision of different learning activities for same-aged children who have different learning needs and preferences (Kulik & Kulik 1997). It allows for differences in both the pace (quantity) and depth (quality) of children's learning (Piirto 1994).

The requirement for a differentiated curriculum does not imply, however, that the whole curriculum should be differentiated (Braggett,

Day & Minchin 1997). Some experiences are equally valuable for all children; others will be suitable for a group of bright children; while still others will be unique to a particular child (Braggett et al. 1997).

Acceleration

The term, *acceleration*, refers to increasing the pace at which the curriculum is presented (Schiever & Maker 1997; Townsend 1996). In the early childhood years, it usually involves moving children up to older groups within a child care centre, allowing them to enter preschool early, or starting them at school early.

Some writers argue that the term *acceleration* is a misnomer since it implies an attempt to speed up the children's development itself (Elkind 1988; Feldhusen 1989; K. Rogers & Kimpston 1992). These writers emphasise that the term really only means providing gifted children with a curriculum which matches their needs and abilities. Therefore, Feldhusen, Van Winkle and Ehle (1996) suggest that we replace the term acceleration with the concept of *appropriate developmental placement*.

The intent of appropriate developmental placement (or acceleration) is to enhance children's achievement by providing a closer match between their needs and abilities and the curriculum which is delivered to them (Benbow 1991). In so doing, the plan is that boredom will be avoided, along with any behavioural difficulties which can result (Holden 1996; Rogers & Kimpston 1992). A second aim is to allow gifted children to mix more successfully socially by placing them with children who differ from them in age but who share similar interests to themselves. It also aims to capitalise early on young children's interests and abilities (Rogers & Kimpston 1992).

Research consistently reports that acceleration meets all of these academic, social and emotional aims (Benbow 1991; Cathcart 1996; Clark 1997; Eales & de Paoli 1991; Harrison 1995; Janos 1987; McCluskey, Massey & Baker 1997; Proctor, Feldhusen & Black 1988; Rimm & Lovance 1992; Robinson & Robinson 1992; Rogers & Kimpston 1992; Sayler & Brookshire 1993; Schiever & Maker 1997; Southern, Jones & Fiscus 1989; Townsend 1996). In fact, *failing to accelerate* gifted children can result in many negative effects on their self-esteem, behaviour, motivation, attitude to school, and achievement levels (Townsend 1996). The overall conclusion is that early school entrance (being one form of acceleration) has far more positive consequences than negative ones, especially for carefully screened children.

Nevertheless, many parents are reluctant for their child to begin school early because they believe its structure is incompatible with young children's social and emotional needs (Kitano 1982). Sometimes, parents or teachers seek to hold a child back because of social or emotional immaturities. But rather than signalling that the child is not ready for school, these behaviours can be a result of being in a socially and educationally inappropriate setting and can improve once the child is more appropriately placed.

These hesitations give rise to an awareness that children and their

Table 25.2: General curriculum guidelines for gifted young children

---

Given gifted learners' advanced thinking skills, the early childhood curriculum will need to offer open-ended activities which:

- encourage higher level thinking skills such as analysis, synthesis, evaluation and problem-solving;
- allow the children to pursue their own interests to a depth which satisfies them;
- involve less repetition and a faster pace than usual for their age;
- promote intellectual risk-taking—that is, creativity;
- offer a high degree of complexity and variety in their content, process and product.

These same guidelines can apply to parents' choice of toys for their young gifted child (Holden, 1996)

---

anticipated school have to be carefully screened before early entry is contemplated. The school has to be willing to accept the child early (Braggett 1993; Mares & Byles 1994), and the classroom which the child is entering needs to be flexibly structured. The child needs to be socially and emotionally mature enough and have sufficient fine motor skills for academic activities such as handwriting (Mares & Byles 1994; Robinson & Robinson 1992). Reading readiness is a crucial factor, as are the child's interest in starting school and the parents' wishes (Braggett 1993; Mares & Byles 1994). It also helps if the child is not small for his or her age so that he or she can participate in the other children's physical games and sports, and does not look physically out of place among older classmates. The child will also need the physical stamina to cope with a longer day (Schiever & Maker 1997). Mares and Byles (1994) also believe that, ideally, children need to have attended an early childhood centre for at least six months prior to school entry so that they can have learned to separate from their parents, delay gratification, cope with conflict with other children using negotiation rather than aggression, and to concentrate.

Nevertheless, the uneven development of gifted children means that few children will be equally mature in all these domains, and so consultation between early childhood staff, parents, and the selected school will be necessary to decide what is best for each individual child (Morelock & Morrison 1996).

Content modifications

Gifted children will need less repetition, revision and consolidation time than less able children (Braggett 1998; Plucker & McIntyre 1996). Therefore, in addition to an increased pace of curriculum delivery (acceleration), they will need a curriculum which offers both *broader* and *deeper* content than is typical for their age. These measures are called curriculum *enrichment* and *extension*.

Their need to pursue topics in depth means that the theme-a-week concept might be inappropriate for gifted children since it might not give them enough time to become absorbed in a topic (Patton & Kokoski 1996).

Process modifications

Gifted children are able to deal with abstract and complex material earlier and gain knowledge in greater depth and breadth than is usual for their age (Morelock & Morrison 1996). Therefore, your curriculum will need to promote their higher level thinking skills such as: being able to apply their knowledge; analyse ideas; synthesise information by creating, inventing and constructing original products; and evaluating outcomes (Braggett 1998).

You will need to encourage learning styles or attitudes such as curiosity, persistence, tolerance of ambiguity, and confidence (especially about taking risks), and to teach self-regulation strategies such as planning, monitoring and evaluation (Berk 1997; Freeman 1995).

Parent collaboration

Whereas many parents are confident that they can meet the needs of typical children, those whose children are gifted might want or need extra suggestions about how to support their young children's learning and emotional adjustment. In reverse, most parents will have valuable insights into their children's interests and abilities, which can inform your curriculum planning and delivery.

In addition to the centre's usual communications with parents, one suggestion to help parents support their children intellectually, is educational backpacks which children take home to complete (Patton & Kokoski 1996). The backpacks contain all the materials which are necessary to complete an activity, along with instructions and suggestions for its extension and elaboration. In this way, parents can be guided to assist their children's learning and also can be encouraged to be involved in their child's early education.

Conclusion

Above all, adults need to be responsive to the signals which young gifted children are sending about their educational, social and emotional needs. Harrison (1995, p. 45) states that, 'Knowledge of the characteristics of giftedness, as well as knowledge of the individual child, can help parents, families and early childhood educators to interpret and respond appropriately to the child's behaviour'. Counselling of children and their families can help young gifted children to understand and cope with their differences from their agemates, and can prevent later underachievement and learning problems (Kitano 1986). When they know the reason for feeling different, most gifted children are able to use their advanced intellectual skills to adjust emotionally and socially. Support from their family and from their early childhood caregiver or teacher can set the scene for a happy and healthy emotional, social and academic life in which gifted children can fully use and appreciate their special abilities.

Suggestions for further reading

Porter, L. (1997), *Young gifted children: Meeting their needs,* AECA Resource Book Series, vol 4, Australian Early Childhood Association, Watson, ACT.

Porter, L. (1999), *Gifted young children,* Allen & Unwin, Sydney.

Harrison, C. (1995), *Giftedness in early childhood,* KU Children's Services, Sydney.

Morelock, M.J. & Morrison, K. (1996), *Gifted children have talents too: Multi-dimensional programmes for the gifted in early childhood,* Hawker Brownlow Education, Highett, Victoria.

Part seven

• • • • • • • • • • •

Caring for adults

The adults in a child care or preschool centre are like the hub of a wheel. You form the core, which shapes all the other features of the centre: its atmosphere; relationships between children, among staff, and with parents; the quality of the program or curriculum . . . and so on.

Increasingly, the care and education of young children is seen to be a mutual concern of their parents and caregiver-teachers. In order to feel empowered to fulfil their respective roles, both partners to this relationship will need support and resources.

In this part, I examine some of the issues which affect the ability of staff to experience satisfaction in your work and to discharge your responsibilities in the best way you know how. This begins with appreciating the perspective of parents and harnessing their skills in caring for their children. Next, it requires that staff, too, are cared for. Your role in caring for and educating young children is a demanding and complex one. Whenever demands are high, supports necessarily must be high also.

Therefore, the chapters in this section examine some of the issues which affect the quality of your working conditions. These, in turn, will affect the quality of the care and education which you are able to provide to the children in your centre.

26

• • • • • • • • • • •

Collaboration with parents

Child care professionals have learned that children are best served when providers have some understanding of the children's primary world at home. They also know that a spirit of partnership with parents promotes a higher quality of child care and that maintaining open lines of communication is an important means to that end.

Kleinman (1988, p. xi)

The relationship between parents and caregivers is an important influence on how well children adjust to child care (McKim 1993; Rolfe, Lloyd-Smith & Richards 1991; Stonehouse 1994b). This is recognised in the accreditation guidelines which, as listed in Appendix A, explicitly address your relationships with parents:

10 There is written and verbal communication with all families about the centre.
11 There is active exchange of information between parents and staff.
12 There is an orientation process for new children and parents.
13 Parents and other family members are encouraged to be involved in the program.
52 Information about the centre's management is readily available to staff and parents.

Rationale for parental participation

The drive towards parental participation is based on a number of assumptions (Sebastian 1989, p. 77):

• parents have the most important and enduring relationship with their children;

- children learn more from their home environment than from any other setting;
- parents' involvement in their child's education contributes to children's attitudes to learning and to themselves as learners (Raban 1997);
- parental involvement in their child's education or care setting promotes mutual respect and understanding and allows for consistency between the home and the program;
- parents can make valuable contributions;
- accountability is more open when parents are involved in their child's program.

Parents can contribute their expertise about their own children, their informed observations of their children over a long period of time and in many circumstances, knowledge of their children's needs, and their skill in reading and responding to their children's cues. When professionals can harness these skills, the child's care can only benefit.

The evolving parent–caregiver partnership

Although working with parents has been an aim of early childhood services for much of their history, over time the concept of a partnership with parents has changed. At first, early childhood services—particularly in America following the Head Start model—were put in place to correct deficiencies in children's home experiences. Many professionals felt they had to rescue or 'save' children from deficient parents.

The next trend limited the responsibility of caregivers and early childhood teachers to *communicating* with parents about the program. The professional was seen to be the one who 'knew what was best' for young children and regarded parents as 'clients' or passive recipients of services (Sebastian 1989).

The next phase in the relationship with parents was to involve them in their child's program when they were available to take part. This *cooperative* relationship is more reciprocal than the one-way flow of information from the centre to home, but it does not necessarily imply a high level of participation (Waters 1996), and might comprise only token involvement such as getting art materials organised or helping to raise funds.

The more recent emphasis is on *collaboration*, which means that caregivers and teachers jointly determine goals and plan strategies along with the children's parents (Hostetler 1991). Parents' participation at this level does not necessarily mean day-to-day assistance in a centre (Arthur et al. 1996)—since many parents use early childhood services because they are employed—and because pressure to participate at a level which is beyond the parents can inadvertently add to the pressure which they already experience in balancing the complex demands of their parenting and other roles (Sebastian 1989). Instead, collaboration is a philosophical stance which implies a shared responsibility for the care and education of young children in which the professional's role is to support parents as they care for their children (Arthur et al. 1996; Fleet & Clyde 1993).

Just like the child-centred perspective, this family-centred perspective relies on observation of and listening to individuals' needs and awareness of their interests and skills. Tinworth describes a family-orientation:

> In such a model, services build from family needs and collaborate . . . to empower the family to make informed choices and control the direction of the service. The approach is sensitive to the family's values, beliefs and aspirations and seeks to construct a service that [they] can identify with and be energised by (1994, p. 28–9).

In order to participate as equally valued partners, parents need to feel that they have something valuable to contribute to a relationship with early childhood professionals. This belief is sometimes termed 'empowerment'. To feel empowered—that is, to feel that they can take action to meet their child's and their family's needs—parents need:

- recognition of their skills;
- encouragement to contribute to their child's care and to decision making;
- information about their options;
- a sense of control over their options;
- time and other resources—such as energy.

Conclusion: The shape of a collaborative partnership

Although you can approach parents in the knowledge that both of you want what is best for their child—even when you have differing ideas about how to achieve this—as consumers of an expensive and important service, parents would be irresponsible if they did not closely question what you offer their child and how you deliver your service (Greenman & Stonehouse 1997). More than being mere consumers or even equal participants in a partnership with you, parents are actually your employers. They pay considerable fees for child care—and considerable taxes for public preschools—and so, as with all employers, you are directly accountable to them for your practices.

This means that, regardless of their manner, the questions which parents ask and the demands they make need to be met with courtesy. Even those 'difficult' parents are not being demanding just to make you jump through hoops: they both *need* and have a *right* to ask questions.

Constraints on collaborative relationships with parents

Empowerment is not a one-way process. Professionals too need to feel that their role is valued and that they have the resources to provide high-quality care to children. Some of the general constraints on the empowerment of early childhood professionals are discussed in the next chapter, but one impediment to working collaboratively with parents is the lack of training for that role for early childhood professionals (McKim 1993).

A second limitation is, of course, the parents' availability and resources for participating actively in the centre's program. However, as I have said already, this is not necessary. Collaboration is a frame of mind, rather than a level of participation.

A third impediment is that professionals are frequently judgmental of parents (Tinworth 1994). They observe parents' interactions with their children during parents' most stressful times of the day—at drop-off and pick-up of their children. The result is that parents can seem to be less competent than they actually are. In addition, there are parents whose skills are difficult to respect. However, respect does not mean having to agree with parents, but it simply means recognising their values and perspective (Caughey 1991).

A fourth impediment is that parents and professions can be keen to convey the 'right' impression to each other (Seligman & Darling 1997). To avoid placing parents under pressure to project a certain image, you will need to find a way to convey that you intend to work alongside the parents, to carry out their wishes for their child, not to judge them or their family.

In terms of your own 'impression management', it can help to remember that being professional does not mean having to be formal and distant with parents. They mainly want an emotionally rich relationship with the professionals with whom they deal, rather than a formal 'expert–client' relationship (Summers et al. 1990). Although you are not ordinarily parents' friends—because being paid to deliver a service is not friendship—you can still be friendly.

Understanding parents' perspective on using child care

When parents feel ambivalent about leaving their children, the children tend to adjust poorly to centre-based care or education. Although some writers (e.g. Stonehouse 1994b) report that many parents are ambivalent about your close relationship with their child, research tells us that this is not so (Galinsky 1990). Most parents are not jealous of early childhood caregivers or teachers, and most parents respect your role with their child.

Restricted care options

However, parents are likely to feel ambivalent about the restricted care options which are available to them. When they are asked whether they are satisfied with the quality of the care their child receives, most parents (85–95 per cent) say that they are. But when they are asked whether they would have used their chosen care option if others had been accessible, over half say that they would not (Galinsky 1989).

Expectations of care

Parents who reluctantly return to the paid work force often see child care as 'a necessary evil'. These parents are more likely to want child care to mirror the nurturing relationships at home (Larner & Phillips 1996). They might try to minimise the amount of time which their child spends in care and so deliver him or her at the latest moment, leaving little time for informal conferences with staff or a relaxed parting from their child. These parents might leave detailed instructions about how they want you to care for their child, and could appear to be very demanding of you.

In contrast, those parents who return to the work force for their own occupational satisfaction are more likely to regard child care as a valuable educational experience and so will be seeking a placement which supplements or complements the experiences which they can offer at home (Larner & Phillips 1996). These parents might be interested in the ratio of adults to children, and the training and experience of staff in a centre.

Either way, most parents choose centres—within the constraints of location, convenience and cost—which will provide safe experiences and nurturing interactions between children and staff (Chick 1996; Tinworth 1994; Williams & Ainley 1994).

Parents' emotions about separation from their child

Even when the parents are highly motivated to return to the work force, their decision still causes them conflict, guilt and sadness (Rolfe et al. 1991). Their subsequent adjustment to being parted from their child is a highly personal and individual process, punctuated with feelings of chronic sadness. These feelings can take some months to resolve (Rolfe et al. 1991). Regardless of the quality of the program, this process of grieving and adjusting is common, although parents' feelings are more readily resolved when they feel safe about the quality of care their child is receiving (Larner & Phillips 1996).

Vulnerability

Parents are painfully aware that they are not likely to be able to anticipate problems which might arise after they have enrolled their child in their chosen care option (Larner & Phillips 1996). Staff changes, the changing needs of a growing child, and other unforeseen changes, can neither be anticipated nor guarded against. This awareness increases their feelings of vulnerability, which are already present because they realise that they cannot actually assess the quality of the care being delivered to their child as they are seldom there to see it.

Their concerns about using child care makes their rapport with their child's caregivers a crucial factor in the parents' choice of care (Larner & Phillips 1996). This makes your acceptance of the child and attitude to parents a fundamental factor in how comfortable parents—and, in turn, their children—will feel in your centre. Sometimes, however, myths about families interfere with forming respectful relationships with those families who depart from the 'ideal' picture of the nuclear family with its two adults and their two biological children. So, let's now examine some of those myths.

Facts and myths about the modern family

The nuclear family has been held up as an ideal type in our society. This ideal is reflected in the language we use about families. For instance, nuclear families are sometimes described as 'intact', while families where the parents do not live together owing to separation or divorce are called 'broken', and discussions about these families often allude to 'family breakdown'. The result is that we regard children in these families as suffering some deprivations and, furthermore, we assume that they are likely to be damaged by these 'inadequacies' in their family.

Family size

Our belief that extended families used to live together and provide mutual support to each other, is actually taken from the landed gentry class in England, where families *had* to remain in the one household in order to maintain the family estate (Bottomley 1983). The short life expectancy in poorer families meant that grandparents—and often parents—were dead before the youngest child left home.

Likewise, although families in the nineteenth century had many children, infant mortality meant that few survived. Then, once contraception became widespread in Australia at the beginning of this century, the average number of children fell to only two to three, just as it is today.

Put together, these two facts debunk some of the myths about modern children being 'over-indulged' because they come from a family with too few children.

Working mothers

The myth that women have not worked outside of home until recently leads to value judgments on parents who do. In one study (Galinsky 1990), one-quarter of caregivers disapproved of working mothers. Yet this ignores the fact that women have always worked. Prior to universal education, both women and children worked out of home. Since then, working class women have always worked, while other women worked out of home during the two World Wars and the 1929–35 depression.

This means that the debate about out-of-home care for children is not about whether it should occur—since it always has—but about the quality of that care (NAEYC 1987), especially for very young infants (Howes 1990). The focus on the quality of care is supported by research which has found that when under-one-year-olds are enrolled in high-quality programs, they display successful social and emotional adjustment and learning behaviours (Howes 1990). This means that when young babies adjust poorly to out-of-home care, this is usually not due to any disruption to the mother-child attachment, but to the low quality of the care they receive (Howes 1990).

Another aspect of the debate about working mothers, is that it assumes that all jobs are the same (Galinsky 1989). If a mother feels satisfied and fulfilled in her work, then she will have a better relationship with her children than a mother who finds her job stressful or unsatisfying.

Single parenthood

Another aspect of family life is the single parent household. The first thing to understand about single-parent families is that, contrary to popular myths of the adolescent single mother, today's single parent is usually a woman who has been in a stable defacto or marital relationship which disintegrated some time after the conception or birth of the youngest child. Teenage births fell from 30500 to 14600 between 1971 and 1991 in Australia (McDonald 1993). In 1990, one in ten Australian women had a child before her 20th birthday, compared with about one in four in 1971. This figure is important, because one of the factors causing stress in children is the youth of their parents (Slee, pers. comm.). Older parents are less stressed—and often less impoverished—than younger parents.

Second, single parenthood is not a modern phenomenon. In Australia, a significant minority of women have always brought up their children alone, as their partners went off to the gold fields, left home to look for work during the 1890s and 1930s depressions, went off to the Boer and two World Wars—and maybe died there. This means that today's figure that 16.6 per cent of families with dependent children have only one parent, is the same as the figure of 100 years ago (16.7 per cent in Victoria in 1891) (McDonald 1993). If modern children are seriously impaired by being brought up in single parent households, then so too have the last five generations of Australian children.

The main effect of single parenthood is on the income of the family unit. Often, marital separation results in a lowering of the family's living standards. If these were already low, then the single parent family can end up living in poverty. It is then the poverty—not the single-parent status—which affects family members. The second effect, of course, is the added work which one adult must perform in the absence of a partner. This gives rise to Raines' (1995) observation that, 'Single parents deserve double praise'.

Divorce

Divorce is usually regarded as a negative phenomenon. However, although the divorce rate is higher now than ever, it has the benefit of allowing adults and children to escape an unhappy home life. It is clear that it is conflict—not divorce—which disturbs children. When a divorce reduces parental conflict, the children are better adjusted in a separated family than they were in an 'intact' but conflict-ridden family (Burns & Goodnow 1985).

Also, despite the modern divorce rate, the chances of marriages lasting many years have increased throughout this century. In 1891, 41 per cent of marriages lasted thirty years or more; in 1991, 53 per cent lasted for longer than thirty years (McDonald 1993). The increase comes about because adults are now living longer. Where death ended a marriage a century ago, now divorce ends it—but less often.

Stepfamilies

Remarriage rates are the same now as they were in the sixteenth and seventeenth centuries (Whelan & Kelly 1986). This means that stepfamilies are as common now as they were then. Of course, stepfamily establishment these days usually follows divorce whereas, centuries ago, it followed the death of one partner. It is likely that this changes the psychological reactions of the new family members. But, nevertheless, stepfamilies as a type are not new and neither are they deficient.

Conclusion: The modern family

Put together, these facts mean that our reverence for the nuclear family as the only 'right' way to bring up children could well be somewhat misplaced. It is clear that many types of families can bring up happy children. The implication of this for caregivers and teachers is that we can respect many family types without regarding them as deficient. This accepting attitude can help us deal more respectfully with individual parents from diverse families.

Implications for practice

Your relationship with parents cannot be rushed. Parents will take time to adjust to having other people sharing the care of their child and for you to earn their trust.

Respect for family diversity

Early childhood professionals are less likely to accept families whose backgrounds are very different from their own (Galinsky 1990). The result is that the families who are least well equipped to care for their children, are the least likely to receive the support they need (Arthur et al. 1996; Galinsky 1988).

A collaborative approach requires that we understand how families are experiencing their lives. So a new way of looking at families who are under stress is to acknowledge that they can survive crises and manage a challenging family situation (Rosenthal & Sawyers 1996). Collaborative relationships will emphasise their inherent strengths and potential contributions.

Empowering parents to select suitable care

Parents who are under stress are more likely to select lower-quality child care. You cannot do anything about the availability of affordable and convenient child care. But you can help parents to choose a centre which most nearly suits their needs. The first thing you can do at an inspection visit before a child enrols is to suggest to the parents that they visit other centres as well. To help them assess what they are seeing, you could supply a list of features to observe and questions they could ask caregivers. This will help all parents—but particularly those who otherwise might select the first centre they visit, regardless of its quality—to make an informed decision about their child's placement and, subsequently, to feel happier about the selection they make.

Delivering sensitive information

There will be occasions when you have concerns about a child's development and need to convey your concerns to the child's parents. When conveying potentially upsetting information about children to their parents, Ginott cautions:

> When a teacher talks to parents about their children, he inevitably intrudes on family dreams . . . What the teacher says about the child touches on deep feelings and hidden fantasies. A concerned teacher is aware of the impact of his words. He consciously avoids comments that may casually kill dreams (1972, p. 277–8).

This means that you will need to plan your meeting very carefully, in order that the parents will feel comfortable and that there is enough time to discuss your concerns and to listen to their reactions (Abbott & Gold 1991). Your main message to the parents will be that you are not certain about their child's needs or abilities and so would like an assessment to examine whether your concerns are warranted and to give you advice about how best you can meet their child's needs. It is not your job to diagnose the child's condition (Abbott & Gold 1991). This message can be supported with samples of the child's products or detailed observations. Parents might be able to add their own information about their child's skills at home but might not necessarily be aware when these skills are atypical.

It will help two-parent families if you can speak with both parents about your concerns. If this cannot be arranged, then you could tape your conversation so that the parent who could not attend can at least listen to the taped conversation. You will need to pass on the invitation for that parent to contact you with any questions that arise from hearing the tape.

Before the meeting, ensure that you have updated your knowledge of which agencies are available to provide the type of assessment the child requires. This information will include waiting time, costs and contact phone numbers. The more specific your information can be, the more easy it will be for the parents to follow up your concerns promptly.

Problem-solving with parents

When a child is experiencing a difficulty—let's say a behavioural difficulty—in your centre, then it is wise to avoid giving advice to the child's parents (Coleman 1991), but rather to collaborate with them to find a solution. You might use the collaborative problem-solving steps which were outlined in chapter 10. However, Heath (1994) asks, 'What if the parents' suggested solutions—such as smacking a child—cannot be implemented?'. If you argue against their suggestion, then you might undermine the parents. But neither can you enact their solution. In this case, Heath suggests that, before selecting which course of action you will follow, the parents and caregiver-teacher could:

- identify the types of solutions which are possible in the circumstances;
- restate your goals for the child;
- identify the relevant characteristics of the child—temperament, age, size (as this affects the child's ability to dominate his or her peers, for instance), interests, responses to earlier disciplinary attempts, and so on;
- identify the needs of the people involved;
- identify the feelings of those who are involved.

In this way, the solution remains compatible with the broader goals for the child. For instance, my overriding goal with behaviour management is to teach children to be considerate rather than compliant. This will mean that options such as time-out—which, as a punishment, is an attempt to force compliance—will not be considered (although, time away could be used—see chapter 15).

Handling complaints

Your first task when parents come to you with a complaint will be to listen. You will need to reflect what they are saying and acknowledge their feelings. When they are expressing these offensively, however, you might have to add an assertive statement such as, 'I accept that you are angry that Simon's clothes have gone missing, although I do not like how you are saying it'. The next step is to state that you have a common interest—namely, providing the best possible care for their child. You might add in what way the meeting is intended to advance that purpose—that is, state the purpose of the meeting: 'I wonder how we could ensure that his clothes do not get lost again'.

Heath (1994) advises that you give yourself time to evaluate parents' complaints, rather than immediately agreeing or becoming defensive or apologetic about them. Take the information, and offer to think about it, or gather more facts from another member of staff about the incident in question, and offer to get back to the parent. This gives the parent time to calm down and for you to decide how to respond.

Referral on

No one knows everything about everything. Part of your work with parents, therefore, will involve referring them to another professional whose job it is to focus on a problem which is outside your field of expertise. This is where your group of parents can act as a very useful resource. By asking their recommendations for practitioners in a range of fields, you can compile a list of local and recommended specialists to whom you can refer parents and children who need specialist help.

Transitions (of parents)

Just as we plan for a child who is moving up to the next age group in the centre to be exposed to the new setting, so too we need to prepare parents for such transitions. Parents are vulnerable and rely heavily on the close and trusting relationship they develop with their child's carers, and so moving on to another group can be a traumatic time for them as well as for their child. It stands to reason that if the parents feel comfortable about the move, then their child is more likely to as well.

Means of communication with parents

There are many occasions when you can exchange information with parents. These include day-to-day informal contacts; brochures about the centre's policies and procedures; formal meetings for intake, to solve problems or routinely review a child's progress; newsletters and bulletin boards; and parent education sessions.

Brochures

A comprehensive brochure which describes your centre's policies and procedures will allow parents to make an informed choice about whether to enrol their child in your centre. Once enrolled, you cannot demand that parents share your centre's values but you can expect that they will abide by them.

Meetings

Whether a meeting is designed to introduce parents to the centre, routinely review a child's response to the program, solve a problem which has arisen, or be part of the centre's management structure, you will need to plan ahead for your conversation with parents. This means gathering examples of the child's activities and your observations and being clear about the purpose of the meeting so that you can be equally clear when the meeting has achieved its purpose.

During meetings, you will be wise to avoid giving advice from an expert's stance, but instead listen to parents and jointly come up with suggestions for handling an issue of concern. This approach was detailed earlier in this chapter.

Newsletters and bulletin boards

It is a challenge to balance giving parents enough information so that they can feel informed about events in the centre, without overwhelming them with paperwork. Handling the paperwork alone can be especially daunting to those parents who do not read easily, but can be demanding for any parents.

Personally, I find the 'hale and hearty' tone of many newsletters patronising to parents. It's as if we are 'jollying them along', almost as if they were young children themselves. In newsletters, I believe that it is important not to praise parents for their efforts within the centre or in bringing up their children, since this implies that you are the judge and you know best. Instead, when you keep in mind that you and the parents are jointly working in their child's interests, you will convey in a respectful tone the information which they need to know in order to fulfil their part of that partnership.

Parent education

The theme of this chapter is that it is not up to us to judge parents for their apparent deficiencies. No one is ever perfect as a parent (Greenman & Stonehouse 1997). In this vein, we cannot assume that parents *need* education in how to bring up their children. However, some might appreciate the chance to discuss issues relating to young children, either with other parents, with staff members or with a specialist whom you invite to deliver a session on a topic which the parents have nominated. How you interact with the children is likely to be your most powerful form of parent 'education' rather than giving advice or holding sessions designed to teach parents some skills which you assume that they lack.

Special populations of parents

Just as you plan for the diversity of needs of the children in your care, so too you need to plan to work collaboratively with parents whose needs are atypical. This is more easily done when you already acknowledge that it is not possible or even desirable to work with every parent in the same way (a'Beckett 1988) and so you are willing to respond to all parents as individuals.

Parents from minority cultures

Parents who do not speak English have the least access to support from early childhood services. Furthermore, their lack of facility with language denies you the information about their child which would assist you in caring for and educating that child. Informal contacts will be more important than written exchanges for parents who speak but are not confident about reading English. Rather than waiting for difficulties to occur and conferences to become formal, it will help if you can locate a professional translator or invite a community volunteer to accompany non-English speaking parents on a regular basis at drop-off or collection times so that you can pass on day-to-day information about their child's care experiences.

Remember that our culture's focus on individual academic achievement is not common to all cultures (Lopez 1996). Many cultures value social cooperation above competition, and social and emotional development over academic achievement. Therefore, clarify parents' goals for their child's participation in your program.

Demonstrate that you accept and honour diversity in the children—with respect to their ages, gender, abilities, interests, personalities and cultures. As discussed in chapter 18, however, avoid a 'tourist curriculum' which trivialises other cultures' festive events and perpetuates stereotypes. This will convey to parents from other cultures that, just as their children are welcome, so too are they.

When I've been ignorant of parents' cultures, I have simply asked them about the practices in their country. I have found that they do not expect me to know the practices of every country in the world and are glad to explain to me some of the values which they hold dear. Asking them about their beliefs also avoids your assuming that they will conform to stereotypes about their culture.

'Difficult' parents

There will be occasions when parents are belligerent, uncooperative, abusive or otherwise disrespectful or overpowering (Boutte et al. 1992). Although at first glance these behaviours can intimidate you, generally the parents feel that they have a valid reason for their behaviour. The notion of collaboration implies that you understand that, from the parents' perspective, their frustration is valid.

The first step to understanding them is not to take their behaviour personally, as it will be triggered by the program and their situation rather than by yourself. You will need to deal with their complaints in the same way as you would any other parental complaints. However, you might need to be more assertive than usual in asking them to moderate how they are talking to you or being more than usually insistent that you will talk with them again about the issue at another time. The intent of building in a delay is to give them time to cool down. They will not be able to listen even to the most reasonable explanation while they are angry (Stanley 1996). A postponement will also avoid having the conflict escalate and will keep you safe from physical abuse or intimidation.

Working with difficult parents will be helped when you look at how the issue seems to them. For instance, if particular parents are frequently late in picking up their child, it could be that they are placed in the unenviable position of having to choose to be obliging by working later at work, even if it means picking their child up late—or else losing their job (Buchanan & Burts 1995). This makes their tardiness more understandable.

Conclusion

Collaboration with parents will not occur by accident. You will need to plan for it, taking into account the differing availability of families to participate in the centre. You will need to ensure that their participation is not just token efforts in fundraising activities or preparing art materials. Parents do not have the time to be involved in ways which do not directly improve the time they can spend with their child (Buchanan & Burts 1995). Instead, parents are more likely to respond to invitations to participate in activities which meet their needs at the same time as meeting the needs of the program (Buchanan & Burts 1995).

Means of facilitating collaboration with parents will need to be written into your centre's policy and procedures document. This policy might also include a statement about the type of inservice training which your staff members might require to equip them to build collaborative relationships with parents.

Suggestions for further reading

Stonehouse, A. (1994), *How does it feel? Child care from a parent's perspective*, Australian Early Childhood Association, Canberra.

Waters, J. (1996), *Making the connection: Parents and early childhood staff*, Lady Gowrie Child Care Centre (Melbourne) Inc., Melbourne.

27

• • • • • • • • • • •

Meeting the needs of staff

> Positive and healthy organizational climates are characterized
> by high energy, openness, trust, a collective sense of efficacy,
> and a shared vision.
>
> Jorde-Bloom (1988, p. 5)

The accreditation guidelines and code of ethics (see Appendix A) attest to how important it is that early childhood professionals take care of themselves and each other. You cannot provide a humane environment for children unless you work within a humane environment yourself. The work which you do is demanding. It requires clear thinking, quick responses and physical stamina.

When individuals feel out of control, their natural tendency is to try harder to take control, both over themselves and others. In care and teaching professions, stressed adults become more concerned with ensuring their own survival than with safeguarding children's needs (Lewis 1997). The result is that exhausted or burnt out caregivers and teachers are more likely to supervise children from a distance, rather than relating to them personally, and tend to focus on controlling children rather than using more appropriate management strategies (Lambert 1994; Lewis 1997).

As well, exhausted staff tend to adopt a clinical attitude to children (Lambert 1994). By this, Lambert might mean a less nurturing attitude, but it also reflects my observations that exhausted staff tend to blame management difficulties on individual children. They seek an explanation for feeling so overwhelmed by problems but, rather than looking at the circumstances under which they are functioning, they sometimes seek a 'clinical' diagnosis of the child which labels that child as having a deficit. (The most popular of these is an 'attention deficit'.)

Specific challenges in early childhood centres

Children are very sensitive to the morale of the people around them. The younger the children, the more reliant they are on the well-being and competence of the adults who care for them (Smith 1990). Therefore, the working conditions in a centre directly affect the children as well as the adults who work there (Doherty-Derkowski 1995; Smith 1996).

Low status

The first hurdle early childhood workers have to face is the popular notion that you are being 'paid to play'. The low status of the child care profession, and the low status of preschool teachers relative to primary and high school teachers, attest to the fact that a profession's status is linked with the status of its clients—and young children have very little status in our society. A profession's status is also low when its members are mainly women. Being women also makes it difficult for workers to balance their professional and personal priorities (Bloom 1982) and places many workers under stress.

The low status given to early childhood professionals makes it difficult for you to advocate for children—be it in conversations with a particular child's parents, or in the wider society.

Anne Stonehouse (1994a) says that the child care profession needs to promote the idea that qualifications are necessary for caregivers, that it needs a career structure in which the upper rungs are further from the bottom than they are at present, and that it needs to have senior early childhood professionals moving into administrative positions in government departments.

Multiple demands

Jorde-Bloom (1988) says that early childhood practitioners make up to 800 decisions a day, many of them 'on the run' or while simultaneously dealing with another issue. In his research into schools, Doyle (1986) found that many characteristics of working with children in groups contribute to worker stress:

- *Multi-dimensionality* refers to the fact that many different people with different interests and abilities are sharing the same space and attempting many tasks.
- *Simultaneity*, as its title implies, refers to the fact that many different things are happening at once.
- *Immediacy* refers to the rapid pace of events, giving you little time to reflect before acting.
- *Unpredictability* refers to the fact that you cannot always predict how a given group of children will respond to a particular activity, necessitating that you be willing to change even a delightful activity if it isn't working at the time.
- *Publicness* means that the action of individual children and your responses are witnessed by other children, colleagues and visitors to

the centre. This has two effects: first, that one child's disruptive behaviour can become contagious—that is, other children might join in; and, second, that any action which you take tells onlookers (both adults and children) about your skills and about how safe they are in the centre.

• *History* refers to the fact that children develop reputations which affect how their behaviour is interpreted by the staff and other children. Staff members develop reputations too, with exemplary practitioners sometimes not acknowledged sufficiently because they always act appropriately; or with staff members whose actions have been questioned frequently in the past, coming under the spotlight and being judged too critically.

Multiple 'clients'

Children are not the only people to whom you are accountable. Their parents are your customers too, and society—which contributes to child care costs through the tax system—expects many things from you as well. These demands are not always clearly stated, however, and even when they are, the needs of one of your 'customers' can compete with the needs of another. For example, a child's need for an afternoon nap can compete with a parent's need for early nights and consequent desire for the child not to sleep at the centre.

Ideology versus evidence

You might have sound theoretical reasons for using a particular approach with the children, and yet you will be aware that there is precious little evidence that your approach is right. This means that when you are challenged you cannot say with conviction why you do what you do, or refute another person's equal conviction that an alternative approach would be better.

Ethical dilemmas

Ethical dilemmas involve choosing between two courses of action, both of which are right, at least to some extent. (If one was right and one was wrong, there would be no dilemma.) A common dilemma is that there can be a tension between being honest and being tactful, between focusing on a child's positive achievements, versus being honest with parents about your concerns about the child's development (Stonehouse 1994a).

Job uncertainty

The wider political climate and economic circumstances make for uncertain job prospects in any human service field—but in child care in particular. As I write, in Australia there is a growing conservative ideology which holds that a mother's place is in the home and that child care is bad for children. Federal policies on funding child care centres have made costs too high for many parents and, as a result, have left many centres financially unviable, with the loss of employment for their staff and the reduction of child care places for needy children and families.

Staff turnover

The high rate of staff turnover in child care centres—which averages 15–30 per cent—is proof that work in this human service is demanding (Bloom 1982). Staff turnover directly affects the rate of interaction between staff and children, the children's attachment to their caregiver-teachers, and the children's language development (Doherty-Derkowski 1995).

Isolation

Staff in early childhood centres are often performing their demanding job in isolation from other professionals with whom they could exchange ideas. Even lunch breaks are taken separately from one's colleagues and there is often a lack of planning for formal staff training (P. Ryan 1988).

Result: Worker burnout

Burn-out comprises emotional and physical exhaustion, disillusionment with one's job and life in general, and self-doubt (Bloom 1982). In turn, these symptoms can cause physical illness, insensitivity to children and their parents, and to feelings of increased isolation as a sufferer feels that everyone else is coping and so it must be her fault (Bloom 1982). Naturally, all these symptoms lead to declining performance on the job (Bloom 1982).

Supports for overcoming these challenges

The following features contribute to a supportive and nurturing organisational climate in which staff can both function more effectively and avoid succumbing to the high demands of their work (Greenman & Stonehouse 1997; Jorde-Bloom 1988).

Leadership

Your team leader, director, or centre owner needs to provide leadership for the whole staff team. But this is not to say that the centre director needs to be a boss. There is a difference between a boss and a leader (Glasser 1992). Whereas a boss gains compliance through having power over others, a leader invites cooperation—and this is willingly given because others recognise the leader's skills and expertise. Leadership involves vision and influence (Rodd 1994).

Your team leader needs to be able to enthuse all the staff to share a common vision of the purpose of the centre; to listen to their ideas for innovations in order that the program responds to children's and parents' changing needs (Broinowski 1994); be skilful at developing a team culture, clear goals and objectives; and have good communication skills (Billman 1995). Team leaders need to be able to delegate duties which are more appropriately done by someone else (Jorde-Bloom 1982), and give caregivers and teachers professional autonomy, while maintaining standards through supervision and program evaluation (Billman 1995). At the same time, leaders need to carry out their administrative function efficiently, to enable other members of staff to carry out their roles effectively (Billman 1995).

Decision-making structure

Staff are more likely to feel valued when the centre director trusts other members of staff and parents to make valuable contributions and wise decisions, rather than imposing decisions on them with little consultation (Clyde 1988; Greenman & Stonehouse 1997; Jorde-Bloom 1982). A consultative authority structure is also more likely to engender a trusting relationship between staff, allowing them to work as a team whose members share even the less desirable tasks, and to support and acknowledge each other's efforts.

Goal consensus

The centre will function more smoothly and staff will feel more satisfied when, as a team, they can agree on the centre's goals and values. The benefits of writing these into a policy document are discussed in the next chapter, which states that the process of arriving at a policy can be as important to teamwork as the resulting guidelines which are generated.

Clarity of roles

When roles are clearly spelled out in policy documents, and procedures are explicit, individual staff members are able to feel confident about what is expected of them and communication between staff is enhanced (Clyde 1988; Greenman & Stonehouse 1997). Nevertheless, these policy documents and other official communications should not be too formal, otherwise they could appear unfriendly and inaccessible.

Collegiality

Collegiality is the extent to which staff support and trust each other and are friendly and caring towards each other (Jorde-Bloom 1988). If you keep pouring out without topping up your emotional store, then you will burn out, like the element of a kettle when water is poured out and not topped-up again. Therefore, the support from other members of your staff team can make a difference to how well you are able to function and how well you feel physically and emotionally.

New workers are particularly likely to feel overwhelmed by the responsibility of caring for such young children, uncertain of how their ideas will be accepted by more experienced staff, and anxious about responding to children's inconsiderate or disruptive behaviour (Brand 1990; Fleet & Clyde 1993). With emotional, practical and professional support from colleagues and a willingness to grow and learn, however, new workers can move from 'survival mode' to a consolidation or assured stage in which they develop confidence and autonomy as professionals (Brand 1990; Clyde 1988; Fleet & Clyde 1993).

Innovation

Staff are certain to become discouraged if their ideas for innovations and improvements are constantly quashed in a centre which dismisses suggestions with a claim that, 'We have always done it this way'. Centres which survive—and retain skilled staff—will be those which are open to new ideas and are willing to take risks in an effort to respond to the changing needs of staff, parents and children.

Openness will also involve regularly reviewing the centre's policies and procedures, and evaluating the effectiveness of its programs in terms of how they are benefiting the children and families.

Work ethic

Staff will respond best to a centre which is achievement-oriented and, at the same time, supports and plans for career advancement for members of staff. Staff who are trusted to use their own initiative will be able to develop self-discipline with respect to their work. This involves being well-prepared and organised; capable in their caring and educational capacities; able to call on a sound and up-to-date theoretical base to guide practice; open to feedback from parents and colleagues; willing to evaluate what they do; and being professionally accountable to children, parents, and the centre as a whole.

In terms of organisational support, staff are helped to be achievement-oriented when they are not burdened with unnecessary tasks (Jorde-Bloom 1988). The centre will need to balance being planned and purposeful, with being obsessed with efficiency (Jorde-Bloom 1988). Procedures are there to serve you, rather than you being a servant to them.

Employment conditions

Although early childhood workers are acknowledged to be underpaid, and a centre is unlikely to be able to pay above-award wages, staff will feel less dissatisfied if they believe that their own centre's policies are fair, and if they feel that their skills are not being taken for granted by management. The occasional social gathering or positive comment about staff members' work can at least partly compensate for the lack of monetary rewards.

As a member of staff you should insist that, for the ultimate good of the children, you need to take care of yourself by taking your allocated breaks—and in a setting which is relaxing (P. Ryan 1988). You need to vary your work, have time to plan and be given time for some duties that are out of direct contact with the children (P. Ryan 1988).

Qualities of staff

Ginott (1972) believes that the most important ingredient for working with children is the adults' self-discipline. This has two parts: emotional self-discipline and disciplined work practices. Central to emotional discipline is that adults express their feelings appropriately and do not humiliate or denigrate children. That is, you must demonstrate the same standards of courtesy and self-discipline that you want the children to observe. Also, you cannot let children determine your own mood or reactions, and must not let the children's behaviour cause you to escalate your response to the point where you are punishing or verbally abusing the children. Instead, it is important to allow children to save face, invite cooperation, and guide them to return to considerate behaviour. In short, you can act spontaneously but not impulsively (Ginott 1972), practising communication skills until they become spontaneous and natural. Ginott believes that workers cannot afford to make scenes and should never use sarcasm. Disciplining from emotion rather than reason is self-indulgent and unhelpful.

Emotional self-discipline will also mean managing your own stress levels, leaving your private worries at home, ensuring that you do not expect the children to meet your emotional needs, and feeling confident enough to provide high quality care and to be emotionally warm with the children. At the same time that you are friendly with children, however, you will not have discernible favourites among the group. (It is natural for you to take more readily to some children than others, but an observer should not be able to notice any difference in your behaviour towards any children.)

A conducive environment

Managing space in the centre is as much for your own benefit as for the children's. The centre is your space too. You have to live there and you deserve to have a pleasant and functional work setting. As I discussed briefly in chapter 1, the quality of the environment directly affects the quality of interactions in a centre (Bloom 1982); it affects how safe the children feel and how much control they can exercise over their own learning; and it can add to or reduce your workload.

Opportunities for professional development

Knowledge is the best stress reducer (Clyde 1988). Therefore, your centre will need to plan for professional development of all staff members based on an assessment of your training needs and the resources available to meet them (Abbott-Shim 1990). Successful staff development will renew your enthusiasm for your work, improve your confidence in your abilities, and allow you to continue to grow professionally (Greenman & Stonehouse 1997).

Supervision of staff at the centre is a naturalistic form of staff development, although it is yet another role for which supervisors receive very little training and, consequently, about which they often experience anxiety (Caruso 1991). Other forms of staff development include staff exchanges with other centres and workshops presented by staff from other centres or community specialists (Abbott-Shim 1990). Hired consultants are the most expensive option but their input can be especially tailored to your centre's needs, which can make their sessions more efficient.

Relationships with children

When you are treated with respect and valued for your contributions, it is easier for you to treat children with respect, relate to them with interest and warmth, guide rather than control them, respond to them individually rather than as a group, and encourage them to be active in their learning. The more engaged you are with the children, the more likely it is that your work with them will be effective and your relationship with them will uplift your own spirits. After all, you work with children because of the joy they can impart and the rewards which you gain from seeing them grow and learn (Brand 1990).

Relationships with parents

When staff are accepted and empowered rather than criticised and denigrated, they are more likely to accord parents this same level of respect. In return, when parents are treated as equal and active partners in the care of their children instead of as passive 'clients' and recipients of a service, they are able to support, respect and appreciate the skills of their child's caregivers and teachers.

Conclusion

Individual centres can do little in the short-term to raise the public perception of the value of early childhood care and education, and will not be able to afford higher pay for workers in the current economic conditions. However, with leadership and commitment, a staff team can create a positive climate in the centre—a tone which supports the children, parents and staff who live and work there (Jorde-Bloom 1988).

Suggestions for further reading

Centre directors might find some useful ideas in:

Broinowski, I. (1994), *Managing child care centres*, TAFE Publications, Collingwood, Victoria.

The following handbook might be of interest to staff who are feeling exhausted by their work:

Lambert, B. (1994), *Beating burnout: A multi-dimensional perspective*, AECA Resource Book Series, vol. 1, no. 2, Australian Early Childhood Association, Watson, ACT.

Given the importance in staff teams of communication skills, I recommend:

Bolton, R. (1987), *People skills*, Simon & Schuster, Sydney.

28

• • • • • • • • • • •

Formulating a centre discipline policy

Your centre will have many policies governing its operations. The purpose of this chapter is to describe what a discipline policy should comprise, and how to go about formulating such a policy.

In general, policies are guidelines which describe what services a centre will offer and how it will deliver them. A policy on discipline expresses how adults and children are expected to behave towards each other so that they can work together productively and caringly (Cowin et al. 1990).

Benefits of formal policies

Written policies have many benefits. These include:

- Their procedures can guide action when a difference of opinion occurs among or between staff, families and management (Farmer 1995).
- Policies offer children, staff and parents safeguards and clear expectations of their roles, rights, and responsibilities.
- Written guidelines help to ensure that decisions about practice are consistent across time and fair to all stakeholders (Farmer 1995).
- The process of formulating policy gives staff and parents the opportunity to clarify their views (Stonehouse 1991b).
- The process of formulation is an opportunity to involve parents and staff collaboratively (Stonehouse 1991b).
- Policy development allows staff to plan in advance how to act, rather than having to make hasty decisions in response to a problem which has already occurred.
- Written documentation helps with familiarising new staff and parents with the philosophy and workings of the centre.

- Written policies assist with evaluation and accountability (Farmer 1995; Stonehouse 1991b).

Components of a policy

Your discipline policy could comprise seven parts (DECS 1990; Farmer 1995): your mandate; direction or goals; a statement of how you intend to achieve these; a theoretical background; statement of your beliefs; a statement of your centre's values; and, finally, a set of procedures or strategies for enacting your policies.

Mandate

Your centre's policy needs to be framed within outside guidelines such as the Quality Improvement and Accreditation Guidelines which are set down by government regulations. In addition, your funding body might have its own sets of policies. Your centre will have to implement these, even if you do not agree with them (Farmer 1995). However, most over-arching policies will be broad and will need to be interpreted for your own specific context.

Direction

Discipline is a process for helping children to learn and to gain personal skills: it is not an end in itself (Jones & Jones 1995). Therefore, a policy statement about discipline will need to state your educational goals for children. For example, my goals—as expressed in this text—comprise developing in children self-discipline, appropriate expression of feelings, cooperation with others, and integrity.

Intention

This is a statement about how you intend to achieve these goals. This section might state your intention to teach children how to behave considerately, rather than to control them. It will emphasise prevention of behavioural difficulties through provision of a culturally, individually and developmentally appropriate curriculum and through ongoing reciprocal contact with the parents of the children in your care.

Theory

This section describes your theoretical base. Your theory will need to be comprehensive—that is, it should help you to understand most instances of children's behaviour and should give you a sound body of information about appropriate preventive and interventive options.

You might evaluate the assumptions and practices of your selected theory on criteria such as:

- Is your theory about discipline consistent with your views about education and child development?

- Does your theory help you figure out how to help children's behaviour to improve, or does it tell you only that they cannot change—for example, by saying that inconsiderate behaviour is due to children's personality, home circumstances, or developmental stage?
- What evidence is there that your chosen theory is more effective and ethical than any others?

Beliefs

This section will detail the philosophy which drives your policy—such as your understandings of behaviour management. In this section, you will state your beliefs about children and how they learn, your purposes of discipline, your explanation of some reasons for inappropriate behaviour, your beliefs about the status of adults compared with children, and your role in guiding appropriate behaviour. These statements might include your beliefs about the disadvantages of the controlling approaches and the benefits of methods which guide children to behave considerately.

Values

This is a statement of the values or ethics which underpin all your actions. You might refer to the accreditation guidelines and early childhood practitioners' code of ethics, specifically referring to those aspects which are relevant to behaviour management. You might also allude to the rights and responsibilities of staff, parents and children in your centre. Examples of these are given in Table 28.1.

Table 28.1: Rights and responsibilities of children, parents and caregiver-teachers

Children's rights	*Children's responsibilities*
To be with people they know and trust.	To be considerate.
Physical and emotional safety and protection.	To learn to care for themselves and others.
Access to interesting materials and resources.	To share equipment.
To learn functional skills that allow them to learn about their world.	To care for equipment (age-appropriately) and use it safely.
To competent care/teaching.	To be cooperative.
Someone to help when they are frightened, frustrated, sad or angry.	To speak out.
Freedom to initiate, explore and experiment with their physical and social world.	Not to dominate individuals or the group.
Gain pleasure, interest and confidence from learning.	To learn accountability for their actions.
Someone to talk to.	

Table 28.1: (*Continued*)

To feel important as people, who have
   the right to be individual and to
   express opinions.
To be treated with dignity.
Opportunities to make choices.
Opportunities to solve their own
   problems.
Familiarity with the day's routines so that
   they can make sense of their day.
Control over pace and involvement in
   activities.
To receive fair treatment.
To have time to be with others.
Time for solitude (moments of peace and
   quiet).
To be protected from the abuses of
   authority.
Access to specialist services as required.
To privacy and confidentiality.
To be free from unnecessary restrictions.
To be free of adult worries.
To have their needs and wants met, not
   denied simply because they are
   children.
Acceptance of their family and culture.
To take intellectual risks (be creative).

Parents' rights

To accessible, affordable and high
   quality services either to support their
   decision to work out of home or to
   provide respite when they care for
   children at home.
To respect from caregivers and teachers.
To flexible services which meet their
   children's needs.
To participate in their child's care
   through:
• Information on programs and activities
• Participation in decision-making
• Receiving and offering information
   about their children's learning and
   behaviour.
To freedom not to participate intensively
   in the administration of the centre.
To expect consistent approaches by
   workers.
To expect non-discriminatory practices.

Parents' responsibilities

To ask for information when
   needed.
To make the time to be involved.
To be open and willing to listen.
To be willing to find workable
   solutions.
To be assertive about their needs
   and rights.
To balance demands on their
   time (e.g. to participate in
   management committees)
   with their child's needs.
To ensure their child does not
   require excessive adult
   attention.
To secure specialist help for their
   child as needed.

Table 28.1: (*Continued*)

Caregivers' and teachers' rights	Caregivers' and teachers' responsibilities
To defend optimal learning environments for all children. To be treated with courtesy. To feel secure in the centre, both emotionally and physically. To expect children to cooperate with reasonable requests which will enhance their growth and will respect workers' and other children's needs. To express an opinion and be heard. To achieve job satisfaction. To respond to disruptive behaviour. To inservice training. To their own style of relating to children (as long as this conveys enjoyment of and respect for children). To contribute to centre policy and procedures. To support from colleagues and administrators. Access to consultants.	To provide for the physical needs of children: good nutrition, comfortable environment, medical care, safety and protection. To provide an environment which is friendly, encouraging, supportive cooperative and stimulating. To be competent. To assist children who need help. To model courteous behaviour. To have reasonable expectations of children, in line with the task demands and the children's developmental levels. To protect children from harm—from themselves, other children, and centre personnel. To listen to children and colleagues. To be fair. To take responsibility for their own feelings, not blaming children for them. To take responsibility for their own actions which could detract from job satisfaction (e.g. stress management). To engage in ongoing learning about their work. To support colleagues. To consult with colleagues and reach agreement. To make an effort to be involved. To establish partnerships with parents.

Source: Porter (1996) and Stonehouse (1994).

As well as meeting children's needs, your discipline policy will need to address how you plan to meet the needs of caregivers and teachers (Good & Brophy 1986; McCaslin & Good 1992). These needs fall into two areas: equipping staff with the skills to work successfully with children and families so that you can experience success and job satisfaction; and receiving personal and professional support (Jones & Jones 1995). The latter need is exacerbated by your isolation from colleagues in other centres, and by the need to 'balance the books' which makes expensive staff development sessions impracticable.

Staff will need to examine their own personal needs—as distinct from their professional goals (Charles 1996)—and examine ways in which they can be satisfied. These personal requirements might include the need for:

- a pleasant physical environment in which to work;
- a measure of order in the room;
- courteous behaviour between children, parents and staff;
- job satisfaction;
- parental and collegial support.

Procedures

The final part of your policy document will describe what procedures are to be used and by whom, in order to enact the principles in your policy. Procedures provide a framework in which systematic action can be taken.

Procedures will focus on how the centre can be organised so that most behavioural difficulties are prevented, and how those which do occur receive a constructive response (Cowin et al. 1990). Procedures must give attention to both prevention and intervention, and must comply with the ethical and other guidelines contained in earlier sections of your policy document.

In terms of intervention, inconsiderate behaviour requires a response which protects the rights of other children and adults in the group and offers the child involved a chance to learn how to make a more skilled choice in the future. Therefore, a policy should include a clear statement about how staff will respond to inconsiderate behaviour. These procedures need to ensure consistent, fair (non-arbitrary) and non-punitive responses to behaviour which is disruptive or which violates a prior agreement.

The procedures will specify a progressive or graded response to disruptions. The first level of response will involve adjusting the program to address possible external causes of disruptions (Cowin et al. 1990). The next level of intervention will involve handling discipline issues in a one-to-one intervention with the child concerned. Finally, the last level will involve consulting with the child's parents and—if necessary—specialists to find a suitable response to the child's behaviour.

Having arrived at some recommended practices, you might ask yourselves the following questions about them (adapted from Cowin et al. 1990; Sharp & Thompson 1994):

- Are your recommended practices realistic?
- Will the staff be willing to carry them out?
- Do you have the skills to do so?
- If not, how could you be equipped with the required skills?
- What advantages do the recommended practices bring?
- What shortcomings do they have?
- Are the endorsed practices consistent with the centre's philosophy, aims, and objectives, with the stated aims of the discipline policy, and with the regulations of licensing and regulatory authorities?

Your procedures will address prevention of behavioural difficulties, intervention with disruptions, how to facilitate parent consultation, how to introduce new and relieving staff to the policy, how to refer children and families to other agencies, and how and when to review the policy. It might also add procedures for dealing with special issues which could affect children's behaviour in the centre—such as child abuse.

Parent consultation

When you formulate your discipline and other policies in consultation with parents, they will have a better understanding of and increased confidence in your practices. At the same time, you can be more confident that you will receive parents' support for your practices.

Referral to consultants

It would be useful to include in the policy a statement about how the centre can use consultants, how and to whom to refer children for help, and in which circumstances a child might be referred. Clear and uncomplicated procedures for making referrals will assist staff in gaining specialist help for children and their families.

Special issues

It may be useful for the policy to mention specific issues such as child abuse. Early childhood professionals are legally obliged to report any suspicions of child abuse to the local child welfare agency. Advising parents of this obligation and detailing issues surrounding child abuse may raise awareness of the issue which in turn may prevent some abuse, or at least can set a foundation for some constructive intervention by centre staff if abuse is suspected.

Evaluation of the plan

The policy will need to include a procedure for routinely reviewing and evaluating its effectiveness. (Your wider policy will include procedures for evaluating the overall quality of your program: this is not the focus of your behaviour management policy.) You might include ways to monitor the effects on children's behaviour, seeking parents' feedback and seeking all staff members' impressions.

Conclusion

Behaviour management is most effective if everyone in the centre agrees on the policy and procedures. This can be promoted if these are arrived at through wide consultation. Although formulating policy is time-consuming, the process gives all participants the opportunity to clarify their values and to become clear about how to enact the procedures which are specified.

Suggestions for further reading

Farmer, S. (1995), *Policy development in early childhood services*, Community Child Care Cooperative Ltd, Newtown, NSW.

Appendix A

• • • • • • • • • •

Standards of care and code of ethics

Quality guidelines

The National Childcare Accreditation Council (1993) Principles are set out below. To be accredited a centre must meet the standard required on each Principle. Core Principles (those in which Good quality is mandatory for accreditation) are indicated with an asterix.

A   Interaction principles

A1   Interactions between staff and children

1* Staff interactions with children are warm and friendly.
2* Staff treat all children equally and try to accommodate their individual needs: they respect diversity of background.
3* Staff treat all children equally and try to accommodate their individual needs: they treat both sexes without bias.
4* Staff use a positive approach in guidance and discipline.
5 Staff are responsive to children's feelings and needs.
6 Staff initiate and maintain communication with children, and their communication conveys respect.
7 Staff show respect for children's developing competence, and foster their self-esteem and independence.
8 Staff interact with children to stimulate their curiosity and thinking.
9 Staff create a pleasant atmosphere.

A2   Interactions between staff and parents

10* There is written and verbal communication with all families about the centre.
11* There is active exchange of information between parents and staff.
12 There is an orientation process for new children and parents.

13   Parents and other family members are encouraged to be involved in the program.

A3 Interactions between staff

14* Staff communicate well with each other.
15   Staff show respect for other members of the team.

B   Program

16* The program is planned to reflect the centre's philosophy and goals.
17* The program incorporates learning experiences appropriate for each child, as indicated by development records maintained by the centre.
18* The program gives children the opportunity to make choices and take on new challenges.
19* The program fosters personal and social development.
20* The program fosters fine and gross motor development.
21* The program fosters creative development and aesthetic awareness.
22* Toileting and nappy changing procedures meet individual needs and are positive experiences.
23* Sleep time and dressing procedures meet individual needs for rest, comfort and self-help.
24* Meal times are pleasant occasions.
25   The program provides a wide range of individual and group experiences.
26   A daily timetable is planned to reflect children's needs, abilities and interests.
27   Procedures for routine activities are flexible and developmentally appropriate.
28   Transitions between activities are smooth.
29   The program fosters intellectual development.
30   The program fosters language development.
31   There is a balanced and developmentally appropriate program.
32   The program provides for children with special needs.
33   The program is regularly evaluated in the light of stated goals.

C   Nutrition, health and safety practices

34* Staff are alert to the health and welfare of each child.
35* Staff try to ensure that children are clothed appropriately for indoor and outdoor play and for sleep.
36   Food and drinks meet children's daily nutritional requirements and are culturally appropriate.
37   Meal times promote healthy nutritional habits.
38   Food is prepared and stored hygienically.
39   Staff adhere to hygiene principles which reduce the spread of infectious diseases.
40   Staff encourage children to follow simple rules of hygiene.
41   Potentially dangerous products are inaccessible to children.
42   Buildings and equipment are safe and hygienic.

43 The centre maintains a record of children's immunisations.
44 The centre has written policies on hygiene, medical, emergency and accident procedures.
45 Staff are familiar with medical, emergency and accident procedures.
46 Staff supervise children at all times.
47 Information on health and other related issues is readily available to the staff.

D Centre management and staff development

48* Staff and parents consult on the program and evaluate it together.
49* New staff are informed about the philosophy and goals of the centre.
50 The centre provides regular learning and training opportunities for staff.
51 The staff roster is arranged to provide continuity of care.
52 Information about the centre's management is readily available to staff and parents.

Source: National Childcare Accreditation Council (1993). Reprinted with permission.

Australian Early Childhood Association Code of ethics

Preamble

A code of ethics is a set of statements about appropriate and expected behaviour of members of a professional group and, as such, reflects its values. The Code that follows was developed by a National Working Party of the Australian Early Childhood Association, with considerable input from the field, and therefore is a Code that is owned by the field, not imposed upon it. The Code has been developed to inform and guide the decisions and behaviour of all personnel involved both directly and indirectly in the provision of early childhood services for children between birth and eight years of age. Although oriented towards those who are in daily contact with children and their families, the Code is also intended as a guide for those who work in other capacities, for example, as tertiary educators, administrators, policy makers and advisory staff. Their work impacts significantly on the ethical behaviour of early childhood personnel in the field.

Young children are especially vulnerable. They have little power over their lives and few skills with which to protect themselves. This places early childhood personnel in a relationship of special trust, one that is powerful, important, and easily violated. The vulnerability and powerlessness of young children and the recognition of the multi-faceted dimensions of the role of early childhood personnel serves to highlight the special importance of a code of ethics. As early childhood personnel carry out their work with and on behalf of young children and their families, they often face situations that involve a conflict of their responsibilities and professional values. A code of ethics is not intended to, and could not possibly, provide easy answers, formulae or prescriptive solutions for the complex professional dilemmas they face in their work. It does provide a basis for critical reflection, a guide for professional behaviour, and some assistance with the resolution of ethical dilemmas.

Adherence to this code necessarily involves a commitment to:

- viewing the well-being of the individual child as having fundamental importance;
- acknowledging the uniqueness of each person;
- considering the needs of the child in the context of the family and culture, as the family has a major influence on the young child;
- taking into account the critical impact of self-esteem on an individual's development;
- basing practice on sound knowledge, research, and theories, while at the same time recognising the limitations and uncertainties of these;
- working to fulfil the right of all children and their families to services of high quality.

I   In relation to children I will:

1 Acknowledge the uniqueness and potential of each child.
2 Recognise early childhood as a unique and valuable stage of life and accept that each phase within early childhood is important in its own right.
3 Honour the child's right to play, in acknowledgment of the major contribution play makes to development.
4 Enhance each child's strengths, competence and self-esteem.
5 Ensure that my work with children is based on their interests and needs and lets them know they have a contribution to make.
6 Recognise that young children are vulnerable and use my influence and power in their best interests.
7 Create and maintain safe, healthy settings that enhance children's autonomy, initiative and self-worth and respect their dignity.
8 Help children learn to interact effectively, and in doing so to learn to balance their own rights, needs, and feelings with those of others.
9 Base my work with children on the best theoretical and practical knowledge about early childhood as well as on particular knowledge of each child's development.
10 Respect the special relationship between children and their families and incorporate this perspective in all my interactions with children.
11 Work to ensure that young children are not discriminated against on the basis of gender, age, race, religion, language, ability, culture or national origin.
12 Acknowledge the worth of the cultural and linguistic diversity that children bring to the environment.
13 Engage only in practices that are respectful of and provide security for children and in no way degrade, endanger, exploit, intimidate, or harm them psychologically or physically.

14 Ensure that my practices reflect consideration of the child's perspective.

II   In relation to families, I will:

1 Encourage families to share their knowledge of their child with me and share my general knowledge of children with them so that there is mutual growth and understanding in ways that benefit the child.
2 Strive to develop positive relationships with families that are based on mutual trust and open communication.
3 Engage in shared decision-making with families.
4 Acknowledge families' existing strengths and competence as a basis for supporting them in their task of nurturing their child.
5 Acknowledge the uniqueness of each family and the significance of its culture, customs, language and beliefs.
6 Maintain confidentiality.
7 Respect the right of the family to privacy.
8 Consider situations from each family's perspective, especially if differences or tensions arise.
9 Assist each family to develop a sense of belonging to the services in which their child participates.
10 Acknowledge that each family is affected by the community context in which it operates.

III   In relation to colleagues, I will:

1 Support and assist colleagues in their professional development.
2 Work with my colleagues to maintain and improve the standard of service provided in my work place.
3 Promote policies and working conditions that are non-discriminatory and that foster competence, well-being and positive self-esteem.
4 Acknowledge and support the use of the personal and professional strengths which my colleagues bring to the work place.
5 Work to build an atmosphere of trust, respect and candour by:
   • encouraging openness and tolerance between colleagues;
   • accepting their right to hold different points of view;
   • using constructive methods of conflict resolution; and
   • maintaining appropriate confidentiality.
6 Acknowledge the worth of the cultural and linguistic diversity which my colleagues bring to the work place.
7 Encourage my colleagues to accept and adhere to this code.

IV   In relation to the community and society, I will:

1 Provide programs which are responsive to community needs.
2 Support the development and implementation of laws and policies that promote the well-being of children and families and that are responsive to community needs.
3 Be familiar with and abide by laws and policies that relate to my work.

4 Work to change laws and policies that interfere with the well-being of children.

5 Promote cooperation among all agencies and professions working in the best interests of young children and families.

6 Promote children's best interests through community education and advocacy.

V   *In relation to* myself as a professional, *I will:*

1 Update and improve my expertise and practice in the early childhood field continually through formal and informal professional development.

2 Engage in critical self-reflection and seek input from colleagues.

3 Communicate with and consider the views of my colleagues in the early childhood profession and other professions.

4 Support research to strengthen and expand the knowledge base of early childhood, and, where possible, initiate, contribute to and facilitate such research.

5 Work within the limits of my professional role and avoid misrepresentation of my professional competence and qualifications.

6 Work to complement and support the child-rearing function of the family.

7 Be an advocate for young children, early childhood services, and my profession.

Source: Australian Early Childhood Association (1991), 'Australian Early Childhood Association code of ethics', *Australian Journal of Early Childhood*, vol. 16, no. 1, pp. 3–6. Reprinted with permission.

Appendix B
• • • • • • • • • •

Activities for children

Cooperative activities

In competitive games, children work against each other so that one can come out as the winner, while many other children become losers. In cooperative games, the children have to work together to achieve the task or to overcome an external obstacle—such as time. The following games can be played with small or larger groups of children.

Cooperative tale

One player starts a story and each child adds a little piece to it, each taking a turn (Arnold 1972, in Sapon-Shevin 1986). This would suit children who are nearing school age.

Cooperative shapes, numbers or letters

A small group of children find a way to form a shape, number or letter, with their bodies (Orlick 1978, in Sapon-Shevin 1986).

Non-elimination musical chairs

This is begun in the same way as the standard version of musical chairs, with one chair fewer than there are children. The children move around the chairs while the music is playing, and then scramble for the chairs when the music stops. However, rather than removing one child at the end of each round, this version of the game calls for the removal of one chair. All of the children remain in the game, having to balance together on the chairs that are left. They must find a way to make room for more and more children on the remaining chairs (Orlick 1978, in Sapon-Shevin 1986).

Barnyard

This is suitable for a larger group of children. They stand in a large group, choose six animals (less for fewer than twenty children) and each child selects one of the six animals to mimic. For young children, an adult could pin an animal picture onto each child. They close their eyes or put on a blindfold, and make the appropriate animal sound. The same animals must find each other by listening for their animal calls and hold hands until everyone is together in their animal groups. It doesn't matter who finishes first (Harrison 1976, in Sapon-Shevin 1986).

Big turtle

A small group of children get onto their hands and knees under a blanket, and have to try to make their 'turtle' move in one direction (Orlick 1978, in Sapon-Shevin 1986).

Big snake

Each child stretches out on his stomach and then clasps the ankles of the child in front. They wriggle like a snake to join up with other snake pairs, until all the children are joined. Then they must figure out how to perform actions without breaking the chain of children. The actions could include rolling over, curling up to go to sleep, or climbing over obstacles or up 'trees' (Orlick 1978, in Sapon-Shevin 1986).

Frozen bean bag

All the children move around, balancing small bean bag pillows on their heads. If a child's bag falls off, she must freeze and she cannot move again until another child replaces the bean bag on her head. The object of the game is to help your friends by keeping them unfrozen (Orlick 1978, in Sapon-Shevin 1986).

Hot or cold

One child looks for an item which has been hidden by the others, and they signal to him when he is getting close to finding it ('hot') or further away ('cold'). They can do this also for blindfolded pin the tail on the donkey, with the group of children clapping hands loudly (for hot) or quietly (for cold) to direct the child to the correct position for the tail (Arnold 1972, in Sapon-Shevin 1986).

Touch blue

The adult calls out 'touch blue' (or any other colour or item) and the children must find this on another child (Harrison 1976, in Sapon-Shevin 1986).

Ha ha

The children lie out in the sun or in a large room. Each child places his head on the stomach of the child next to him. The first says, 'ha', the second says, 'ha ha' and the third says, 'ha ha ha' and so on, increasing the number of ha's. The laughter is contagious (Harrison 1976, in Sapon-Shevin 1986).

Raindrops

Each child stands behind a friend. The child in front bends forward from the waist. The child behind rests her hands gently on his back. She pretends that her fingertips are raindrops and taps lightly down the other child's back from his head to his bottom. Next, she can let the raindrops fall gently on his head. She can ask her friend how it feels. If he would like it harder, she can pretend that her fingers are hailstones. Then the children change places with their partner (Belknap 1989).

A fun touching activity

Back rub/pat/scratch. The children stand in a circle one behind the other, so that each person can put her hands on the shoulders of the person in front of her. One child begins by rubbing, patting or scratching the back of the child in front of her, while he rubs, pats or scratches the back of the child in front of him. This continues until all the children are rubbing, patting or scratching the back of the child who is in front of them. The circle could then reverse.

Relaxation activities for children[1]

Total body

Rag doll. This activity can be done with one or more children. Show the children a rag doll and demonstrate how it moves and what happens to the rag doll's limbs when the legs and arms are lifted and then let go. Have the children lie down and pretend to be floppy rag dolls. Go around the group and check out how relaxed they are. Raise limbs a few centimetres (an inch or two) and then let go so that the limbs fall back to the floor. See how floppy the children can be. (Don't drop a leg very far or the children will become tense!)

As the children learn to relax while they are lying down, see if they can gain skill in locating just the muscles they need; that is, they can sit up while keeping their arms and head relaxed. Then have them try standing. Eventually add music.

Breathing. Diaphragmatic (belly) breathing encourages the use of our full breathing capacity, filling the lungs entirely with air. It also emphasises long slow exhalation and is thus relaxing. The following exercise teaches children how to relax. It can be used almost any time or anywhere. Have the children follow these steps:

1 Get comfortable. Move your arms and legs around to make your muscles loose.
2 Close your eyes. (Very young children might not be able to close their eyes, so don't insist.)

---

1   Many of these relaxation activities were first suggested to me by Gaye McAllister, private practising psychologist, Bower Place, Adelaide.

3 Take a deep breath in while you count slowly: one . . . two . . . three . . . four.
4 Let the air out very slowly, counting one . . . two . . . three . . . four . . . five . . . six.
5 Repeat this breathing, but this time place your hands on your stomach and feel it filling up with air (pushing out) when you breathe.
6 Breathe in deeply: one . . . two . . . three . . . four.
7 Let the air out slowly: one . . . two . . . three . . . four . . . five . . . six. (Feel your stomach pull back in).
8 Repeat this a few more times.
9 Open your eyes.
10 Now how do you feel?

To get enough practice at breathing deeply, children will need a few minutes' practice each day. The breathing technique can be used alone or in combination with other relaxation exercises such as progressive muscle relaxation or visualisation. This form of breathing can also be encouraged with the balloon-blowing activity.

Balloon blowing. Ask the children to pretend that they have a balloon to blow up: 'Take a big breath . . . hold it . . . and then blow up your balloon until all that air goes into the balloon. Now another big breath', and so on. 'Now let your balloon go and watch all the air come out and watch the balloon disappear into the clouds'.

The belly balloon. Tell the children to lie down comfortably. (They can close their eyes if they want to, although some will find that difficult.) Then say the following: 'Place a hand on your tummy. Breathe into your tummy and feel your hand move up and down. Pretend you have a balloon inside your tummy. As you breathe in, blow up the balloon. (Long pause). As you breathe out, empty the balloon. (Long pause). Blow up the balloon again. Let the air leak out through your teeth with a long slow hiss. Blow up the balloon again. Imagine sticking a pin into the balloon. Let the air out through your mouth with a sudden pop. Notice how relaxed you are' (Belknap 1989).

Trees in the breeze. Instruct the children: Stand with your feet a little apart. Breathe in and lift your arms over your head. Join your thumbs together. Imagine you are a tall tree on the beach, and sway from side to side in the breeze. (Long pause). Now you are an oak tree in summertime. Stretch your leafy branches out and down to your side. (Long pause). Pretend you are a weeping willow by the river. Bend your trunk and branches forward over the river in front of you. (Long pause). Stand up and pretend you are an apple tree with your branches heavy with fruit. Some children come by and shake you so your apples fall to the ground. Let them shake you a little harder. (Long pause).

The children can suggest other trees which they can be, such as a tall pine tree or a Christmas tree being decorated, and move like them (Belknap 1989).

Monster mask. The instructions for this game are: 'Sit comfortably and close your eyes. Imagine you're a very ugly monster. Squeeze everything in your face toward the end of your nose. Wriggle your mouth and chin from side to side. Make wrinkles in your forehead and around your eyes. Open your mouth wide and stick out your tongue. Make an ugly monster sound. Now say goodbye to the monster. Let all the muscles in your face go smooth and soft. Rest your whole face' (Belknap 1989).

Simon says. When giving an instruction which begins with, 'Simon says', you ask the children to relax various muscle groups, using instructions such as:

Head: Try to make your eyebrows touch your hair.
    Squeeze your eyes shut.
    Wrinkle up your nose.
    Press your lips together.
    Press your tongue against the roof of your mouth.
Shoulders and back: Lift your shoulders, and try to touch your ears.
    Bring your shoulders back as far as they will go.
Hands and arms: Make your fist as tight as you can.
    Show me your arm muscles.
Stomach: Make your stomach as hard as you can; pull it way in.
Upper legs: Lift your legs and feet off the floor.
    Press your knees together.

Unlike the original 'Simon says' game, no one is excluded from this version of the game for doing incorrect actions or for following instructions which have not been preceded by 'Simon says'.

Mirrors. One child copies the actions of another child.

Iceblock. Pretend that you are an iceblock in the freezer—all hard and cold . . . Now pretend someone has taken you out into the sun. What's happening? Slowly, slowly you are melting. The top of your head is melting, then your neck is becoming floppy and your arms and shoulders too. The longer you stand, the more you melt, you flop at the waist, your knees wobble until finally you melt into a puddle on the floor.

Fast/slow/stop. An outdoor game. Use a percussion instrument or recorded music which by its beat regulates the speed with which the children move. When it stops, the children must stop. A noise which corresponds to 'flopping' can also be included, so that the children flop to the ground when they hear that sound.

Moon walking. Have the children do moon walking in a slow and exaggerated movement which requires them to go slowly.

Animal movements. Have the children makes movements like different animals, ending with the slow and calm movements of, say, a turtle, Clydesdale horse or elephant.

Statues. A group of children moves to music and then stops when the music stops. This can give them an appreciation of the tension of holding muscles still.

Balloon. The children crouch down low, and with each large breath they swell up bigger and taller. They hold that position for a moment until you clap your hands, upon which they pop and fall to the ground. Or, you can have them let their balloon go, so that the air pours out of them gradually and they run around before dropping to the ground.

Face and nose

Fly. Here comes a pesky old fly. He has landed on your nose. Try to get him off without using your hands. That's right, wrinkle up your nose. Make as many wrinkles in your nose as you can. Scrunch your nose up really hard. Good. You've chased him away. Now you can relax your nose . . . Oops, here he comes back again. Shoo him off. Wrinkle it up hard. Hold it just as tight as you can. Okay, he flew away. You can relax your face. Notice that when you scrunch up your nose that your cheeks and your mouth and your forehead and your eyes all help you, and they get tight, too. So when you relax your nose, your whole face relaxes too, and that feels good. Oh-oh! This time that old fly has come back, but this time he's on your forehead. Make lots of wrinkles. Try to catch him between all those wrinkles. Hold it tight, now. Okay, you can let go. He's gone for good. Now you can just relax. Let your face go smooth, no wrinkles anywhere. Your face feels nice and smooth and relaxed.

Big eyes and little eyes. Open your eyes up big and then make them little so that you can see only a little bit. Then snap them shut. Slowly open them big again.

Sneeze. Wrinkle up your nose as if you are going to sneeze. Hold it. . . . ready now . . . SNEEZE!

Frown. Make a big frowning face and then a happy face—repeat.

Jaw

Bubble gum. You have a giant jawbreaker bubble gum in your mouth. It's very hard to chew. Bite down on it. Hard! Let your neck muscles help you. Now relax. Just let your jaw drop. Okay, let's tackle that jawbreaker again now. Bite down. Hard! Try to squeeze it out between your teeth. That's good. You're really tearing that gum up. Now relax again. Just let your jaw drop off your face. It feels so good just to let go and not have to fight that bubble gum. Okay, one more time. We're really going to tear it up this time. Bite down. Hard as you can. Harder. Oh, you're really working hard. Good. Now relax. Try to relax your whole body. You've beaten the bubble gum. Let yourself go as loose as you can.

Poking tongue. Poke your tongue out as far as you can. Put it back inside your mouth and relax. Repeat. This activity is fun for children because they're being allowed to do something normally forbidden. It is also excellent for relaxing jaw muscles.

Shoulders and neck

Yawn. Keep your mouth closed, and have a yawn with your lips together. Notice how your neck feels relaxed afterwards.

Turtle. Now pretend you are a turtle. You're sitting out on a rock by a nice, peaceful pond, just relaxing in the warm sun. It feels nice and warm and safe here. Oh-oh! You sense danger. Pull your head into your shell. Try to pull your shoulders up to your ears and push your head down into your shoulders. Hold on tight. It isn't easy to be a turtle in a shell. (Pause.) The danger is past now. You can come out into the warm sunshine and, once again, you can relax and feel the warm sunshine. (Pause.) Watch out now! More danger. Hurry, pull your head back into your house and hold it tight. You have to be closed in tight to protect yourself. Okay, you can relax now. Bring your head out and let your shoulders relax. Notice how much better it feels to be relaxed than to be all tight. One more time, now. Danger! Pull your head in. Push your shoulders way up to your ears and hold tight. Don't let even a tiny piece of your head show outside your shell. Hold it. Feel the tenseness in your neck and shoulders. Okay. You can come out now. It's safe again. Relax and feel comfortable and safe. There's no more danger. Nothing to be afraid of. You feel good.

Arms and shoulders

Lazy cat. Pretend you are a furry, lazy cat. You want to stretch. Stretch your arms out in front of you. Raise them up higher over your head. Way back. Feel the pull in your shoulders. Stretch higher. Now just let your arms drop back to your side. Okay, cat, stretch again. Stretch your arms out in front of you. Raise them over your head. Pull them back, way back. Pull hard. Now let them drop quickly. Good. Notice how your shoulders feel more relaxed. This time let's have a great big stretch. Try to touch the ceiling. Stretch your arms way up. Notice the tension and pull in your arms and shoulders. Hold tight, now. Great. Let them drop very quickly and feel how good it is to be relaxed. It feels good and warm and lazy.

Rubber band. Hold your hands out in front, palms facing. Pretend there's a rubber band around them. See how hard you can pull them, pull, pull and now stop pulling against the rubber band and feel your arms and hands go soft.

Weight lifting. Bend down and pretend to pick up something heavy off the ground. Bend your knees and use your hands to pick it up, slowly stand up again bringing the heavy object up to your tummy and then up over your head. Then slowly, slowly put it down on the ground again.

Hands and arms

Ball squeeze. Pretend you have a ball in your hand. Now squeeze it hard. Try to make it flat. Feel how tight your hand and arm are as you squeeze. Now drop the ball. Notice how your hand feels.

Toothpaste. Pretend you are squeezing the toothpaste tube.

Shredded paper. The child can shred paper into a trough.

Balloon puppets. Fill deflated balloons with flour and draw faces on them with permanent textas (felt-tipped pens). The puppet can be squeezed, forming unusual faces.

Play dough. The child can squeeze, or imagine squeezing, play dough through her fingers.

Finger paint. The child could experience manipulating finger paints. For children who dislike getting dirty or those with disabilities who become overwhelmed by sensory input (those who are 'tactile defensive') the paint can be sealed in a plastic bag or under plastic wrap and can still be manipulated.

Lux flakes. The child can squeeze soap flakes in thick foam through her fingers. (If a child is tactile-defensive and becomes overwhelmed by having the mixture on her hands, then you could put it in a sealed plastic bag or on a table and then cover it with plastic wrap.)

Cooking. The child can help to cook meatballs, squid, fish or to bake bread or biscuits which require kneading.

Stomach

Baby elephant. Hey! Here comes a cute baby elephant. But he's not watching where he's going. He doesn't see you lying there in the grass, and he's about to step on your stomach. Don't move. You don't have time to get out of the way. Just get ready for him. Make your stomach very hard. Tighten up your stomach muscles real tight. Hold it. It looks like he is going the other way. You can relax now. Let your stomach go soft. Let it be as relaxed as you can. That feels so much better. Oops, he's coming this way again. Get ready. Tighten up your stomach. Really hard. If he steps on you when your stomach is hard, it won't hurt. Make your stomach into a rock. Okay, he's moving away again. You can relax now. Settle down, get comfortable, and relax. Notice the difference between a tight stomach and a relaxed one. That's how we want it to feel: nice and loose and relaxed. You won't believe this but this time he's really coming your way and no turning around. He's headed straight for you. Tighten up. Tighten hard. Here he comes. This is really it. You've got to hold on tight. He's stepping on you. He's stepped over you. Now he's gone for good. You can relax completely. You're safe. Everything is okay, and you can feel nice and relaxed.

Squeeze. This time imagine that you want to squeeze through a narrow fence and the boards have splinters on them. You'll have to make yourself very skinny if you're going to make it through. Suck your stomach in. Try to squeeze it up against your backbone. Try to be as skinny as you can. You've got to get through. Great—you made it! Now relax. You don't have to be skinny now. Just relax and feel your stomach being warm and loose. Settle back and let your stomach come back out where it belongs. You can feel really good now. (Repeat.)

Legs and feet

Mud puddle. Now pretend that you are standing barefoot in a big, fat mud puddle. Squish your toes down deep into the mud. Try to get your feet down to the bottom of the mud puddle. You'll probably need your legs to help you push. Push down, spread your toes apart, and feel the mud squish up between your toes. Now step out of the mud puddle. Relax your feet. Let your toes go loose and feel how nice that is. It feels good to be relaxed. You feel warm and tingly. (Repeat.)

Autumn leaves. Imagine you are walking or running through autumn leaves. Hear them crunching and crackling. Swish your legs back and forth to make the leaves rustle, and kick the leaves around.

This activity can be done for real also, teaching the children these sensations so that they can imagine them later. Likewise, the shredded paper activity can be extended into allowing the children to kick piles of the paper which they have shredded.

Appendix C

• • • • • • • • • • •

Diagnostic criteria for the attention-deficit disorders (ADD and ADHD)

To receive the diagnosis of ADD or ADHD, a child's symptoms must begin prior to seven years of age; continue for at least six months—and longer in the early childhood age range; be present in at least two situations; result in significant impairment of the child's social or academic functioning; and not be the result of other conditions.

The primary or diagnostic criteria as listed in the DSM-IV (American Psychiatric Association 1994, pp. 83–5) comprise the following:

1. Inattentive symptoms

The child displays six or more of the following behaviours for at least six months to a degree that is maladaptive and inconsistent with his or her developmental level:

- often fails to give close attention to details or makes careless mistakes in school work, work, or other activities;
- often has difficulty sustaining attention in tasks or play activities;
- often does not seem to listen when spoken to directly;
- often does not follow through on instructions and fails to finish school work, chores, or duties in the workplace (not due to oppositional behaviour or failure to understand instructions);
- often has difficulty organising tasks and activities;
- often avoids, dislikes, or is reluctant to engage in tasks that require sustained mental effort (such as school work or homework);
- often loses things necessary for tasks or activities (e.g., toys, school assignments, pencils, books, tools);
- is often easily distracted by extraneous stimuli;
- is often forgetful in daily activities.

2. Hyperactivity

The following symptoms of hyperactivity–impulsivity have persisted for at least six months and to a degree that is maladaptive and inconsistent with developmental level:

- often fidgets with hands or feet or squirms in seat;
- often leaves seat in classroom or in other situations in which remaining seated is expected;
- often runs about or climbs excessively in situations in which it is inappropriate (in adolescents or adults, may be limited to subjective feelings of restlessness);
- often has difficulty playing or engaging in leisure activities quietly;
- is often 'on the go'; or often acts as if 'driven by a motor';
- often talks excessively.

Impulsivity

- often blurts out answers before questions have been completed;
- often has difficulty awaiting his or her turn;
- often interrupts or intrudes on others (e.g., butts into conversations or games).

Children will be diagnosed with ADD when they meet the criteria in section 1; they might have the hyperactive–impulsive symptoms (section 2) alone; or they will be determined to have ADHD when they meet the criteria in both sections.

Source: American Psychiatric Association (1994), *Diagnostic and statistical manual of mental disorders*, 4th edn, pp. 83–5, author, Washington, DC. Reprinted with permission.

Appendix D

• • • • • • • • • •

Characteristics of young gifted children

Cognitive (thinking) skills
- early achievement of developmental milestones;
- quick learning;
- keen observation of their environment;
- active in eliciting stimulation from their environment;
- may read, write or use numbers in advanced ways;
- advanced preferences for books and films, unless too sensitive to their older themes;
- quick and accurate recall;
- can remember skills and information introduced some time ago;
- have deeper knowledge than other children;
- can teach other children;
- understand abstract concepts such as death or time;
- imaginative, creative;
- have a keen sense of humour.

Learning style
- motivated, curious, in search of understanding;
- intense focus on an area of interest, as long as they are presented with sufficient challenge;
- wide-ranging interests;
- alert, sometimes to the point of having a poor sleeping pattern;
- respond to novel stimuli;
- longer than usual concentration span on challenging topics of interest; in contrast, may 'flit' from one activity to another if activities are not challenging enough;
- early use of metacognitive skills to manage their own thinking processes;

- clear understanding of cause-and-effect;
- good planning skills;
- internal locus of control;
- reduced impulsivity;
- independent work at challenging, non-routine tasks;
- logical thinking.

Speech and language skills

- show early comprehension;
- have advanced speech—in terms of vocabulary, grammar and clear articulation;
- use metaphors and analogies;
- spontaneously make up songs or stories;
- modify their language for less mature children;
- use language for a real exchange of ideas and information at a young age;
- carry out instructions to do several things in succession.

Motor abilities

- early motor development, particularly in skills which are under cognitive control;
- can locate themselves within their environment;
- early awareness of left and right;
- fine motor skills may lag behind other developmental domains;
- can put together new or difficult puzzles;
- can take apart and reassemble objects with unusual skill;
- make interesting shapes or patterns with objects;
- have high levels of physical energy.

Social skills

- less egocentric;
- highly developed empathy for others;
- leadership skills;
- advanced play interests;
- can play games with rules early;
- form one or two close friendships;
- may seek out older children or adults for companionship;
- might withdraw to solitary play if intellectual peers are not available;
- are frequently sought out by other children;
- develop moral reasoning and judgment early;
- show an early interest in social issues involving injustices.

Emotional and behavioural characteristics

- emotionally sensitive, intense and responsive;
- develop fears early;

- develop early a self-concept and awareness of being different;
- are self-confident in their strong domains;
- can be perfectionist—in the sense of striving for the high standards of which they are capable;
- may be over-sensitive to criticism;
- become frustrated, which can lead to emotional or behavioural outbursts;
- accept responsibility usually given only to older children;
- are non-conformist.

Sources: Baska 1989; Borkowski & Peck 1986; Chamrad & Robinson 1986; Chan 1996; Clark 1997; Damiani 1997; Davis & Rimm 1998; Delisle 1992; Gross 1993; Haensly & Reynolds 1986; Jackson 1992; Jackson & Butterfield 1986; Kanevsky 1992; Kitano 1990; Klein 1992; Knight 1995; Lewis & Louis 1991; Mares 1991; McClelland et al. 1991; Mendaglio 1994; Miller et al. 1994; Moltzen 1996; Morelock & Morrison 1996; Moss 1990 1992; Parker & Adkins 1995; Parker & Mills 1996; Rabinowitz & Glaser 1985; Renzulli 1986; Roedell et al. 1980; Silverman 1993; Sternberg & Lubart 1991 1992; Tannenbaum 1983 1992 1997; Whitmore 1980.

Appendix E

• • • • • • • • • •

Resource books for children and adults

Children's books can help give you some appropriate words to discuss difficult topics, they can help a child come to terms with an everyday challenge without preaching, and they can be good fun. These titles are suggestions only: new publications become available frequently. A specialist children's book store would be a likely place to locate these and other titles. Those that have gone out of print might still be available in libraries.

Feelings

Anger

Carle, *The bad tempered ladybird*
Hitte, *Boy was I mad*
Mayer, *I was so mad*
Oram, *Angry Arthur*
Preston, *The temper tantrum book*
Viorst, *Alexander and the terrible, horrible, no good, very bad day*

Night terrors

Gleeson & Greder, *Sleep time*
Grindley, *Knock knock who's there*
Hayward, *I had a bad dream*
Hill, *One night at a time*
Mayer, *There's a nightmare in my cupboard*
Mayer, *There's an alligator under my bed*
Mayer, *There's something spooky in my attic*
Salmon, *Scroggy: The monster who was scared of the dark*
Snell, *Danny is afraid of the dark*

Self-esteem

Ashley, *Cleversticks*
Browne, *Willy the champ*
Carlson, *I like me*
Crary, *My name is not dummy*
Diestel-Fedderson, *No one quite like me*
Fox, *Tough Boris*
Harper & Hellard, *It's not fair*
Haze, *Growing up is hard sometimes*
Hutchins, *Happy birthday, Sam*
Jennings, *Tom's tail*
Knowles, *Edward the emu*
McSpedden, *The mouse with the too long tail*
Wold, *Well, why didn't you say so?*

Shyness

Garland, *Going to playschool*
Wells, *Shy Charles*
Wold, *Tell them my name is Amanda*

Friendship

Browne, *Willy and Hugh*
Hilton, *Andrew Jessup*
Oram, *Just like us*
Stevenson, *No friends*
Stones, *No more bullying?*
Timlock, Basil, *The loneliest boy in the block*
Wild & Huxley, *Mr Nick's knitting*

Families

Adoption

Blomquist, *Zachary's new home*
Miller, *Did my first mother love me*
Patterson, *Twice upon a time*

Siblings

Anholt, *Sophie and the new baby*
Blume, *The pain and the great one*
Clark, *Along came Eric*
Cooper, *Little monster did it*
De Lynam, *Stop copying me*
Foreman, *Ben's baby*
Hains, *My baby brother*
Holabird, *Angelina's baby sister*
Hutchins, *The very worst monster*
Hutchins, *Silly Billy*
Morris, *My friends*
Prater, *Along came Tom*
Smith, *Jenny's baby brother*

Waddell, *When the teddy bears came*
Wilhelm, *Let's be friends again*

The only child

Smith, *The lonely only mouse*

Twins

Aliki, *Jack and Jake*
Anholt, *Twins: Two by two*

Family violence

Davis, *Something is wrong at my house: A book for children about parents' fighting*
Paris, *Mommy and Daddy are fighting*

Marital separation

Ballard, *Gracie*
Berry, *About divorce: Good answers to tough questions.* Suitable for older children.
Boegehold, *Daddy doesn't live here anymore*
Brown & Brown, *Dinosaur's divorce*
Galloway, *Jennifer has two daddies*
Heegaard, *When Mom and Dad separate*
Nystom, *Mike's lonely summer.* The tale of a child's reactions to his parents' decision
    to divorce.
Osman, *Where has Daddy gone?*
Shaw, *So Mum and Dad split up: Coping when parents separate and divorce.* Suitable for
    older children.
Simon, *I wish I had my father.* Describes a child's reactions to Fathers' Day when he
    has no contact with his father.
Sonneborn, *Friday night is papa night.* Tells of intermittent parent absence.
Stanek, *I won't go without a father*
Wild, *Sam's Sunday Dad* (Out of print during 1996)

Single parent families

Lindsay, *Do I have a Daddy?*
McGinnis & Paterson, *If Daddy only knew me*
Storrie, *Living with Mum*

Stepfamilies

Boyd, *Sam is my half brother* (Out of print in 1996)
Berry, *About stepfamilies: Good answers to tough questions.* Suitable for school-aged
    children.
Cook, *Room for a stepdaddy*
Vigna, *She's not my real mother.* Tells of a child's response to his stepmother.

Death

Althea, *When uncle Bob died*
Berry, *About death: Good answers to tough questions.*
Brown & Brown, *When dinosaurs die*

Carrick, *The accident*. Tells of the death of a child's pet dog.

Catterwell & Argent, *Sebastian lives in a hat*

De Paola, *Nana upstairs and Nana downstairs*. Tells of the death of a child's great grandmother.

De Paola, *Now one foot, now the other*

Fox, *Sophie*

Heegaard, *When someone very special dies*

Hubner, *Grandmother*

Hughes, *Dogger*. The child loses his favourite soft toy, which is recovered when all hope is lost.

Juneau, *Sad but OK: My Daddy died today*

Lucas & Lewis, *A new star* (about SIDS)

McGough, *The kite and Caitlin*. Tells of a child who is dying.

Mellonie & Ingpen, *Lifetimes (Beginnings and endings with lifetimes in between)*. Useful for introducing the concepts of living and dying although not so useful for a child who is already grieving.

Munsch, *Love you forever*

Old, *Stacy had a little sister*

Palmer, *I wish I could hold your hand . . . A child's guide to grief and loss*

Perkins, *Remembering Mum*

Smith, *A taste of blackberries*. A boy's friend dies, and he tells of his reactions.

Spelman, *After Charlotte's Mom died*

Stanley, *China's plum tree*. A child's pet cat dies.

Van Loon, *I remember Georgie*. Tells of the death of a child's elderly neighbour.

Varley, *Badger's parting gifts*. Badger knows he is old and will die soon, and gives all his friends a gift.

Viorst, *The tenth good thing about Barney*

Vogel, *My twin sister Erika*. Tells of the death of a child's twin sister.

Warland, *Our baby died*

Wild, *Old pig*. The grandmother pig prepares herself and her grand-daughter for her coming death.

Wild, *Remember me*

Wild, *The very best of friends*

Wild, *Toby*

Wilhelm, *I'll always love you*

Books for adults about death and divorce

Ahrons, *The good divorce: Keeping your family together when your marriage falls apart*

Foster & Smith, *Brief lives: Living with the death of a child*

Johnson, *Children die, too*. An excellent booklet for parents grieving at the loss of their child.

Kubler-Ross, *On death and dying*

McKissock & McKissock, *Coping with grief*

Schaefer, *How do we tell the children?*

Teyber, *Helping children cope with divorce*

Westberg, *Good grief*

Child protection

Bass, *I like you to make jokes with me, but I don't want you to touch me*. The child practises telling a man in a shop that she doesn't want him to touch her. When she tells him this, he accepts it readily.

Elliott, *Feeling happy, feeling safe*

Fox, *Hattie and the fox*. Tells of Hattie the hen noticing a fox in the bushes and trying to warn the other animals who ignore her. A lesson in persistence, and in noticing unsafe feelings.

Freeman, *Loving touches*. Discusses the needs of a young child, including the need for loving touches. Introduces the topic of touch, allowing for further discussion of all types of touches.

Freeman, *It's my body*. Describes how a child's body is personal, and that children can choose who and how they touch.

Johnsen, *The trouble with secrets*. Excellent discussion of different types of secrets: surprises, breaking someone else's possession, medical examinations, unsafe touches.

Responding to abuse

Picture books for young children

Hessell, *What's wrong with bottoms?* A child's uncle asks him to engage in sexual play. The child reports this to his mother, who explains what is wrong with the uncle's suggestion. The story is matter-of-fact and non-threatening.

Kehoe, *Something happened and I'm scared to tell: A book for young victims of abuse*

Otto, *Tom doesn't visit us anymore*

Parent-child manuals

Adams & Fay, *No more secrets: Protecting your child from sexual assault*

McGrath, *Safe start, safe future*

Freeman, *It's my body: A book to teach young children how to resist uncomfortable touch*

Gordon & Litt (Eds.), *Try again red riding hood*. An activity book for children by children about keeping safe.

Gordon & Dawson, *Keeping children safe from abuse*

Hart-Rossi, *Protect your child from sexual abuse: A parent's guide*

Kehoe, *Helping abused children*. Directed at those who work with sexually abused children but suitable for parents also. Individual chapters discuss facts of abuse, prevention, identification, and treatment.

Lenett, & Crane, *It's O.K. to say no!* A parent–child manual for the protection of children.

Self-help manuals for adults

Bass & Davis, *Beginning to heal: A first guide for female survivors of child sexual abuse*

Brinegar, *Breaking free from domestic violence*

Daugherty, *Why me? Help for victims of child sexual abuse (even if they are adults now)*

Farmer, *Adult children of abusive parents*

Hunter, *Abused boys: The neglected victims of sexual abuse*

Kelly, *Surviving sexual abuse*

Marecek, *Breaking free from partner abuse: Voices of battered women caught in the cycle of domestic violence*

Matthews, *Breaking through: No longer a victim of child abuse*

Bibliography

● ● ● ● ● ● ● ● ● ●

a'Beckett, C. (1988), 'Parent/staff relationships', in A. Stonehouse (ed.), *Trusting toddlers: Programming for one to three year olds in child care centres*, Australian Early Childhood Association, Watson, ACT.

Abbott, C.F. & Gold, S. (1991), 'Conferring with parents when you're concerned that their child needs special services', *Young Children*, vol. 46, no. 4, pp. 10–14.

Abbott, D. & Meredith, W. (1986), 'Strengths of parents with retarded children', *Family Relations*, vol. 35, pp. 371–5.

Abbott-Shim, M.S. (1990), In-service training: A means to quality care, *Young Children*, vol. 45, no. 2, pp. 14–18.

Adler, R., Rosenfeld, L., & Towne, N. (1995), *Interplay: The process of interpersonal communication*, 6th edn, Harcourt Brace College Publishers, Fort Worth.

Ahrons, C. (1995), *The good divorce: Keeping your family together when your marriage falls apart*, Bloomsbury, London.

Alberto, P.A. & Troutman, A.C. (1995), *Applied behavior analysis for teachers*, 4th edn, Merrill, Columbus, Ohio.

Allen, K.E. & Marotz, L. (1994), *Developmental profiles: Pre-birth through eight*, 2nd edn, Delmar, Albany, NY.

American Psychiatric Association (1994), *Diagnostic and statistical manual of mental disorders*, 4th edn, author, Washington, DC.

Anastopoulos, A.D. & Barkley, R.A. (1992), 'Attention deficit-hyperactivity disorder', in C.E. Walker & M.C. Roberts (eds), *Handbook of clinical child psychology*, 2nd edn, John Wiley & Sons, New York.

Arnold, L.E. (1996), 'Sex differences in ADHD: Conference summary', *Journal of Abnormal Child Psychology*, vol. 24, no. 5, pp. 555–69.

Arthur, L., Beecher, B., Dockett, S., Farmer, S., & Richards, E. (1996), *Programming and planning in early childhood settings*, 2nd edn, Harcourt Brace, Sydney.

Asher, S.R. & Parker, J.G. (1989), 'Significance of peer relationship problems in childhood', in B.H. Schneider, G. Attili, J. Nadel & R.P. Weissberg (eds.), *Social competence in developmental perspective*, Kluwer Academic Publishers, Dordrecht.

Asher, S.R. & Renshaw, P.D. (1981), 'Children without friends: Social knowledge and social skills training', in S.R. Asher & J.M. Gottman (eds), *The development of children's friendships*, Cambridge University Press, Cambridge.

Australian Early Childhood Association (1986), 'What is quality?', *Australian Early Childhood Association Newsletter*, February.

—(1991), Australian Early Childhood Association code of ethics, *Australian Journal of Early Childhood*, vol. 16, no. 1, pp. 3–6.

Bailey, D.B. & Wolery, M. (1992), *Teaching infants and preschoolers with disabilities*, 2nd edn, Merrill, Columbus, Ohio.

Balson, M. (1992), *Understanding classroom behaviour*, 3rd edn, ACER, Melbourne.

—(1994), *Becoming better parents*, 4th edn, ACER, Melbourne.

Bandura, A. (1986), *Social foundations of thought and action*, Prentice Hall, Englewood Cliffs, NJ.

Barkley, R.A. (1988), 'Attention deficit disorder with hyperactivity', in E.J. Mash & L.G. Terdal (eds), *Behavioral assessment of childhood disorders*, 2nd edn, Guilford, New York.

Baska, L.K. (1989), 'Characteristics and needs of the gifted', in J. Feldhusen, J. Van Tassel-Baska & K. Seeley (eds), *Excellence in educating the gifted*, Love Publishing, Denver.

Baumrind, D. (1967), 'Child care practices anteceding three patterns of preschool behavior', *Genetic Psychology Monographs*, vol. 75, pp. 43–88.

Bay-Hinitz, A.K., Peterson, R.F., & Quilitch, R. (1994), 'Cooperative games: A way to modify aggressive and cooperative behaviors in young children', *Journal of Applied Behavior Analysis*, vol. 27, no. 3, pp. 435–6.

Beck, A. (1976), *Cognitive therapy and the emotional disorders*, International Universities Press, New York.

Belknap, M. (1989), *Taming your dragons*, D.O.C., New York.

Benbow, C.P. (1991), 'Meeting the needs of gifted students through use of acceleration', in M.C. Wang, M.C. Reynolds & H.J. Walberg (eds), *Handbook of special education: Research and practice*, Pergamon Press, Oxford.

Benson, A.J. & Presbury, J.H. (1989), 'The behavioral tradition in schools (and miles to go before we sleep)', in J.N. Hughes & R.J. Hall (eds), *Cognitive-behavioral psychology in the schools*, Guilford, New York.

Berk, L. (1997), *Child development*, 4th edn, Allyn and Bacon, Boston.

Bergen, D. (1994), 'Should teachers permit or discourage violent play themes?', *Childhood Education*, vol. 70, no. 5, pp. 300–1.

Berne, P.H. & Savary, L.M. (1996), *Building self-esteem in children*, (exp. edn), Crossroad Publishing, New York.

Biddulph, S. (1993), *The secret of happy children*, rev. edn, Bay Books, Sydney.

Billman, J. (1995), 'Child care program directors: What skills do they need? Results of a statewide survey', *Early Childhood Education Journal*, vol. 23, no. 2, pp. 63–70.

Birch, L.L., Johnson, S.L., & Fischer, J.A, (1995), 'Children's eating: The development of food-acceptance patterns', *Young Children*, vol. 50, no. 2, pp. 71–8.

Bland, L.C., Sowa, C.J., & Callahan, C.M. (1994), 'Overview of resilience in gifted children', *Roeper Review*, vol. 17, no. 2, pp. 77–80.

Bloom, P.J. (1982), *Avoiding burnout: Strategies for managing time, space, and people in early childhood education*, New Horizons, Lake Forest, Illinois.

Blum, N.J. & Mercugliano, M. (1997), 'Attention-deficit/hyperactivity disorder', in M.L. Batshaw (ed.), *Children with disabilities*, 4th edn, MacLennan & Petty, Sydney.

Bolton, R. (1987), *People skills*, Simon & Schuster, Sydney.

Borkowski, J.G. & Peck, V.A. (1986), 'Causes and consequences of metamemory in gifted children', in R.J. Sternberg & J.E. Davidson (eds), *Conceptions of giftedness*, Cambridge University Press, Cambridge.

Borland, J.H. (1986), 'IQ tests: Throwing out the bathwater, saving the baby', *Roeper Review*, vol. 8, no. 3, pp. 163–7.

Bottomley, G. (1983), 'Review of historical and sociological models of "the family"', in A. Burns, G. Bottomley & P. Jools (eds), *The family in the modern world*, Allen & Unwin, Sydney.

Boutte, G.S., Keepler, D.L., Tyler, V.S., & Terry, B.Z. (1992), 'Effective techniques for involving "difficult" parents', *Young Children*, vol. 47, no. 3, pp. 19–22.

Braggett, E.J. (1993), 'Acceleration: What, why, how and when?', in D. Farmer (ed.), *Gifted children need help? A guide for parents and teachers*, New South Wales Association for Gifted and Talented Children Inc, Sydney.

—(1994), *Developing programs for gifted students*, Hawker Brownlow, Melbourne.

—(1998), 'Gifted and talented children', in A. Ashman & J. Elkins (eds), *Educating children with special needs*, 3rd edn, Prentice Hall, Sydney.

Braggett, E., Day, A., & Minchin, M. (1997), *Differentiated programs for primary schools*, Hawker Brownlow, Melbourne.

Brand, S.F. (1990), 'Undergraduates and beginning preschool teachers working with young children: Educational and developmental issues', *Young Children*, vol. 45, no. 2, pp. 19–24.

Briggs, F. (1993), *Why my child? Supporting the families of victims of child sexual abuse*, Allen & Unwin, Sydney.

Broinowski, I. (1994), *Managing child care centres*, TAFE Publications, Collingwood, Vic.

Brown, B. (1986), 'We can help children to be self-reliant', *Children Today*, Jan–Feb, pp. 26–8.

Buchanan, T. & Burts, D. (1995), 'Getting parents involved in the 1990s', *Day Care and Early Education*, vol. 22, no. 4, pp. 18–22.

Bullock, J.R. (1993), 'Lonely children', *Young Children*, vol. 48, no. 6, pp. 53–7.

Burns, A. & Goodnow, J. (1985), *Children and families in Australia*, 2nd edn, Allen & Unwin, Sydney.

Burns, R.B. (1982), *Self-concept development and education*, Holt, Rhinehart & Winston, London.

Butterworth, D. (1991), 'The challenge of day care: Liberation or constraint?' *Australian Journal of Early Childhood*, vol. 16, no. 2, pp. 20–3.

Carter, F. & Cheesman, P. (1988), *Anxiety in childhood and adolescence: Encouraging self-help through relaxation training*, Croom Helm, New York.

Caruso, J.J. (1991), 'Supervisors in early childhood programs: An emerging profile' *Young Children*, vol. 46, no. 6, pp. 20–6.

Cathcart, R. (1996), 'Educational provisions: An overview', in D. McAlpine & R. Moltzen (eds), *Gifted and talented: New Zealand perspectives*, ERDC Press, Palmerston North.

Caughey, C. (1991), 'Becoming the child's ally—observations in a classroom for children who have been abused', *Young Children*, vol. 46, no. 4, pp. 22–8.

Chamrad, D.L. & Robinson, N.M. (1986), 'Parenting the intellectually gifted preschool child', *Topics in Early Childhood Special Education*, vol. 6, no. 1, pp. 74–87.

Chan, L.K.S. (1996), 'Motivational orientations and metacognitive abilities of intellectually gifted students', *Gifted Child Quarterly*, vol. 40, no. 4, pp. 184–94.

Chandler, P.A. (1994), *A place for me: Including children with special needs in early care and education settings*, National Association for the Education of Young Children, Washington, DC.

Charles, C.M. (1996), *Building classroom discipline: From models to practice*, 5th edn, Longman, New York.

Chick, K.A. (1996), 'Caregivers of quality: One mother's search for child care', *Early Childhood Education Journal*, vol. 23, no. 3, pp. 149–51.

Chitwood, D.G. (1986), 'Guiding parents seeking testing', *Roeper Review*, vol. 8, no. 3, pp. 177–9.

Clark, B. (1997), *Growing up gifted*, 5th edn, Merrill, New York.

Clewett, A.S. (1988), 'Guidance and discipline: Teaching young children appropriate behaviour', *Young Children*, vol. 43, no. 4, pp. 26–31.

Clyde, M. (1988), 'Staff burnout—the ultimate reward?', in A. Stonehouse (ed.), *Trusting toddlers: Programming for one to three year olds in child care centres*, Australian Early Childhood Association, Watson, ACT.

Coady, M. (1994), 'Ethical and legal issues for early childhood practitioners', in E.J. Mellor & K.M. Coombe (eds), *Issues in early childhood services: Australian perspectives*, WCB, Dubuque, Iowa.

Coie, J.D., Christopoulos, C., Terry, R., Dodge, K.A., & Lochman, J.E. (1989), 'Types of aggressive relationships, peer rejection, and developmental consequences', in B.H. Schneider, G. Attili, J. Nadel & R.P. Weissberg (eds), *Social competence in developmental perspective*, Kluwer Academic Publishers, Dordrecht.

Cole, P. & Chan, L. (1990), *Methods and strategies for special education*, Prentice Hall, New York.

Coleman, M. (1991), 'Planning for the changing nature of family life in schools for young children', *Young Children*, vol. 46, no. 4, pp. 15–20.

Compas, B.E. (1987), 'Coping with stress during childhood and adolescence', *Psychological Bulletin*, vol. 101, no. 3, pp. 393–403.

Cook, R.E., Tessier, A., & Klein, D. (1996), *Adapting early childhood curricula for children in inclusive settings*, 4th edn, Merrill, Englewood Cliffs, NJ.

Coopersmith, S. (1967), *The antecedents of self-esteem*, W.H. Freeman, San Francisco.

Coplan, R.J., Rubin, K.H., Fox, N.A., Calkins, S.D., & Stewart, S.L. (1994), 'Being alone, playing alone and acting alone: Distinguishing among reticence and passive and active solitude in young children', *Child Development*, vol. 65, no. 1, pp. 129–37.

Corey, G. (1996), *Theory and practice of counseling and psychotherapy*, 5th edn, Brooks/Cole, Monterey, CA.

Cornell, D.G. (1989), Child adjustment and parent use of the term 'gifted', *Gifted Child Quarterly*, vol. 33, no. 2, pp. 59–64.

Cowin, M., Freeman, L., Farmer, A., James, M., Drent, A., & Arthur, R. (1990), *Positive school discipline: A practical guide to developing policy*, rev. edn, Narbethong Publications, Boronia, Vic.

Crary, E. (1992), 'Talking about differences children notice', in B. Neugebauer (ed.), *Alike and different: Exploring our humanity with young children*, (rev. edn), National Association for the Education of Young Children, Washington, DC.

Creaser, B. & Dau, E. (1995), *The anti-bias approach in early childhood*, Harper Educational, Pymble, NSW.

Cupit, C.G. (1989), *Socialising the superheroes*, Watson, ACT, Australian Early Childhood Association.

Curry, N.E. & Johnson, C.N. (1990), *Beyond self-esteem: Developing a genuine sense of human value*, National Association for the Education of Young Children, Washington DC.

Damiani, V.B. (1997), 'Young gifted children in research and practice: The need for early childhood programs', *Gifted Child Today*, vol. 20, no. 3, pp. 18–23.

Davis, G.A. & Rimm, S.B. (1998), *Education of the gifted and talented*, 4th edn, Allyn & Bacon, Boston.

Dawkins, M. (1991), 'Hey dudes, what's the rap? A plea for leniency towards superhero play', *Australian Journal of Early Childhood*, vol. 16, no. 2, pp. 3–8.

Delisle, J.R. (1992), *Guiding the social and emotional development of gifted youth*, Longman, New York.

Department for Education and Children's Services (1990), *Guidelines for policy development*, author, Adelaide.

—(1995), *Quality matters: A learning manual for quality assurance in early childhood services*, author, Adelaide.

—(1996), *Foundation areas of learning*, author, Adelaide.

Dengate, S. (1997), 'Dietary management of attention deficit disorder', *Australian Journal of Early Childhood*, 22, no. 4, pp. 29–33.

Derevensky, J. & Coleman, E.B. (1989), 'Gifted children's fears', *Gifted Child Quarterly*, vol. 33, no. 2, pp. 65–8.

Derman-Sparks, L. (1992), ' "It isn't fair!" Antibias curriculum for young children', in B. Neugebauer (ed.), *Alike and different: Exploring our humanity with young children*, rev. edn, National Association for the Education of Young Children, Washington DC.

Derman-Sparks, L. & the ABC Task Force (1989), *Anti-bias curriculum: Tools for empowering young children*, National Association for the Education of Young Children, Washington DC.

Dickey, J.P. & Henderson, P. (1989), 'What young children say about stress and coping in school', *Health Education*, Feb–March, pp. 14–17.

Dinkmeyer, D. & McKay, G. (1989), *Systematic training for effective parenting*, 3rd edn, American Guidance Service, Minnesota.

Dinkmeyer, D., McKay, G. & Dinkmeyer, D. (1980), *Systematic training for effective teaching*, American Guidance Service, Minnesota.

Dobson, K.S. & Pusch, D. (1993), 'Towards a definition of the conceptual and empirical boundaries of cognitive therapy', *Australian Psychologist*, vol. 28, no. 3, pp. 137–44.

Dodge, K.A. (1985), 'Facets of social interaction and the assessment of social competence in children', in B.H. Schneider, K.H. Rubin & J.E. Ledingham (eds), *Children's peer relations: Issues in assessment and intervention*, Springer-Verlag, New York.

Doherty-Derkowski, G. (1995), *Quality matters: Excellence in early childhood programs*, Addison-Wesley, Don Mills, Ontario.

Doyle, W. (1986), 'Classroom organization and management', in M.C. Wittrock (ed.), *Handbook of research on teaching*, 3rd edn, Macmillan, New York.

Dyck, M.J. (1993), 'New directions in cognitive-behaviour therapy', *Australian Psychologist*, vol. 28, no. 3, pp. 133–6.

Eales, C. & de Paoli, W. (1991), 'Early entry and advanced placement of talented students in primary and secondary schools', *Gifted Education International*, vol. 7, no. 3, pp. 140–4.

Ebbeck, M.A. (1991), *Early childhood education*, Longman Cheshire, Melbourne.

Edwards, C.H. (1997), *Classroom discipline and management*, 2nd edn, Macmillan, New York.

Elicker, J. & Fortner-Wood, C. (1995), 'Adult-child relationships in early childhood programs', *Young Children*, vol. 51, no. 1, pp. 69–78.

Elkind, D. (1988), *The hurried child: Growing up too fast too soon*, (rev. edn), Addison-Wesley Publishing Co., Massachusetts.

Farmer, S. (1995), *Policy development in early childhood services*, Community Child Care Cooperative Ltd, Newtown, NSW.

Farquhar, S.E. (1990), 'Defining quality in the evaluation of early childhood programs', *Australian Journal of Early Childhood*, vol. 15, no. 4, pp. 16–23.

Feldhusen, J.F. (1989), 'Synthesis of research on gifted youths', *Educational Leadership*, vol. 46, no. 6, pp. 6–11.

Feldhusen, J.F., Van Winkle, L., & Ehle, D.A. (1996), 'Is it acceleration or simply appropriate instruction for precocious youth?', *Teaching Exceptional Children*, vol. 28, no. 3, pp. 48–51.

Fields, M.V. & Boesser, C. (1997), *Constructive guidance and discipline: Preschool and primary education*, 2nd edn, Merrill, Upper Saddle River, NJ.

Fischer, M., Barkley, R.A., Fletcher, K.E., & Smallish, L. (1993), 'The adolescent outcome of hyperactive children: Predictors of psychiatric, academic, social and emotional adjustment', *Journal of the American Academy of Child and Adolescent Psychiatry*, vol. 32, no. 2, pp. 324–32.

Fleet, A. & Clyde, M. (1993), *What's in a day? Working in early childhood*, Social Science Press, Wentworth Falls, NSW.

Fox, A.M. & Rieder, M.J. (1993), 'Risks and benefits of drugs used in the management of the hyperactive child', *Drug Safety*, vol. 9, no. 1, pp. 38–50.

Fraser, N. (1996), 'Parenting', in D. McAlpine & R. Moltzen (eds), *Gifted and talented: New Zealand perspectives*, ERDC Press, Palmerston North.

Freeman, J. (1995), 'Annotation: Recent studies of giftedness in children', *Journal of Child Psychology and Psychiatry*, vol. 36, no. 4, pp. 531–47.

Frosh, S. (1983), 'Children and teachers in schools', in S. Spence & G. Shepherd (eds), *Developments in social skills training*, Academic Press, London.

Furman, R.A. (1995), 'Helping children cope with stress and deal with feelings', *Young Children*, vol. 50, no. 2, pp. 33–41.

Galbraith, J. (1985), 'The eight great gripes of gifted kids: Responding to special needs', *Roeper Review*, vol. 8, no. 1, pp. 15–18.

Galinsky, E. (1988), 'Parents and teacher-caregivers: Sources of tension, sources of support', *Young Children*, vol. 43, no. 3, pp. 4–12.

—(1989), 'A parent/teacher study: Interesting results', *Young Children*, vol. 45, no. 1, pp. 2–3.

—(1990), pp. 'Why are some parent/teacher partnerships clouded with difficulties?', *Young Children*, vol. 45, no. 5, pp. 2–3, 38–9.

Gardner, H. (1983), *Frames of mind: The theory of multiple intelligences*, Basic Books, New York.

Gartrell, D. (1994), *A guidance approach to discipline*, Delmar, New York.

Gerber, M. (1981), 'What is appropriate curriculum for infants and toddlers?', in B. Weissbourn & J. Musick (eds), *Infants: Their social environments*, National Association for the Education of Young Children, Washington DC.

Gestwicki, C. (1995), *Developmentally appropriate practice: Curriculum development in early education*, Delmar, Albany, NY.

Ginott, H. (1972), *Teacher and child*, New York: Macmillan.

Glasser, W. (1977), 'Ten steps to good discipline', *Today's Education*, vol. 66, pp. 61–3.

—(1986), *Control theory in the classroom*, Harper & Row, New York.

—(1992), *The quality school*, 2nd edn, Harper & Row, New York.

—(1993), *The quality school teacher*, Harper & Row, New York.

Goldstein, M. & Goldstein, S. (1995), 'Medications and behavior in the classroom', in S. Goldstein (ed.), *Understanding and managing children's classroom behavior*, John Wiley & Sons, New York.

Goldstein, S. (1995), 'Attention deficit hyperactivity disorder', in S. Goldstein (ed.), *Understanding and managing children's classroom behavior*, John Wiley and Sons, New York.

Good, T.L. & Brophy, J.E. (1986), 'School effects', in M.C. Wittrock (ed.), *Handbook of research on teaching*, 3rd edn, Macmillan, New York.

Goodenow, C. (1993), 'The psychological sense of school membership among adolescents: Scale development and educational correlates', *Psychology in the Schools*, vol. 30, no. 1, pp. 79–90.

Goodman, S.H., Brumley, H.E., Schwartz, K.R. & Purcell, D.W. (1993), 'Gender and age in the relation between stress and children's school adjustment', *Journal of Early Adolescence*, vol. 13, no. 3 pp. 329–45.

Gordon, T. (1970), *Parent effectiveness training*, Plume, New York.

—(1974), *Teacher effectiveness training*, Peter H. Wyden, New York.

—(1991), *Teaching children self-discipline at home and at school*, Random House, Sydney.

Gotts, E.E. (1988), 'The right to quality child care', *Childhood Education*, vol. 64, no. 5, pp. 268–75.

Green, C. & Chee, K. (1997), *Understanding ADHD: A parent's guide to attention-deficit hyperactivity disorder in children*, Random House, Sydney.

Greenberg, P. (1992), 'Ideas that work with young children: How to institute some simple democratic practices pertaining to respect, rights, roots and responsibilities in any classroom (without losing your leadership position)', *Young Children*, vol. 47, no. 5, pp. 10–17.

Greenman, J. (1988), *Caring spaces; learning spaces: Children's environments that work*, Exchange Press, Redmond, WA.

Greenman, J. & Stonehouse, A. (1997), *Prime times: A handbook for excellence in infant and toddler programs*, Longman, South Melbourne.

Grey, K. (1995), 'Not in praise of praise', *Child Care Information Exchange*, vol. 7, pp. 56–9.

Gronlund, G. (1992), 'Coping with ninja turtle play in my kindergarten classroom', *Young Children*, vol. 48, no. 1, pp. 21–5.

Gross, M.U.M. (1993), *Exceptionally gifted children*, Routledge, London.

Grossberg, I.N. & Cornell, D.G. (1988), 'Relationship between personality adjustment and high intelligence: Terman versus Hollingworth', *Exceptional Children*, vol. 55, no. 3, pp. 266–72.

Guralnick, M.J., Connor, R.T., Hammond, M., Gottman, J.M., & Kinnish, K. (1995), 'Immediate effects of mainstreamed settings on the social interactions and social integration of preschool children', *American Journal on Mental Retardation*, vol. 100, no. 4, pp. 359–77.

Hadaway, N. & Mareh-Schroer, M.F. (1992), 'Multidimensional assessment of the gifted minority student,' *Roeper Review*, vol. 15, no. 2, pp. 73–7.

Haensly, P.A., Reynolds, C.R., & Nash, W.R. (1986), 'Giftedness: Coalescence, context, conflict, and commitment', in R.J. Sternberg & J.E. Davidson (eds), *Conceptions of giftedness*, Cambridge University Press, Cambridge, NY.

Harrison, C. (1995), *Giftedness in early childhood*, KU Children's Services, Sydney.

Harrison, J. (1996), *Understanding children: Towards responsive relationships*, 2nd edn, ACER, Melbourne.

Hart, E.L., Lahey, B.B., Loeber, R., Applegate, B., & Frick, P.J. (1995), 'Developmental change in attention-deficit hyperactivity in boys: A four-year longitudinal study', *Journal of Abnormal Child Psychology*, vol. 2, no. 6, pp. 729–49.

Hartup, W.W. (1979), 'Peer relations and social competence', in M.W. Kent & J.E. Rolf (eds), *Social competence in children*, University Press of New England, Hanover, New Hampshire.

Hay, I. (1993), 'Motivation, self-perception and gifted students', *Gifted Education International*, vol. 9, no. 1, pp. 16–21.

Heath, H.E. (1994), 'Dealing with difficult behaviors: Teachers plan with parents', *Young Children*, vol. 49, no. 5, pp. 20–4.

Herbert, M. (1987), *Behavioural treatment of children with problems: A practice manual*, 2nd edn, Academic Press, London.

Hill, S. & Hill, T. (1990), *The collaborative classroom: A guide to cooperative learning*, Eleanor Curtin, Melbourne.

Hill, S. & Reed, K. (1989), 'Promoting social competence at preschool: The implementation of a cooperative games programme', *Australian Journal of Early Childhood*, vol. 14, no. 4, pp. 25–31.

Hilliard, A.G. (1985), 'What is quality care?', in B.M. Caldwell & A.G. Hilliard III (eds), *What is quality care?*, National Association for the Education of Young Children, Washington DC.

Hinshaw, S.P. & Erhardt, D. (1991), 'Attention-deficit hyperactivity disorder', in P.C. Kendall (ed.), *Child and adolescent therapy: Cognitive-behavioral procedures*, Guilford, New York.

Hitz, R. & Driscoll, A. (1988), 'Praise or encouragement? New insights into praise: implications for early childhood teachers', *Young Children*, vol. 43, no. 5, pp. 6–13.

Hohmann, M. & Weikart, D.P. (1995), *Educating young children*, High/Scope Press, Ypsilanti, Michigan.

Holden, B. (1996), 'Educational provisions: Early childhood', in D. McAlpine & R. Moltzen (eds), *Gifted and talented: New Zealand perspectives*, ERDC Press, Palmerston North.

Honig, A.S. (1986), 'Stress and coping in children (Part 1)', *Young Children*, vol. 41, no. 4, pp. 50–63.

Hostetler, L. (1991), 'Collaborating on behalf of young children', *Young Children*, vol. 46, no. 2, pp. 2–3.

Howes, C. (1990), 'Can the age of entry into child care and the quality of child care predict adjustment in kindergarten?' *Developmental Psychology*, vol. 26, no. 2, pp. 292–303.

Humphrey, J.H. & Humphrey, J.N. (1985), *Controlling stress in children*, Charles C. Thomas, Illinois.

Hundert, J. (1995), *Enhancing social competence in young students: School-based approaches*, Pro-ed, Austin, Texas.

Irwin, M. (1994), 'Medication treatment in ADHD', in D.L. Wodrich (eds), *Attention deficit hyperactivity disorder. What every parent wants to know*, Paul H. Brookes, Baltimore, MD.

Jackson, N.E. (1992), 'Precocious reading of English: Origins, structure, and predictive significance', in P.S. Klein & A.J. Tannenbaum (eds), *To be young and gifted*, Ablex, Norwood, NJ.

Jackson, N.E. & Butterfield, E.C. (1986), 'A conception of giftedness designed to promote research', in R.J. Sternberg & J.E. Davidson (eds), *Conceptions of giftedness*, Cambridge University Press, Cambridge, NY.

Jakubowski, P. & Lange, A.J. (1978), *The assertive option: Your rights and responsibilities*, Research Press, Illinois.

Janos, P.M. (1987), 'A fifty-year follow-up of Terman's youngest college students and IQ-matched agemates', *Gifted Child Quarterly*, vol. 31, no. 2, pp. 55–8.

Jenkins-Friedman, R. & Murphy, D.L. (1988), 'The Mary Poppins effect: Relationships between gifted students' self-concept and adjustment', *Roeper Review*, vol. 11, no. 1, pp. 26–30.

Johnson, D.W. & Johnson, R.T. (1991), *Learning together and alone*, 3rd edn, Allyn & Bacon, Boston.

Johnson, D.W., Johnson, R.T., & Holubec, E.J. (1990), *Circles of learning: Cooperation in the classroom*, 3rd edn, Interaction Books, Minnesota.

Jones, V.F. & Jones, L.S. (1995), *Comprehensive classroom management: Creating positive learning environments for all students*, 4th edn, Allyn & Bacon, Boston.

Jorde-Bloom, P. (1988), 'Teachers need "TLC" too', *Young Children*, vol. 43, no. 6, pp. 4–8.

Kamii, C. (1985), 'Autonomy: The aim of education envisioned by Piaget', *Australian Journal of Early Childhood*, vol. 10, no. 1, pp. 3–10.

Kanevsky, L. (1992), 'The learning game', in P.S. Klein & A.J. Tannenbaum (eds), *To be young and gifted*, Ablex, Norwood, NJ.

Katz, L.G. (1988a), *Early childhood education: What research tells us*, Phi Delta Kappa Educational Foundation, Bloomington, Indiana.

—(1988b), 'What should children be doing?' *Rattler*, Spring, pp. 4–6.

—(1995), *Talks with teachers of young children*, Ablex, Norwood, NJ.

Katz, L.G., Evangelou, D., & Hartman, J.A. (1990), *The case for mixed-age grouping in early education*, National Association for the Education of Young Children, Washington, DC.

Kendall, P.C. (ed.), (1991), *Child and adolescent therapy: Cognitive-behavioral procedures*, Guilford, New York.

Kendall, P.C. & Panichelli-Mindel, S.M. (1995), 'Cognitive-behavioral treatments', *Journal of Abnormal Child Psychology*, vol. 23, no. 1, pp. 107–24.

Kerr, M. & Nelson, M. (1998), *Strategies for managing behavior problems in the classroom*, 3rd edn, Merrill, Columbus, Ohio.

King, H.E. (1992), 'The reactions of children to divorce', in C.E. Walker & M.C. Roberts (eds), *Handbook of clinical child psychology*, 2nd edn, Plenum, New York.

Kitano, M. (1982), 'Young gifted children: Strategies for preschool teachers', *Young Children*, vol. 37, no. 4, pp. 14–24.

—(1986), 'Counseling gifted preschoolers', *Gifted Child Today*, vol. 9, no. 4, pp. 20–5.

—(1990), 'A developmental model for identifying and serving young gifted children', *Early Child Development and Care*, vol. 63, pp. 19–31.

Klein, P.S. (1992), 'Mediating the cognitive, social, and aesthetic development of precocious young children', in P.S. Klein & A.J. Tannenbaum (eds), *To be young and gifted*, Ablex, Norwood, NJ.

Knight, B.A. (1995), 'The influence of locus of control on gifted and talented students', *Gifted Education International*, vol. 11, no. 1, pp. 31–3.

Knight, T. (1991), 'Democratic schooling: Basis for a school code of behaviour', in M.N. Lovegrove & R. Lewis (eds), *Classroom discipline*, Longman Cheshire, Melbourne.

Koegel, R.L., Shriebman, L., Loos, L.M., Dirlich-Wilhelm, H., Dunlap, G., Robbins, F.R., & Plienis, A.J. (1992), 'Consistent stress profiles in mothers of children with autism', *Journal of Autism and Developmental Disorders*, vol. 22, no. 2, pp. 205–16.

Kohler, F.W. & Strain, P.S. (1993), 'The early childhood social skills program', *Teaching Exceptional Children*, vol. 25, no. 2, pp. 41–2.

Kontos, S. & Wilcox-Herzog, A. (1997), 'Teachers' interactions with children: Why are they so important?', *Young Children*, vol. 52, no. 2, pp. 4–12.

Koralek, D.G., Colker, L.J., & Dodge, D.T. (1993), *The what, why, and how of high-quality early childhood education: A guide for on-site supervision*, National Association for the Education of Young Children, Washington DC.

Kotzman, A. (1989), *Listen to me, listen to you*, Penguin Books, Ringwood.

Kulik, J.A. & Kulik, C-L.C. (1997), 'Ability grouping', in N. Colangelo & G.A. Davis (eds), *Handbook of gifted education*, 2nd edn, Allyn & Bacon, Boston.

Lady Gowrie Child Centre Melbourne Inc. (1987), *Aspects of quality day care: An evaluative summary of recent literature*, author, North Carlton, Victoria.

Lambert, B. (1990), 'Hyperactivity: A review of research', *Australian Journal of Early Childhood*, vol. 15, no. 2, pp. 43–8.

—(1994), 'Beating burnout: A multi-dimensional perspective', *AECA Resource Book Series*, vol. 1, no. 2, Australian Early Childhood Association, Watson, ACT.

Larner, M. & Phillips, D. (1996), 'Defining and valuing quality as a parent', in P. Moss & H. Penn (eds), *Transforming nursery education*, Paul Chapman Publishing, London.

Lee, C. (1993), 'Cognitive theory and therapy: Distinguishing psychology from ideology', *Australian Psychologist*, vol. 28, no. 3, pp. 156–60.

Levy, F. (1993), 'Side effects of stimulant use', *Journal of Paediatric Child Health*, vol. 29, pp. 250–4.

Lewis, M. & Louis, B. (1991), 'Young gifted children', in N. Colangelo & G.A. Davis (eds), *Handbook of gifted education*, Allyn and Bacon, Boston.

Lewis, R. (1997), *The discipline dilemma*, 2nd edn, ACER, Melbourne.

Lopez, A. (1996), 'Creation is ongoing: Developing a relationship with non-English speaking parents', *Child Care Information Exchange*, vol. 107, pp. 56–9.

Luthar, S.S. & Zigler, E. (1991), 'Vulnerability and competence: A review of the research on resilience in childhood', *American Journal of Orthopsychiatry*, vol. 6, pp. 6–22.

MacMullin, C.E. (1988), Assessment of children's social skills: Identifying social situations that are problematic for children at school, University of Connecticut: Unpublished doctoral thesis.

MacMullin, C.E. & Napper, M. (1993), Teachers and inclusion of students with disabilities: Attitude, confidence, or encouragement?, Paper presented to the Australian Early Intervention Association (SA Chapter), Conference, Adelaide, June 1993.

Mallory, B.L. & New, R.S. (1994), 'Introduction: The ethic of inclusion', in B.L. Mallory & R.S. New (eds), *Diversity and developmental appropriate practices: Challenges for early childhood education*, Teachers College Press, New York.

Mares, L. (1991), *Young gifted children*, Hawker Brownlow Education, Melbourne.

Mares, L. & Byles, J. (1994), *One step ahead: Early admission of, and school provisions for, gifted infants*, Hawker Brownlow Education, Melbourne.

McCaslin, M. & Good, T.L. (1992), 'Compliant cognition: The misalliance of management and instructional goals in current school reform', *Educational Researcher*, vol. 21, no. 3, pp. 4–17.

McClelland, R., Yewchuk, C., & Mulcahy, R. (1991), 'Locus of control in underachieving and achieving gifted students', *Journal for the Education of the Gifted*, vol. 14, no. 4, pp. 380–92.

McCluskey, K.W., Massey, K.J., & Baker, P.A. (1997), 'Early entrance to kindergarten: An alternative to consider', *Gifted and Talented International*, vol. 12, no. 1, pp. 27–30.

McCollum, J.A. & Bair, H. (1994), 'Research in parent–child interaction. Guidance to developmentally appropriate practice for young children with disabilities', in B.L. Mallory & R.S. New (eds), *Diversity and developmentally appropriate practices: Challenges for early childhood education*, Teachers College Press, New York.

McDonald, P. (1993), *Family trends and structure in Australia*, Australian Institute of Family Studies, Victoria.

McKim, M.K. (1993), 'Quality child care: What does it mean for individual infants, parents and caregivers?', *Early Child Development and Care*, vol. 88, pp. 23–30.

McKissock, M. & McKissock, D. (1995), *Coping with grief*, 3rd edn, ABC, Sydney.

Mendaglio, S. (1994), 'Gifted sensitivity to criticism', *Gifted Child Today*, vol. 17, no. 3, pp. 24–5.

—(1995), 'Children who are gifted/ADHD', *Gifted Child Today*, vol. 18, no. 4, pp. 37–40.

Meyer, D.J. (1993), 'Lessons learned: Cognitive coping strategies of overlooked family members' in A.P. Turnbull, J.M. Patterson, S.K. Behr, D.L. Murphy, J.G. Marquis & M.J. Blue-Banning (eds), *Cognitive coping, families and disability*, Paul H. Brookes, Baltimore.

Miller, N.B., Silverman, L.K., & Falk, R.F. (1994), 'Emotional development, intellectual ability, and gender', *Journal for the Education of the Gifted*, vol. 18, no. 1, pp. 20–38.

Mitchell, G. (1993), *Help! What do I do about . . ?*, Scholastic, New York.

Mize, J. (1995), 'Coaching preschool children in social skills: A cognitive-social learning curriculum', in G. Cartledge & J.F. Milburn (eds), *Teaching social skills to children: Innovative approaches*, 3rd edn, Allyn & Bacon, Boston.

Mize, J. & Ladd, G.W. (1990), 'Toward the development of successful social skills training for preschool children', in S.R. Asher & J.D. Coie (eds), *Peer rejection in childhood*, Cambridge University Press, Cambridge.

Moltzen, R. (1996), 'Characteristics of gifted children', in D. McAlpine & R. Moltzen (eds), *Gifted and talented: New Zealand perspectives*, ERDC Press, Palmerston North.

Moody, K. (1980), *Growing up on television: The TV effect: A report to parents*, Times, New York.

Moon, S.M., Kelly, K.R., & Feldhusen, J.P. (1997), 'Specialized counseling services for gifted youth and their families: A needs assessment', *Gifted Child Quarterly*, vol. 41, no. 1, pp. 16–25.

Morelock, M.J. & Morrison, K. (1996), *Gifted children have talents too: Multi-dimensional programmes for the gifted in early childhood*, Hawker Brownlow Education, Highett, Victoria.

Moss, E. (1990), 'Social interaction and metacognitive development in gifted preschoolers', *Gifted Child Quarterly*, vol. 34, no. 1, pp. 16–20.

—(1992), 'Early interactions and metacognitive development of gifted preschoolers', in P.S. Klein & A.J. Tannenbaum (eds), *To be young and gifted*, Ablex, Norwood, NJ.

Mullins, J.B. (1987), 'Authentic voices from parents of exceptional children', *Family Relations*, vol. 36, pp. 30–3.

National Association for the Education of Young Children (1983), 'Four components of high quality early childhood programs: Staff–child interaction, child–child interaction, curriculum, and evaluation', *Young Children*, vol. 38, no. 6, pp. 46–52.

—(1984), Criteria for high quality early childhood programs, Position paper from National Academy of Early Childhood Programs, pp. 3–13.

—(1987), 'Ideas that work with young children: Infants and toddlers away from their mothers', *Young Children*, vol. 42, no. 4, pp. 40–2.

National Childcare Accreditation Council (1993), *Putting children first: Quality improvement and accreditation system handbook*, National Childcare Accreditation Council, Sydney.

Ochiltree, G. (1994), *Effects of child care on young children: Forty years of research*, Australian Institute of Family Studies, Melbourne.

O'Donnell, C. & Craney, J. (1982), 'Incest and the reproduction of the patriarchal family', in C. O'Donnell & J. Craney (eds), *Family violence in Australia*, Longman Cheshire, Melbourne.

Oehlberg, B. (1996), *Making it better: Activities for children living in a stressful world*, Redleaf Press, St Paul, MN.

Orlick, T. (1982), *The second cooperative sports and games book*, Pantheon, New York.

Parker, W. & Adkins, K.K. (1995), 'Perfectionism and the gifted', *Roeper Review*, vol. 17, no. 3, pp. 173–6.

Parker, W. & Mills, C.J. (1996), 'The incidence of perfectionism in gifted students', *Gifted Child Quarterly*, vol. 40, no. 4, pp. 194–9.

Patton, M.M. & Kokoski, T.M. (1996), 'How good is your early childhood science, mathematics, and technology program?: Strategies for extending your curriculum', *Young Children*, vol. 51, no. 5, pp. 38–44.

Perry, D. & Bussey, K. (1984), *Social development*, Prentice Hall, Englewood Cliffs, NJ.

Phillips, D.A. & Howes, C. (1987), 'Indicators of quality child care: Review of research', in D. Phillips (ed.), *Quality in child care: What does research tell us?*, National Association for the Education of Young Children, Washington DC.

Piirto, J. (1994), *Talented children and adults*, Merrill, Upper Saddle River, NJ.

Plucker, J.A. & McIntyre, J. (1996), 'Academic survivability in high-potential, middle school students', *Gifted Child Quarterly*, vol. 40, no. 1, pp. 7–14.

Pope, A.W., McHale, S.M., & Craighead, E.W. (1988), *Self-esteem enhancement with children and adolescents*, Pergamon, New York.

Porteous, M.A. (1979), 'A survey of the problems of normal 15-year-olds', *Journal of Adolescence*, vol. 2, no. 4, pp. 307–23.

Porter, L. (1996), *Student behaviour: Theory and practice for teachers*, Allen & Unwin, Sydney.

—(1997a), *Children are people too: A parent's guide to young children's behaviour*, 2nd edn, author, Adelaide.

—(1997b), *Young gifted children: Meeting their needs*, AECA Resource Book Series, vol. 4, no. 1, Australian Early Childhood Association, Watson, ACT.

—(1999), *Gifted young children*, Allen & Unwin, Sydney.

Proctor, T.B., Feldhusen, J.F., & Black, K.N. (1988), 'Guidelines for early admission to elementary school', *Psychology in the Schools*, vol. 25, no. 1, pp. 41–3.

Pugh, G. & Selleck, D.R. (1996), 'Listening to and communicating with young children', in R. Davie, G. Upton & V. Varma (eds), *The voice of the child: A handbook for professionals*, Falmer Press, London.

Putallaz, M. & Wasserman, A. (1990), 'Children's entry behavior', in S.R. Asher & J.D. Coie (eds), *Peer rejection in childhood*, Cambridge University Press, Cambridge.

Raban, B. (1997), 'What counts towards quality provision?', *International Journal of Early Childhood*, vol. 29, no. 1, pp. 57–63.

Rabinowitz, M. & Glaser, R. (1985), 'Cognitive structure and process in highly competent performance', in F.D. Horowitz & M.O'Brien (eds), *The gifted and talented: Developmental perspectives*, American Psychological Association, Washington, DC.

Raines, S. (1995), *Never ever serve sugary snacks on rainy days: The official little instruction book for teachers of young children*, Gryphon House, Beltsville, MD.

Readdick, C.A. (1993), 'Solitary pursuits: Supporting children's privacy needs in early childhood settings', *Young Children*, vol. 49, no. 1, pp. 60–4.

Renzulli, J.S. (1986), 'The three-ring conception of giftedness: A developmental model for creative productivity', in R.J. Sternberg & J.E. Davidson (eds), *Conceptions of giftedness*, Cambridge University Press, Cambridge, NY.

Rimm, S.B. & Lovance, K.J. (1992), 'How acceleration may prevent underachievement syndrome', *Gifted Child Today*, vol. 15, no. 2, pp. 9–14.

Robinson, N.M. & Robinson, H. (1992), 'The use of standardized tests with young gifted children', in P.S. Klein & A.J. Tannenbaum (eds), *To be young and gifted*, Ablex, Norwood, NJ.

Rodd, J. (1996), *Understanding young children's behaviour*, Allen & Unwin, Sydney.

Roedell, W.C., Jackson, N.E., & Robinson, H.B. (1980), *Gifted young children*, Teachers College, Columbia University, New York.

Rogers, C. (1951), *Client-centred therapy*, Constable, London.

—(1978), *On personal power*, Constable, London.

Rogers, C.R. & Freiberg, H. (1994), *Freedom to learn*, 3rd edn, Merrill, Columbus, Ohio.

Rogers, K.B. & Kimpston, R.D. (1992), 'Acceleration: What we do vs. what we do not know', *Educational Leadership*, vol. 50, no. 2, pp. 58–61.

Rogers, W. (1991), 'Decisive discipline', in M.N. Lovegrove & R. Lewis (eds), *Classroom discipline*, Longman Cheshire, Melbourne.

—(1994), *Behaviour recovery*, ACER, Melbourne.

—(1998), *'You know the fair rule' and much more: Strategies for making the hard job of discipline and behaviour management in school easier*, ACER, Melbourne.

Rolfe, S., Lloyd-Smith, J., & Richards, L. (1991), 'Understanding the effects of infant care: The case of qualitative study of mothers' experiences', *Australian Journal of Early Childhood*, vol. 16, no. 2, pp. 24–32.

Rose, S.R. (1983), 'Promoting social competence in children: A classroom approach to social and cognitive skill training', in C.W. LeCroy (ed.), *Social skills training for children and youth*, Haworth Press, New York.

Rosenthal, D.M. & Sawyers, J.Y. (1996), 'Building successful home/school partnerships: Strategies for parent support and involvement', *Childhood Education*, vol. 72, no. 4, pp. 194–200.

Rubin, Z. (1980), *Children's friendships*, Harvard University Press, Massachusetts.

Rutter, M. (1985), 'Resilience in the face of adversity: Protective factors and resistance to psychiatric disorder', *British Journal of Psychiatry*, vol. 147, pp. 598–611.

—(1990), 'Psychosocial resilience and protective mechanisms', in J. Rolf, A.S. Masten, D. Cicchetti, K.H. Nuechterlein & S. Weintraub (eds), *Risk and protective factors in the development of psychopathology*, Cambridge University Press, New York.

Ryan, N.M. (1989), 'Stress-coping strategies identified from school age children's perspective', *Research in Nursing and Health*, vol. 12, pp. 109–22.

Ryan, P. (1988), 'The context of care: Staff', in A. Stonehouse (ed.), *Trusting toddlers: Programming for one to three year olds in child care centres*, Australian Early Childhood Association, Watson, ACT.

Saifer, S., Clark, S., James, H., & Kearns, K. (1993), *Practical solutions to practically every problem*, Pademelon, Sydney.

Sapon-Shevin, M. (1986), 'Teaching cooperation', in G. Cartledge and J.F. Milburn (eds), *Teaching social skills to children: Innovative approaches*, 2nd edn, Pergamon, New York.

Sayler, M.F. & Brookshire, W.K. (1993), 'Social, emotional, and behavioral adjustment of accelerated students, students in gifted classes, and regular students in eighth grade', *Gifted Child Quarterly*, vol. 37, no. 4, pp. 150–4.

Scarr, S., Eisenberg, M., & Deater-Deckard, K. (1994), 'Measurement of quality in child care centres', *Early Childhood Research Quarterly*, vol. 9, 131–51.

Schiever, S.W. & Maker, C.J. (1997), 'Enrichment and acceleration: An overview and new directions', in N. Colangelo & G.A. Davis (eds), *Handbook of gifted education*, 2nd edn, Allyn & Bacon, Boston.

Schneider, B.H. (1989), 'Between developmental wisdom and children's social skills training', in B.H. Schneider, G. Attili, J. Nadel & R.P. Weissberg (eds), *Social competence in developmental perspective*, Kluwer Academic Publishers, Dordrecht.

Sebastian, P. (1989), *Handle with care: A guide to early childhood administration*, 2nd edn, Jacaranda Press, Milton, QLD.

Sebastian-Nickell, P. & Milne, R. (1992), *Care and education of young children*, Longman Cheshire, Melbourne.

Sekowski, A. (1995), 'Self-esteem and achievements of gifted students', *Gifted Education International*, vol. 10, no. 2, pp. 65–70.

Seligman, M. (1975), *Helplessness: On depression, development and death*, W.H. Freeman and Co., San Francisco.

—(1995), *The optimistic child*, Random House, Sydney.

Seligman, M. & Darling, R.B. (1997), *Ordinary families; Special children*, 2nd edn, Guilford, New York.

Sharp, S. & Thompson, D. (1994), 'The role of whole-school policies in tackling bullying behaviour in schools', in P.K. Smith & S. Sharp (eds), *School bullying: Insights and perspectives*, Routledge, London.

Shimoni, R., Baxter, J., & Kugelmass, J. (1992), *Every child is special: Quality group care for infants and toddlers*, Addison-Wesley, Don Mills, Ontario.

Silverman, L.K. (1993), 'The gifted individual', in L.K. Silverman (ed.), *Counselling the gifted and talented*, Love Publishing, Denver.

—(1994), 'The moral sensitivity of gifted children and the evolution of society', *Roeper Review*, vol. 17, no. 2, pp. 110–16.

Silverman, W.K., La Greca, A.M., & Wasserstein, S. (1995), 'What do children worry about? Worries and their relation to anxiety', *Child Development*, vol. 66, pp. 671–86.

Simons, J. (1986), *Administering early childhood services*, Sydney College of Advanced Education, Sydney.

Slaby, R.G., Roedell, W.C., Arezzo, D., & Hendrix, K. (1995), *Early violence prevention: Tools for teachers of young children*, National Association for the Education of Young Children, Washington DC.

Slee P.T. (1991), 'What stresses Australian children?', *Children Australia*, vol. 16, no. 3, pp. 12–14.

—(1993), 'Children, stressful life events and school adjustment: An Australian study', *Educational Psychology*, vol. 23, no. 1, pp. 3–10.

Smith, A.B. (1990), 'Early childhood on the margins', *Australian Journal of Early Childhood*, vol. 15, no. 4, pp. 12–15.

Southern, W.T., Jones, E.D., & Fiscus, E.D. (1989), 'Practitioner objections to the academic acceleration of gifted children', *Gifted Child Quarterly*, vol. 33, no. 1, pp. 29–35.

Spirito, A., Stark, L.J., Grace, N., & Stamoulis, D. (1991), 'Common problems and coping strategies reported in childhood and early adolescence', *Journal of Youth and Adolescence*, vol. 20, no. 5, pp. 531–44.

Stanley, D. (1996), 'How to defuse an angry parent' *Child Care Information Exchange*, vol. 108, pp. 34–5.

Sternberg, R.J. (1997), 'A triarchic view of giftedness: Theory and practice', in N. Colangelo & G.A. Davis (eds), *Handbook of gifted education*, 3rd edn, Allyn & Bacon, Boston.

Sternberg, R.J. & Lubart, T.I. (1991), 'An investment theory of creativity and its development', *Human Development*, vol. 34, pp. 1–31.

—(1992), 'Creative giftedness in children', in P.S. Klein & A.J. Tannenbaum (eds), *To be young and gifted*, Ablex, Norwood, NJ.

Stonehouse, A. (ed.), (1988), *Trusting toddlers: Programming for one to three year olds in child care centres*, Australian Early Childhood Association, Watson, ACT.

—(1991a), *Our code of ethics at work*, Australian Early Childhood Association, Watson, ACT.

—(1991b), *Opening the doors: Child care in a multi-cultural society*, Australian Early Childhood Association, Watson, ACT.

—(1994a), *Not just nice ladies: A book of readings on early childhood care and education*, Pademelon Press, Sydney.

—(1994b), *How does it feel? Child care from a parent's perspective*, Australian Early Childhood Association, Canberra.

Stonehouse, A. & Creaser, B. (1991), 'A code of ethics for the Australian early childhood profession: Background and overview', *Australian Journal of Early Childhood*, vol. 16, no. 1, pp. 7–10.

Summers, J.A., Dell'Oliver, C., Turnbull, A.P., Benson, H.A., Santelli, E., Campbell, M., & Siegal-Causey, E. (1990), 'Examining the individualised family service plan process: What are family and practitioner preferences?', *Topics in Early Childhood Special Education*, vol. 10, no. 1, pp. 78–99.

Swetnam, L., Peterson, C.R., & Clark, H.B. (1983), 'Social skills development in young children: Preventive and therapeutic approaches', in C.W. LeCroy (ed.), *Social skills training for children and youth*, Haworth Press, New York.

Tannenbaum, A.J. (1983), *Gifted children: Psychological and educational perspectives*, Macmillan, New York.

—(1992), 'Early signs of giftedness: Research and commentary', in P.S. Klein & A.J. Tannenbaum (eds), *To be young and gifted*, Ablex, Norwood, NJ.

—(1997), 'The meaning and making of giftedness', in N. Colangelo & G.A. Davis (eds), *Handbook of gifted education*, 2nd edn, Allyn & Bacon, Boston.

Teyber, E. (1992), *Helping children cope with divorce*, Jossey-Bass, San Francisco.

Theilheimer, R. (1993), 'Something for everyone: Benefits of mixed-age grouping for children, parents, and teachers', *Young Children*, vol. 48, no. 5, pp. 82–7.

Thompson, B.J. (1993), *Words can hurt you: Beginning a program of anti-bias education*, Addison-Wesley, Menlo Park, California.

Thompson, C.L. & Rudolph, L.B. (1996), *Counseling children*, 4th edn, Brookes/Cole, Pacific Grove, CA.

Tinworth, S. (1994), 'Conceptualising a collaborative partnership between parents and staff in early childhood services', in E.J. Mellor & K.M. Coombe (eds), *Issues in early childhood services: Australian perspectives*, William C. Brown, Dubuque, Iowa.

Townsend, M.A.R. (1996), 'Enrichment and acceleration: Lateral and vertical perspectives in provisions for gifted and talented children', in D. McAlpine & R. Moltzen (eds), *Gifted and talented: New Zealand perspectives*, ERDC Press, Palmerston North.

Turnbull, A.P. & Turnbull, H.R. (1997), *Families, professionals and exceptionality: A special partnership*, 3rd edn, Upper Saddle River, NJ: Merrill.

Turnbull, H.R., Guess, D., & Turnbull, A.P. (1988), 'Vox populi and baby Doe', *Mental Retardation*, vol. 26, no. 3, pp. 127–32.

Umansky, W. & Hooper, S.R. (eds), (1998), *Young children with special needs*, 3rd edn, Merrill, Upper Saddle River, NJ.

van Boxtel, H.W. & Mönks, F.J. (1992), 'General, social, and academic self-concepts of gifted adolescents', *Journal of Youth and Adolescence*, vol. 21, no. 2, pp. 169–86.

Van Tassel-Baska, J. (1997), 'What matters in curriculum for gifted learners: Reflections on theory, research and practice', in N. Colangelo & G.A. Davis (eds), *Handbook of gifted education*, 2nd edn, Allyn & Bacon, Boston.

Wangmann, J. (1992), 'Accreditation: A right for all Australia's young children or a waste of time and money', in B. Lambert (ed.), *Changing faces: The early childhood profession in Australia*, Australian Early Childhood Association, Watson, ACT.

Waters, J. (1996), *Making the connection: Parents and early childhood staff*, Lady Gowrie Child Centre (Melbourne), Inc., Melbourne.

Weinreb, M.L. (1997), 'Be a resiliency mentor: You may be a lifesaver for a high-risk child', *Young Children*, vol. 52, no. 2, pp. 14–20.

Weissberg, R.P. (1989), 'Challenges inherent in translating theory and basic research into effective social competence promotion programs', in B.H. Schneider, G. Attili, J. Nadel & R.P. Weissberg (eds), *Social competence in developmental perspective*, Kluwer Academic Publishers, Dordrecht.

Westberg, G.E. (1992), *Good grief*, rev. edn, Fortress, Melbourne.

Whelan, T. & Kelly, S. (1986), *A hard act to follow: Step-parenting in Australia today*, Penguin, Ringwood.

White, C.S. (1985), 'Alternatives for assessing the presence of advanced intellectual abilities in young children', *Roeper Review*, vol. 8, no. 2, pp. 73–5.

Whitmore, J.R. (1980), *Giftedness, conflict, and underachievement*, Allyn & Bacon, Boston.

Williams, G. & Ainley, M. (1994), 'Participant perceptions of quality child care', *Australian Journal of Early Childhood*, vol. 19, no. 2, pp. 43–7.

Wodrich, D.L. (1994), *Attention deficit hyperactivity disorder. What every parent wants to know*, Paul H. Brookes, Baltimore, MD.

Wolfle, J. (1989), 'The gifted preschooler: Developmentally different, but still 3 or 4 years old', *Young Children*, vol. 44, no. 3, pp. 41–8.

Wragg, J. (1989), *Talk sense to yourself: A program for children and adolescents*, ACER, Melbourne.

Yong, F.L. (1994), 'Self-concepts, locus of control, and Machiavellianism of ethnically diverse middle school students who are gifted', *Roeper Review*, vol. 16, no. 3, pp. 192–4.

Young, B.B. (1995), *Stress and your child*, Harper Collins, Sydney.

Young, M.E. (1992), *Counseling methods and techniques: An eclectic approach*, Merrill, New York.

Zentall, S.S. (1989), 'Self-control training with hyperactive and impulsive children', in J.N. Hughes & R.J. Hall (eds), *Cognitive-behavioral psychology in the schools*, Guilford, New York.

Zimmerman, M.A. & Arunkumar, R. (1994), 'Resiliency research: Implications for schools and policy', *Social Policy Report*, vol. 8, no. 4, pp. 1–17.

Index

Child's Play
Revisiting Play in Early Childhood Settings

Edited by
Elizabeth Dau

Through a range of topical issues explored by practitioners and educators in the child care field, *Child's Play—Revisiting Play in Early Childhood Settings* uncovers the intricate relationship between play and learning.

The role of play in furthering young children's social, cognitive and emotional development is examined, with a particular focus on the acquisition of social skills and the development of attitudes. Central to the text is its 'anti-bias' theme, which is specifically highlighted in chapters addressing gender boundaries, cultural variance and the differing abilities of young children.

Using both personal accounts and informed, theoretical discourse *Child's Play—Revisiting Play in Early Childhood Settings* covers the nature and purpose of play, types and stages of play, appropriate materials and resources, and the role of the adult. The discussion questions in each chapter are designed to prompt students and practitioners alike to analyse their own perceptions and attitudes, and ultimately guide them in developing programs that recognise play as a powerful learning experience.

A matrix at the back of the book provides a correlation between the chapters and the National Child Care Competency Standards.

0-86433-141-X

Also available from MacLennan + Petty

Children with Disabilities 4ed.

Edited by
Mark L. Batshaw, MD

Professionals, families and students can rely on this fully illustrated, comprehensive resource for all of their disability reference needs. Along with extensive coverage of genetics, heredity, pre- and postnatal development, specific disabilities, family roles, and intervention, this edition features new chapters on substance abuse, AIDS, Down syndrome, fragile X syndrome, behaviour management, transitions to adulthood, and health care in the 21st century. It also reveals the causes of many conditions that can lead to developmental disabilities. The convenient selection of appendices includes a new one that describes the properties and uses of a wide variety of medications.

For personal, professional or academic use, this informative classic has a place on the desk of everyone who works with, cares for, or loves a child with disabilities.

0-86433-137-1